Advance Praise for
Intuition at Work

"Intuition is the difference between average and excellent decisions. The best leaders know this. This book opens the door to excellence. *Intuition at Work* is the right subject at the right time. All future leaders should get acquainted with this vast and proactive subject."
— John R. O'Neil, president
California School of Professional Psychology
author, *The Paradox of Success*

"*Intuition at Work* reveals once again the amazing fecundity of the American mind. Whatever it seizes, it unfolds it in its minutest details. This is a volume, therefore, meant for all those who are interested in better management of the affairs of the world."
— Dr. S.K. Chakraborty, convenor
Management Centre for Human Values
Indian Institute of Management Calcutta

"Includes many practical techniques for developing the intuitive capability inherent in each of us, while demystifying the nature of intuition."
— John D. Adams
Education Manager
Sun Microsystems, Inc.

"The external and thence internal challenges facing tomorrow's business require fresh perception and new approaches, slavish and mechanistic processes to delight the customer, excellence in product innovation, and in supply line services, coupled with the inclusion of the interests of other key stakeholders will only work inadequately. The requisite perception and integrated opportunity for tomorrow's business can be compared with that of humankind, opened by intuition and creativity, honed by intellect and knowledge, and developed by practice and lifelong learning. This book opens the door."
— Michael JE Frye, CEO
B. Elliott, plc, London

"*Intuition at Work* magnificently demonstrates the great value of the intuitive approach. It shows business people how to be productive while remaining human."
> — Meryem LeSaget, author
> *Le Manager Intuitif* (winner of Paris-Dauphine Prize for best business book in 1993)

"In the years of leading Medtronic, Inc., and in my work now in retirement, I have operated by the slogan 'Ready, Fire, Aim.' *Intuition at Work* has shown me that I was really leading by intuition. This is a wonderful book that helps one understand this important business tool."
> — Earl E. Bakken, founder and director emeritus
> Medtronic, Inc.

"*Intuition at Work* offers a breakthrough in our understanding of human powers. The editors and authors show how we all share the common wisdom that unifies a bountiful universe."
> — William E. Halal, George Washington University
> author, *The New Management: Democracy and Enterprise are Transforming Organizations*

"In *Intuition at Work*, editors Roger Frantz and Alex Pattakos immerse us in the lore of intuition—its intellectual as well as practical manifestations. They move us closer to a decision model that responds to essential elements of the workplace. Given the phenomenal changes in both work and workers characteristic in today's workplace, something new is needed. Frantz and Pattakos fill that need in. In doing so they do a service to both leaders and the millions of workers in today's corporations who are seeking better ways of leading others in an increasingly chaotic workplace. Well done!"
> — Gil Fairholm, author
> *Capturing the Heart of Leadership: Spirituality and Community in the New American Workplace* (forthcoming)

"There are lots of books about business. This is a book about how people can access what is inside of them to transform business. *Intuition at Work* is important and indeed groundbreaking in its approach. It goes right to the heart of how to change a system that needs changing."
> — Lawrence Perlman, chairman and CEO
> Ceridian Corporation

"New Leaders Press has done it again! *Intuition at Work* is a masterpiece: a valuable and exciting work organized like an artichoke; the taste and texture of each chapter brings you close to the 'heart' of the matter. It makes a compelling case for the use of intuition as a highly leveraged tool for the information age. And, the good news is we all have it...we just need to use it more consistently. The book is filled with guidelines, suggestions, and exercises designed to sharpen the reader's ability to use intuition in all areas of our lives; personal and professional. It's a 'must read' as we approach the 21st Century."

— W. Mathew Jeuchter, CEO
ARC International Ltd.

"*Intuition at Work* is what we all need. Get this book onto your desk and into your heart!"

— Laurie Beth Jones
The Jones Group

"A book long awaited. Highly informative and practical. I recommend it to everyone interested in the future of work and business."

— Rolf Österberg,
author, *Corporate Renaissance*
co-author, *The Search for Meaning in the Workplace*

"I tend to ignore 'collections' or 'anthologies'; usually, they are a hodgepodge of ideas, a kind of intellectual goulash. *Intuition at Work* changed my mind. It is a coherent and seminal work that describes and illustrates the transformation of our conceptions of management thought and practice. Listening to the 'inner voice'— trusting the inner voice—is one of the most important lessons of leadership that I've learned. In fact, following what Emerson called the 'blessed impulse' is basic to understanding what leadership and organizations are all about. This collection of readings is the single best source I know of that deals directly, concretely, and lucidly with this powerful idea."

— Warren Bennis, author
Organizing Genius: The Secrets of Creative Collaboration (forthcoming)

Intuition At Work
Pathways to Unlimited Possibilities

Featuring writings by

Joanne Badeaux • Joanne Black • Susan Collins
Gigi Van Deckter • Sharon Franquemont
Roger Frantz • Linda A. Garrett • Suzie Hightower
Edith Jurka • Joel Levey • Jaime Licauco
Gary D. Markoff • Jeffrey Mishlove
Michael W. Munn • Laurie Nadel
Jan Newman-Seligman • Alex N. Pattakos
John Pehrson • Michael Ray • Elle Collier Re
Christine Roess • Nancy Rosanoff
Kymn Harvin Rutigliano • Gary Zukav

Editors: Roger Frantz and Alex N. Pattakos

NewLeadersPress

STERLING &
STONE, INC.

Sterling & Stone
New Leaders Press

San Francisco

New Leaders Press/Sterling & Stone, Inc.
1668 Lombard St.
San Francisco, CA 94123
Tel: 415.928.1473; Fax: 415.928.3346; email: staff@newleadersnet.org

To purchase additional copies or inquire about bulk discounts for multiple
orders, contact the publisher at 1.800.928.LEAD.

Bookstores and wholesalers, please contact National Book Network, 4720
Boston Way, Lanham, MD 20706; Tel: 301.731.9515, 1.800.462.6420; Fax:
301.459.2118.

 Printed in the United States of America on recycled paper.

Library of Congress Catalog Card Number: 96-070867

Intuition at Work. Edited by Roger Frantz, PhD and Alex N. Pattakos, PhD

ISBN 0-886710-00-7
First Edition

Contents

"The really valuable thing is intuition."

—Albert Einstein

Foreword

Business Discovers Intuition

Willis W. Harman

Willis W. Harman, PhD, is president of the Institute of Noetic Sciences and a co-founder of World Business Academy. He is also the author of many books including Global Mind Change *and* Creative Work *(with John Hormann).*

This book is about intuition and its relationship to business. Only since the late 1970s have business journals and books included reference to "hunches," "gut feelings," and intuition in decision making. Prior to then, not only was intuition absent from the practical businessman's lexicon (even the prudent businesswoman's public speech), one was unlikely to find the word used anywhere without its being preceded by the adjective "feminine."

The idea of arriving at insight directly, noetically, without the intervention of reason or analysis, was profoundly disturbing in a time when "rational man" was the ideal model. It was not a concept that the tough-minded business executive talked about comfortably. Yet it is now an open secret that the most successful business executives have learned to trust their intuition—and have further learned that in the trusting, it becomes more reliable and accurate, until in the end it proves to be the most trustworthy guide available. The rational mind, still useful, is put in a secondary role with respect to the deep intuition.

Whether we focus on these new insights of executive functioning, or on what Nobel laureate Roger Sperry termed the

coming "consciousness revolution" in science—or both together—
the implications are the same. Modern society appears to be going
through one of the most fundamental shifts in history. At the
deepest level of that shift is a change in worldview rivaling that of
the scientific revolution and the ending of the Middle Ages. It
amounts to a departure from the objectivist, positivist, reduction-
ist assumptions that have dominated Western science (and hence
influenced "common sense") for over three centuries. These metaphysical assumptions are being replaced by a worldview that
emphasizes wholeness, interconnectedness, and "inner knowing." This cultural change amounts to the recognition that posi-
tivistic, reductionistic science intrinsically comprises no more
than a partial and inadequate understanding of the universe we
live in and of our place in it.

By the latter part of the 20th Century it was becoming
apparent that, however useful prediction-and-control-focused
science might be for some purposes, most notably generation of
manipulative technologies, it had a serious negative effect on our
understanding of values. This effect was to undermine the common religious base of values and to replace it with a stance of
moral relativism. Into the vacuum came, as a kind of "pseudo-
values," economic and technical criteria—material progress, efficiency, productivity, economic growth, return on investment,
discounted future value, and so on. Decisions that would affect
the lives of billions of people around the globe, and countless
generations to come, were decided on the basis of short-term
economic considerations. The "technological imperative" to develop and deploy any technology that could turn a profit or
destroy an enemy endangered both the life-support systems of
the planet and human civilization.

Spirituality and religiosity did not disappear, of course. The
churches still played a role in people's lives, and, privately, many
a scientist guided his or her life by deep spiritual beliefs. But
modern society was attempting the impossible. That was to
manage society, and the planet, on the basis of two conflicting
and mutually contradictory pictures of reality—the mechanistic
universe of conventional science, and the spiritual universe
assumed in society's religious traditions.

By mid-century, science had become increasingly adept at
exploring the external, physical world, and society had become
increasingly neglectful of the world of inner experience. This was

extremely serious, because it is from this deep intuitive experience that all individuals and all societies have always derived their sense of ultimate meanings and eternal values. Industrial society was becoming more and more like a ship with ever-increasing speed, but no compass and charts to guide it.

This all began to change in the 1960s. Just as the modern perception of reality differed from the medieval, so a growing band of individuals (now estimated in the many tens of millions) are betting their lives on a different picture of reality than that of reductionistic science. It is not just that some "New Age" values are spreading through the populace. Rather, a fundamentally different and competing picture of reality infuses holistic health care approaches, "deep ecology," new concepts of business management, and people seeking to replace the lost meaning in their lives.

Growing public interest in such areas as Eastern religious philosophies, yoga and meditation, spiritual traditions of indigenous peoples, paranormal phenomena, channeling and near-death experiences, imagery-based approaches to healing and education, etc., has made clear how widespread is the dissatisfaction with the scientists' exclusive claim to valid truth-seeking.

In the historical development of science there were good reasons for an initial limiting of the scope of the new inquiry to those aspects of reality that are physically measurable, and to explanations that are non-teleological and reductionistic. Nevertheless there were consequences. One of those consequences has been that a tremendous amount of effort has gone into defending the barricades against, or explaining away, a host of phenomena that don't fit within those limits. These outcasts included miraculous healings and psychic phenomena, and impressive evidence that death is better viewed as a change of state than a termination—as well as more ordinary experiences such as volition, intention, selective attention, conscious awareness, synchronicity, and creative insight.

By the second half of the last decade of this millennium, things had begun to change. Serious conferences were being held in North America, Europe, and Japan to raise these questions about the problems with scientific epistemology, and to explore what would be needed to create a true "science of consciousness" that would deal in appropriate ways with the unlimited richness of our inner experience. The "transpersonal" movement was no longer a tiny group with a strange enthusiasm, but a vital social movement.

What are the implications of the fact that our society has apparently decided to honor intuition, in business and other practical sectors of society? There are several:

1. It brings a new approach to decision making. Using intuition (together with the rational mind) amounts to using more of the mind. Because the "more" turns out to be extremely competent, decision making should be more successful in terms of long-range concerns, well-being of the whole, and anticipating "unforeseen" consequences.

2. It has implications with regard to values. Our most important value commitments have their origins in the inclinations of the deep intuitive mind. Paying more attention to this brings about challenges to the economic and technical values which hold sway over modern society, and so strongly influence social choices. The influence of these values will tend to decline, as the valence of other values increases—particularly, cooperative, nurturing, altruistic, humane, ecological, aesthetic, and spiritual values.

3. It amounts to a reassessment of the role of business. As more and more of those involved in the business enterprise— executives, employees, customers—experience changes in the value emphases that govern their lives, the basic questions of the role of business, the role of speculation (vs. true investment), relationships with the populations of the "developing" countries, business involvement in the arms trade, etc. will all be reassessed.

4. It amounts to a reassessment of the basic metaphysical assumptions that underlie modern industrial society. Insofar as it does so, it amounts to the end of the modern era, just as surely as the shift in assumptions that comprised the scientific revolution meant the end of the medieval era. The late 21st Century will be, it is now clear, as different from modern times as these are from the Middle Ages.

We all experience an understandable psychological resistance to the proposition that our internalized assumptions about reality must change. It is not a comfortable feeling to be aware that some kind of fundamental change is essential, and not know just what that is going to do to our accustomed way of life, our assumed "security," or indeed, our basic convictions about "how things are." (Each of us reading this book has undoubtedly gone through some experiencing of this kind of discomfort.)

Thus, on the one hand, we can see an exhilarating time ahead. Business will be finding new roles; unsolvable problems will be appearing in a new and more tractable light; we will be discovering new freedoms to take charge of our own lives, and discovering that we receive assistance from the universe in unexpected and mysterious ways. Task number one is global mind change, and many of us will feel ourselves to be at the vibrant heart of that change. On the other hand, this fundamental shift is going to feel threatening to a lot of people, and some of them will be responding to it irrationally. The things we do to keep down the level of anxiety will be very important, because that affects the amount of human misery and social carnage involved as society goes through what could be an extremely wrenching transformation.

Thus, all things considered, the current interest in intuition undoubtedly goes much deeper than surface appearances. Indeed, "intuition" turns out to be a code word for referring to a major transformation of modern society.

Willis W. Harman
Sausalito, California
August 1996

*"The intuitive mind
will tell the thinking
where to look next."*

—Jonas Salk

Preface

The vision and collaboration demonstrated by everyone associated with the creation, development, and publication of this incredible collection of writing has been a marvel to observe. The concept for an anthology on the subject of intuition in business began during an exploratory conversation with Stanford's Michael Ray, publisher John Renesch, and Intuition Network director Jeffrey Mishlove at Shasta Lake in Northern California in July of 1994. The concept was polished a bit and an editor selected to work with the publisher—Roger Frantz, professor of economics at the San Diego State University.

Invitations to prospective authors started going out in November of that year and an exciting group of contributors developed over the following months.

Alex Pattakos came aboard the team in the summer of 1995, offering to help with the editing portion of the project and work with Roger in confirming some additional authors.

As the production phase of this anthology began, futurist Willis Harman was asked to write a foreword, which he generously did, and the entire package was finally ready for author checks and advance previews. And then, at last, it became a book—ready for you the reader.

It's been quite a journey—filled with miracles, laughter, difficulties, upsets, and more miracles. And here we are—a fabulous collection of writings, arranged for you to read sequentially or, if you prefer, at random.

The rich content everyone has brought to you represents the best and latest thinking about intuition and its place in organizational life, particularly in business.

The book has been organized by the editors in six parts, following their Introduction. Twenty-two essays follow as the contributing authors explore the frontier of intuition, with anecdotes, scientific explanation, technology, methods and processes, and personal experience.

Acknowledgments

Intuition at Work has been a collaboration involving many people besides the authors, editors, and publisher.

Several authors wish to express their appreciation and gratitude for people who supported them in their creative process.

First and foremost, Joel Levey would like to acknowledge his wife, Michelle Levey, who has collaborated in this work and so skillfully crafted this chapter with him. Heartfelt thanks also to Roger Frantz, Alex Pattakos, Bill Veltrop, Jon Dunnington, Shirley Swink, Peter and Trudy Johnson-Lenz, Chris Thorsen, Ruth Thorsen, Richard Moon, Jack Cirie, Bill Gough, Robert O. Becker, Duane Elgin, and Robert Lawlor, and our many mentors for their inspiration in this inquiry. Thanks also to the "all star" teams who have helped us to validate and demonstrate the profound synergy of innerwork and intuition at work: Hewlett-Packard, Weyerhaeuser, The Travelers, Group Health Cooperative, AT&T, SRI, MIT, PetroCanada, TransAlta Utilities, U.S. Army Green Berets, P.E.A.R. at Princeton University, and NASA.

Susan Collins is deeply grateful to the serendipitous nature of her life for forcing her—in order to survive—to develop intuition and creativity early on. And along her winding path she was happy to meet up with John Shearer of the Leadership Trust who led her to this book. She offers special thanks to Roger Frantz and Alex Pattakos for pulling her out from behind a huge mound of galleys for *Our Children Are Watching* and on to what was next.

Linda Garrett wants to especially thank Olga Fernandez and Steven A. Schmitz for helping with various phases of this writing process. "Olga, thanks for your creativity, patience, flexibility, and understanding, as well as for keeping an open heart. And thanks for the opening lines. Steve, thanks for helping me get started as well as coming up with a great title!" She also wants to thank Alex Pattakos for being a catalyst for this writing project; Larry Brunnetti and Mark Falconer for sharing their insights, experiences and feelings about the uses of intuition in the workplace; Lynda Davis and Robert St. Germain for giving her support during the "final" review; and Juliane Ziegart, as well as her daughter, Katie Garrett, for helping her access her own intuition more confidently.

Kymn Harvin Rutigliano expresses her appreciation to co-editor Alex Pattakos for his steadfast encouragement and generous guidance, to Tom Prewitt for his partnership and courage in championing love and spirit at AT&T, and to her husband Vince and all others who have encouraged her in being Love's messenger.

Joanne Badeaux acknowledges two people who contributed directly to her essay. She was relieved when writer Dale Napier was able to add clarification and explanations to her otherwise abstract writing. She was ecstatic when artist Richard Horridge was able, in one day, to visually illustrate her article through sketches. Further, she humbly thanks Unity Church for all of its teachings which allow her to continually access her intuition. She dedicates her essay to her son, whose presence in her life reminds her that love is real.

Suzie Hightower acknowledges some exceptional people who have made significant contributions to her life and her story. Grateful acknowledgments and many thanks to her mother, Ann Pottorff, for her unconditional love, constant support and encouragement, and for teaching her to embrace her intuition. She thanks God daily for loving her so beautifully through her. She has been a most precious gift and she loves her dearly. Her spiritual daughter, Cherri Bowe, for her kindness and compassion. She is most grateful that she came into her life. To Alex Pattakos, PhD, friend and colleague, who touched her life so deeply and invited her to contribute to this anthology. There are many types of partnerships. This is one of divine intervention. To her dear friend, Randy Gillespie, for always having faith in her. To Terry Sullivan for his friendship and genuine interest in her life. To Jim Peters for sharing so much and introducing her to *The Road Less Traveled*. To her professional mentors, Norman Brinker and Rick Berman, for giving her incredible opportunities and support in the business world. To her dear friend, Jane

Christensen, for her love and support. To her beloved friends Ellen Glickman, Linda Hooser, and Gloria Rechner for their excitement in and enthusiasm for all things spiritual. To her colleagues at PPA and members of the Association. Special thanks to Ted Olson and Doug Heath for believing in her and allowing her to spread her wings.

Grateful acknowledgment is made for permission to reproduce the Mindful Meditation technique explained by Deepak Chopra, M.D., in his book *Journey Into Healing*, copyright 1994 by Harmony Books, a division of Crown Publishers, Inc. Profound gratitude to Dr. Chopra for his insights on mind–body medicine and human potential. She owes a special debt of gratitude to all the health care professionals who participated in her healing process. In particular to Ken Killen, M.D., Roby Mize, M.D., and Tamra Drexler, R.N., who honored her holistic approach to mind–body medicine and for expressing such a genuine concern for her complete recovery. And everyone else who has helped her along the way.

Roger Frantz wishes to thank John Renesch for trusting in his abilities to edit this book, the entire staff of New Leaders Press and especially Claudette Allison for their assistance, Alex Pattakos for breathing life into the project at a very critical juncture, and the contributing authors for loving the project.

Co-editor Alex N. Pattakos wishes first to thank his son, Nick, for teaching him lessons about intuition at work that could never be learned from a book. He also wants to thank all the authors for sharing their intuitive wisdom and for some wonderful discussions and dialogue. A learning community we did become! Roger Frantz, his co-editor, deserves special recognition for supporting him through the various stages of the acquisition and editing process. An extra special thanks also must go to the two people at New Leaders Press who made this book a reality: John Renesch and Claudette Allison. Thank you both for your faith in me and for giving me the opportunity to play "Spartacus." To John, moreover, thanks for "letting go" and demonstrating the courage to try some new things with me. I certainly learned a lot from our association and from this experience. My heartfelt thanks also go to several close friends, colleagues, partners, and kindred spirits in the "Big Sky" who provided me with ongoing inspiration and support during our virtual whitewater rafting trip: Manuella Buell, Linda A. Garrett, and Jack Peterson. I hope you enjoyed the ride as much as I did. I love you all.

Jan Newman-Seligman wants to thank Roger Frantz for being such a wise and compassionate editor; Cherie Diamond who is a gem of a writer, thinker, artist, and friend; Helice Bridges from Difference Makers International for paving the way for her self-esteem; Dr. Anne Hanley for modeling teaching the way it really should be; and her mother who has always given her the support she needs to be all that she can.

New Leaders Press thanks everyone associated with this project, most prominently all the contributing authors, knowing that coordinating the efforts of so many people requires much cooperation and organizational focus as well as the talent for expression. In addition thanks go to the book's co-editors, Roger Frantz and Alex Pattakos, the publisher John Renesch, New Leaders staff members Claudette Allison and Tatiana Roegiers, and Amy Kahn who was involved in the very beginning of the project. Deep appreciation also goes out to the production and design people, namely Carolynn Crandall and Karen Deist and their team at Select Press for typography, Sue Malikowski of Autographix for cover design and production, and Lyle Mumford and Alan Smart of Publishers Press, our printers.

Special thanks also go to Jeffrey Mishlove, director of the Intuition Network, who was involved in the original conceptualization of this book. Kazimierz "Kaz" Gozdz, Ben Mancini, and Michael Ray also deserve thanks for their roles in the conceptualization of this book aboard *Utopia* on Shasta Lake. To Willis Harman who wrote the foreword of this collection we owe profound gratitude.

The advisory board of New Leaders Press/Sterling & Stone, Inc. has been invaluable as a continuing resource and we wish to acknowledge each of them: Pat Barrentine, David Berenson, William Halal, Willis Harman, Paul Hwoschinsky, William Miller, Shirley Nelson, Christine Oster, Steven Piersanti, Catherine Pyke, James O'Toole, Michael Ray, Stephen Roulac, Jeremy Tarcher, Peggy Umanzio, and Dennis White.

Finally, on behalf of authors, editors, and the publishing staff, a special "thank you" goes to those individuals who agreed to preview this collection and provide us with their comments before we went to press. These people are: John D. Adams, Mary Anderson, Angeles Arrien, Earl E. Bakken, Richard Barrett, Warren Bennis, Lorna Catford, S.K. Chakraborty, Gil Fairholm,

Michael JE Frye, William E. Halal, W. Mathew Jeuchter, Laurie Beth Jones, Meryem LeSaget, Loretta McCarthy, John R. O'Neil, Rolf Österberg, and Lawrence Perlman.

Roger Frantz, PhD, (left) is a professor of economics at San Diego State University. He is the director of Intuition 2000, a conference on intuition held annually at San Diego State University. He teaches intuition training classes and provides intuitive-based consulting through his company, Profits and Sense. He is also a "coach" for the Self Expression and Leadership Program offered by Landmark Education.

Alex N. Pattakos, PhD, (right) is a pracademic, avid martial artist, and cybernaut. He is also a former president of Renaissance Business Associates, an international nonprofit networking association "committed to demonstrating the power and effectiveness of integrity through elevating the human spirit at work," is on the advisory board of the Innovation Network, and chairs a national working group on technology for the American Society for Public Administration.

Pattakos is a contributing author to *Managing in Organizations that Learn* and *Rediscovering the Soul of Business: A Renaissance of Values*.

Introduction

Understanding The Magician's Journey

Roger Frantz and Alex N. Pattakos

While this book is about "intuition," the reader will find that it is also about creativity and spirit. Indeed, most discussions about creativity would be remiss if they did not in some way touch upon the topic of intuition. To many, in fact, unleashing the creative spirit is simply another way of animating one's intuition. As we shall see throughout this book, intuition cuts at the very core of our individuality and may actually be the final arbiter of how each of us manifests who we really are as living beings. In this respect, intuition represents the essence of our personal and collective identities and contains the spark of life energy that we often refer to as "spirit."

Intuition as spirit is certainly not a new concept. On the contrary, it is deeply rooted in a variety of philosophical traditions—both Eastern and Western. In this connection, Rudolf Steiner, an Austrian-born scientific, literary, and philosophical scholar, asserted that free spiritual activity, which he basically understood as the human ability to think intuitively, is the appropriate cognitive path for human beings to take in order to express fully their "freedom" as individuals. To Steiner, by experiencing and living intuitive thinking, that is, "the conscious experience of a purely spiritual content," true freedom as a creative force for socially responsible action would become manifest. Intuition in this way can be viewed as a source of animation providing the energy that brings the cartoon characters we call humans "alive."

Intuition at work, then, is about being alive, wherever one may be. Speaking of the creative spirit in the workplace, Anita Roddick, CEO of The Body Shop, observed that "all people want is to be alive in the workplace." While this may not appear to be rocket science, in many respects, it is a concept that is more difficult to understand and practice than rocket science. In rocket science, one plus one equals two. The dynamics of human affairs, on the other hand, offer little assurance that such principles can be applied consistently and with any degree of precision. The mystery surrounding topics like intuition makes it difficult for many people, particularly those concerned with "traditional" business practices, to rely on them—at least consciously—as identifiable elements of the mental models that guide their methods of operation. In the final analysis, even though all decisions are ultimately made "intuitively"—irrespective of the data used to support them—contemporary schools of management thought are only just beginning to recognize intuition as a legitimate dimension of business practice.

Where does intuition come from, how do we access it, and how can we apply it? These are just some of the questions that are addressed in this comprehensive collection of essays. In short, this book endeavors to unravel the mysteries surrounding intuition by accommodating a broad array of perspectives, some grounded in science, others tied perhaps more to the strings of faith than reason. Our primary objective is to paint a tapestry that mirrors as much of what we know about intuition as possible. At the same time, we recognize that, as blind people trying to describe an elephant, we are never quite certain that we have included all necessary points of view. Intuition, as we will see, reflects more a process than it does a product. This book, because it tries to accomplish in a finite collection of words what each of us can only experience in "real-time" and on multiple levels of awareness, provides only a context or template for understanding the mysteries of intuition. It is the responsibility of each reader to complete and personalize the tapestry presented here.

The chapters in this collection demonstrate quite clearly that intuition is as much a process of self-discovery as it is a tool for decision making. Moreover, because this process is grounded in personal experience, it is the individual who is responsible for charting his or her course towards increased intuitive awareness. At times, the path may seem unclear and the journey may appear unpleasant. Then, almost like magic, the force of intuitive knowledge becomes evident and new expressions of self emerge. For perhaps only an instant, we are able to experience a manifestation of "intuition at work" and our faith in the process is renewed.

Is this really magic? And, if so, must we become magicians or wizards in order to tap into this mystical resource? How does one do that anyway? Again, the essays in this anthology resonate with these questions and offer conceptual and practical guidance across many dimensions along the path of personal and organizational transformation. For starters, we believe that everyone is "creative," that everyone is "intuitive," and that everyone is a "magician." Intuitive thinking, which Steiner has described as a "philosophy of freedom," is indeed a magical journey. Carol S. Pearson and Sharon Seivert, in their recent book, *Magic at Work,* underscore that "magic happens not just because of what we do but because of what we are willing to become." To begin the journey within, they stress that one must engage in activities that "free your intuition" and "increase your creative receptivity." This book contains numerous examples of these kinds of activities. Furthermore, it offers snapshots of the evolutionary path of consciousness which comprises the sine qua non of intuition "at work."

According to popular author Dr. Deepak Chopra, "A wizard exists in all of us. This wizard sees and knows everything." Becoming a wizard is certainly a spiritual path, in Dr. Chopra's view, and he outlines many lessons along the way as part of the requisite training in alchemy to foster human development. Since wizards are essentially "seers," they are also more likely to see reality as a whole rather than simply a collection of many parts.

Wizards, by definition, also do not "see" boundaries. This is especially significant when we consider the normal way we use our "senses" to process information in our environments. What about our so-called "sixth sense"? How do we factor it into the equation that creates what we perceive as life? More dramatically, how can we be so sure that our "senses" actually function the way that we think they do? If we add the sixth sense, commonly referred to as intuition, to the phenomenon of sensory fusion, what does this really say about human capacity to "know" anything? With the growing interest in virtual organizations, networking organizations, and boundaryless organizations, the possibilities for unleashing human potential within these new organizational forms are unlimited. This book explores pathways that may lead to the fulfillment of such possibilities.

The journey to build the "Camelots" in our lives is going to involve an evolution of consciousness—individually as well as collectively—of magical proportions. Each one of us already has the capacity to do the "magic" that is necessary to transform ourselves and our institutions on a continuous basis. Some of us just don't know that yet.

Oystein Skalleberg, the founder of Skaltek, a major equipment manufacturer in Stockholm, Sweden, described his philosophy concerning how best to cultivate creativity in the workplace:

> Every human being is a Leonardo da Vinci. The
> only problem is that he doesn't know it. His
> parents didn't know it, and they didn't treat him
> like a Leonardo. Therefore he didn't become like
> a Leonardo. That's my basic theory.

It is going to take a shift in awareness for this potential to be realized and for the intended personal and collective transformations to occur. Indeed, as Chicago Bulls basketball coach Phil Jackson has so astutely observed, "Being aware is more important than being smart." To the extent that this book helps to increase this level of awareness, we feel that it will have made a difference in fostering intuition at work.

Part One

SPINNING THE WEB

What is Intuition?
Jeffrey Mishlove

Sources, Brain Routes, And Manifestations Of Intuition
Edith Jurka

Mind Treasure:
Intuitive Wisdom And The Dynamics Of
Mystery And Mastery at Work
Joel Levey

Jeffrey Mishlove, PhD, is director of the Intuition Network, an international organization of thousands of professionals in business, government, science, health and education who are dedicated to cultivating and applying intuitive abilities.

A clinical psychologist, he is also host of *Thinking Allowed,* a weekly public television interview series that has appeared throughout North America since 1988. In this capacity he has interviewed hundreds of leading, creative thinkers in philosophy, psychology, health, science and spirituality.

Mishlove is the author of *The Roots of Consciousness: The Classic Encyclopedia of Consciousness Studies, Revised and Expanded, Thinking Allowed,* an anthology of interviews from the television series, and *Psi Development Systems,* an analysis of methods for training intuitive abilities.

1

What Is Intuition?

Jeffrey Mishlove

According to the *American Heritage Dictionary,* intuition is "the act or faculty of knowing without the use of rational processes; immediate cognition. A capacity for guessing accurately; sharp insight." Antecedents include the Middle English "intuycion," meaning contemplation; the Latin "intueri," meaning to look at or toward, contemplate, to watch or protect; and the Indo-European "teu," to pay attention, to turn to.

The word intuition suggests a paradox—conventionally it means knowing something without knowing how you know. Many people in business identify intuition with a "gut feeling" or a "hunch." However, other people both in and out of the business arena say that, for them, if it is a hunch or a gut-feeling, then it cannot be a real intuition! Intuition is a beautiful word precisely because it includes so many possibilities. A variety of approaches to intuition have been put forth from both the religious and scientific communities.

Yet how can we select among them without an overview of the many existing approaches? At the Intuition Network, we have encountered literally hundreds of distinct applications of the term "intuition." In this chapter applications and uses of the term intuition are grouped into seventeen different definitions for purposes of providing an overview of the field.

1. A Personality Trait

According to the great Swiss psychiatrist Carl Gustav Jung, intuition is one of the four basic functions of the human mind (along with thinking, feeling, and sensation). It reflects, therefore, a cognitive style that has become widely recognized and measured in such well-known test instruments as the Myers-Briggs Personality Inventory. Businesses can use these instruments to identify which of their employees has highly cultivated intuitive skills. These employees can then be assigned to tasks such as new product development for which intuitive skills are a prerequisite. Jung defines the intuitive function as follows:

> The primary function of intuition...is simply to transmit images, or perceptions of relations between things, which could not be transmitted by the other functions, or only in a very round-about way. These images have the value of specific insights which have a decisive influence on action whenever intuition is given priority.... The intuitive is never to be found in the world of accepted reality-values, but he has a keen nose for anything new and in the making.

Many intuition trainers, such as Marcia Emery, have developed processes for cultivating this variety of intuition through the use of mental imagery such as visualization.

2. Mental Imagery

Virtually everybody experiences mental imagery in the form of dreams, reveries, visualizations, and imagination. Brain researchers have documented that, in Western culture, logical-linear thought is a product of the brain's left hemisphere while mental imagery occurs when the right hemisphere of the cerebral cortex is active. Mental imagery of this sort has long been associated with intuition, that is, with both holistic solutions to problem solving and with extrasensory information. Research even suggests that visualization can result in dramatic creative breakthroughs among those considered to have learning difficulties and other forms of mental impairment.

3. Common Sense and Social Conditioning

One common-sense view of intuition is that it is simply the unconscious unthinking product of unquestioned habits and social forces. This is what some scientists refer to when they delight in having made a "counter-intuitive" discovery—they are pleased in having discovered the weakness in conventional habits of thought.

4. Subliminal Computation

This is the cognitive science definition that has been promoted by Nobel Laureate Herbert A. Simon who notes that we now have "expert" computer systems that can and do perform a substantial number of human tasks at a professional level: diagnosing illnesses, designing electric motors and transformers, judging credit risks, playing chess, and many others. He suggests that many of these systems simulate the operation of the human brain. This line of reasoning leads him to postulate that the very complex behaviors of human experts—especially their intuitions—can be reduced to a small number of simple computational processes. In an article in *American Psychologist*, he explains expert intuition in the following manner:

> First the expert needs a large memory (some millions of chunks) indexed by a discrimination net (EPAM net) that recognizes a corresponding number of different kinds of stimuli. All studies show that it takes a motivated person at least 10 years of intensive study and practice to acquire this memory store and reach "world-class" level in any domain of expertise. Second the expert needs the ability to solve problems by selective (heuristic) search through spaces of possibilities, using such general heuristic "tricks" as means-ends analysis and such specific ones as the calculus or diagrams or legal reasoning.

In effect, Simon suggests that all of this information processing is taking place at a subconscious level—which is why our intuitions appear mysterious to us. Simon believes that cognitive research has taken the mystery out of intuition. His definition of intuition is consistent with the commonly held notion in many professions that intuition means having the experience and knowledge that provides an overview perspective.

5. Empathy

In psychotherapy as well as in many spiritual traditions, intuition refers to insight, empathy, compassion, and being in the present moment. This means letting go, at least temporarily, of theoretical considerations in order to be able to appreciate what is new and unique in each situation. It means being willing to be vulnerable oneself to the possibility of sharing the emotional pain of another human being. It also means risking the possibility of being seen in one's vulnerability—rather than as an idealized and almost godlike professional. In their chapter later in this volume, Roger Frantz and Alex Pattakos write about Adam Smith, the "founder" of economics, who stated quite clearly that empathy is the moral basis for capitalism and its ability to serve both private and public interests at the same time.

6. Intuitive Software

The computer industry has made wide use of the above definition of intuition in their product descriptions. Here "intuition" refers to products that people can easily use because they conform to current habits of behavior. Computer users, unlike scientists, prefer not to encounter time-consuming, "counterintuitive" discoveries in their new software.

7. Being in the Flow, Perfect Timing, Effortless Humor, Joy, Grace

In sports, intuition often means entering a zone where the correct decisions come effortlessly, powerfully, and without thought. Other traditions suggest that conscious human effort actually interferes with intuition—in a paradoxical way. All seem to agree on the usefulness of discipline and education in cultivating intuition. Yet, the time must come when all rituals, books, and exercises are set aside. This is the time of relaxation and unconscious incubation which is just as necessary for intuitive breakthroughs as is conscious striving.

8. Extrasensory Perception, Clairvoyance, Precognition, Telepathy, etc.

While the existence of ESP abilities is socially controversial, the scientific evidence for such abilities is substantial, if not incontrovertible. The Parapsychological Association, an organization of some 250 scientific researchers, has been affiliated with the American Association for the Advancement of Science since 1969. The U.S. government has been funding research in this field, obtaining consistently positive results continuously for over two decades.

Although we have scientifically established the existence of extrasensory perception, we know very little about how it operates. There is every reason to think that ESP and psi are related to intuition—especially those instances where intuitive knowledge takes on a truly uncanny quality. We also now have a growing body of evidence that extrasensory abilities can be applied for many practical purposes in business and science.

9. Instinct

In biology, intuition refers to our tendency to satisfy our various survival drives. Thus, it is through a process akin to intuition that spiders know how to spin their complex webs; that birds, fish, and butterflies all know how to migrate over vast distances; that chameleons know when and how to change their skin coloring; and that ants and bees know how to form colonies.

10. Pattern Recognition

In criminology and detective work, intuition refers to the ability to notice minute bits of evidence and to make skillful inductive and deductive inferences. A similar skill is required in future forecasting, financial forecasting, and business analysis. In each of these cases, intuition refers to the gift of spotting trends and patterns before they are noticed by others. This ability may result from experience, but in many cases it seems to result from an uncanny "sixth sense" and may actually be an application of extrasensory perception that is still generally unexplored—even by psi researchers.

11. Understanding Language

In linguistics, it is through intuition that we know how to form words and sentences, and how to understand language itself. In normal discourse, we do not consciously decide how to pronounce each individual word and how to string words together into sentences. Nor do we consciously strain to understand the meaning of other native speakers. These things occur automatically at a deep, intuitive level of the brain. They are fundamental to consciousness itself.

12. Apprehension of First Principles

In philosophy, it is from intuition that we develop the premises for our arguments. It is also through intuition that we apprehend space, time, mind, purpose, matter, energy, causation, identity and all a priori principles. In metaphysics and cosmology, intuition provides the means by which we grasp the deep principles that unify the apparent diversity of the manifest world. In political discourse, intuition is sometimes used to refer to following one's best moral and political judgments. These principles—such as justice, equality, freedom, interconnectedness, compassion, beauty, truth, wisdom, loyalty, and goodness—are not at all apparent to the senses. Nor can they be contained within systems of logic. They are transcendental and are best grasped with the heart or with the intuitive mind.

13. Grasping Mathematical Relations

In mathematics, intuition involves visualizing or otherwise apprehending the magical world of numeric and platonic relationships. Such things as pure numbers, ratios, and geometrical shapes are abstractions that do not exist in the material world. Yet, to scientists and mathematicians, these abstractions have a more profound reality than the visible appearances that we experience with our senses. Some mathematicians are even known to have the ability to visualize geometrical shapes in more than three dimensions of space. In fact, the exploration of higher dimensions of space and time seems to be a highly intuitive enterprise that is already promising to solve the major remaining mysteries of unifying the known forces of physics.

14. Connection With One's Essence, Destiny, Purpose, Inner Self

This definition is fundamental to our understanding of intuition, as it pinpoints the primary quest of each individual. Yet, such an inquiry is outside the boundaries of conventional scientific thinking. "Essence, destiny, purpose and inner-self" are concepts that are not recognized as useful by science or by modern, positivist philosophy and behaviorist thought. Thus, an exploration of intuition necessitates an openness to transpersonal, idealistic, and even mystical realms of thought and experience.

15. Mystical Identification With the External World

A corollary to the first definition is the view of yoga philosophy that understanding the essence of an external object follows from the inner process of a mystical identification with the object in a state like dhyana or samadhi. In classical Hindu philosophy, such intuitive states of awareness are described in great detail and precision. The Yoga Sutras of Patanjali refer to discrete states of consciousness in which the disciplined yogi attains an awareness of the essence of things by loosening the normal restrictions of egoic awareness and, in effect, merging with the object of contemplation.

16. Divine Inspiration

A related idea is that of divine inspiration in the arts and sciences, philosophy, and religion. In religion, theology, and spiritual traditions, intuition refers to the apprehension of our relationship to the divine purpose of the universe, to the spirit of creation, and to the mysteries of life. Many individuals of genius also attribute their intuitive inspirations to a divine source outside of normal consciousness—whether a muse, a daemon, an angel, a saint, a spirit guide, or a deity. Modernistic thinking might consider such an attribution to be quaint or superstitious. Yet, modernism itself is a contemporary fad whose social impact is being severely impinged upon by both religious traditionalism and the growing movement toward spiritual creativity. To the extent that a spiritual approach to intuitive creation works, businesses are justified in remaining open-minded. And, if history is any guide, we have every reason to expect that a flexible, spiritual approach to intuition can foster an enormous creative vitality.

17. The Intuitive Balancing Act

Intuition is often a matter of balancing the competing claims on our time and attention, of discovering our values and determining our priorities. These claims are not only external to ourselves, but may also represent the different organ systems of our body, and even the competing structures within our own psyche. It is in this sense that intuition is the expression of our coherence, our oneness, our self.

The seventeen definitions of intuition listed above can be divided into several categories: philosophical, spiritual, and scientific. It is not my intention here to determine which of these approaches is correct or true. From the perspective of the theme of this anthology, I think it is most appropriate to look at the practical consequences of each definition. It turns out, from this analysis, that the different definitions of intuition yield very different heuristic outcomes.

For example, if we take the perspective that intuition reflects a personality trait or style then we will likely favor the tactics developed by management professors Weston Agor (the founder of the Intuition Network) and William Taggart, that suggest we can identify highly intuitive employees in a large organization through a process of personality testing. Such employees can then be given special assignments that require rapid problem solving and creativity. In addition, strategies can be developed to shield such employees from the negativism of their fellow employees who may not share or understand the unconventional thought processes utilized by those who achieve high scores on the various intuitive measurement scales.

On the other hand, the model proposed by Herbert Simon that what we call intuition is a reflection of subliminal mental calculations has very different practical outcomes. This approach provides encouragement for those who would build robots and computers that can simulate human styles of expertise. The proponents of "expert systems," artificial intelligence, and robotics are almost all unanimous in their view that mechanical systems will be developed that can simulate human intuition in every way. Another corollary of this view, held by Dr. Daniel Cappon, is that by subjecting intuition to microscopic analysis, we will develop more effective techniques for helping non-intuitive individuals cultivate these abilities.

I am especially fascinated by the definition that relates intuition to research in clairvoyance, precognition, and telepathy. When we can probe the farther reaches of the human mind, we are exploring the very limits of human nature, and come to learn a great deal about ourselves in the process. However, the practical applications of psi abilities have significant, and very real, short-term consequences for our social and business interests. Today, there are about a dozen small organizations offering psi consulting services to government and business. The services they provide range from military intelligence operations to financial forecasting to aiding police departments find missing persons. The situation is analogous to the state of the computer industry fifty years ago or the automobile industry one hundred years ago.

My reading of the reliability and validity of psi research suggests that the aforementioned analogy is especially apt. Therefore, I conclude that in the next fifty to one hundred years, we will see our society changed by psi-related, intuitive technologies at least as much as automobiles and computers have already changed our civilization. The Intuition Network is interested in playing a significant role in the development of this new industry. For example, a successful pilot study of psi-related, intuitive application in financial forecasting written by four members of the Intuition Network Advisory Board was published in the *Journal of Scientific Exploration* in 1995. This research implies the possibility that, after over one hundred years, psi research is well-positioned for a breakthrough that will bring it squarely into the mainstream of our culture. If so, this perspective on intuition will assume enormous importance during the next fifty years.

The viewpoint that intuition is part of the soul's deepest wisdom suggests a direction whose practical applications are probably noticeable only in the long term. Those who cultivate the spiritual aspects of intuition within the workplace may find themselves concerned more with the thrust and purpose of their entire career than with innovative problem solving. They are the ones who will be taking a stance on issues relating to the environment, to compassion for all social classes, and to the importance of ethics and integrity in business. They will be less concerned with improving our present ways of doing business then with developing entire new industries and lifestyle options. Ultimately, in my view, it is this definition of intuition that is likely to have the greatest impact upon our culture.

Edith Jurka, MD, is a physician, board certified in Psychiatry and Neurology. Her work has included psychotherapy in New York City. Her patients have often been high achievers in their work, who realized that they were not achieving their full potential and had problems in their emotional relationships. Helping these patients requires an understanding of the unconscious mind, which is also the messenger of intuition.

Jurka developed an individualized program to train a lifestyle maximizing intuition, and even built a house with special facilities for this program, including a Faraday Cage. It includes physical exercise programs, brain wave function and training, psychological patterns, and meditation techniques, as well as knowledge about intuition. Among her other qualifications, she studied physical chemistry with a Nobel Prize winner, then received her degree in medicine from the Yale University School of Medicine, where she has been given a Distinguished Alumni Award. She is also listed in *Who's Who in America*.

2

Sources, Brain Routes, And Manifestations Of Intuition

Edith Jurka

This essay explores the origins of intuition and the many forms that it can take in coming to our attention. It also approaches the sources of intuition from a number of different perspectives, and tries to help the reader determine which avenues for manifesting intuition are most natural for him or her. Because the author is a medical doctor trained in psychiatry and neurology, the essay contains material drawn from both disciplines and draws heavily from the author's clinical and related experiences.

Languages Of Intuition

The vehicle for intuition is obviously the brain, but also the body and the mind, and largely the unconscious mind. Of the three evolutionary developments of the brain (as we shall discuss in more detail later), that in reptiles, in animals, and in humans, it is the second stage, i.e., the *limbic brain*, that is the main source of intuition. It is here where emotional memories are stored, and where connections with the physiological processes of the body are made. There is still another source of intuition, variously referred to as the universal mind or consciousness. In this essay, the reader will become acquainted with the many forms which intuition can take, including the

17

various paths in the brain which intuition uses.

Thousands of years ago people understood the function of intuition as protection. The concept of intuition, in fact, is derived from its Latin and old French roots: in = inside, and *tuicion* = to watch, guard, protect. Our modern definition, according to *Webster's* dictionary, is "immediate cognition; the power of knowing without recourse to inference or reasoning." A dictionary definition of *tuition* is the "act of teaching or instruction," or more usually now, the payment for the instruction. Bringing the ideas of instruction from the inside and the power derived from intuition fits our experience that knowledge is power. Moreover, information can be an important source of protection, even if, in the case of intuition, we somehow cannot see where it comes from. Intuitive people tend to perceive and understand much more of what is going on around them than others, most of it going into their memories unconsciously. Intuition, then, is an unconscious, specialized source of information. Some of it comes from putting together information already in our unconscious minds, but not all of it.

In modern times, there are many occasions when intuition has warned people of danger, so they avoided travel on a certain day or meeting with certain people. I had an experience which illustrates the idea that intuition protects. It also helps illustrate an important source of intuition, which is information from what many call universal intelligence or universal consciousness, a concept Carl Jung promoted.

Once I was in Cairo, Egypt, planning to go to an important appointment in London. Two days before my flight, the idea entered my head that the plane I was to take would crash in France. I didn't know whether to believe it or not. Here is where past experience with one's intuition can be a help. Sometimes what seems like intuition is really the expression of a hope or fear, and not intuition at all. I have never had a fear of flying. Also, this wasn't just a feeling that the plane would crash. It was *specific* information that the plane would crash over France. As you can imagine, it makes sense not to take the risk. I went to a travel agent to see if I could fly to London via Spain or Denmark. But there were no such flights from Cairo. On the scheduled morning I went to the Cairo Airport, hoping my warning was not valid intuition. As I entered I heard an announcement that the flight I was to take had been delayed. Well, that is not unusual. But all day, while I was waiting in that hot, crowded, dirty airport, sitting on an iron bench, they kept repeating, without any explanation, that the flight was delayed. Finally, about 6 p.m., they announced that the plane had left London, was flying to Cairo, would refuel, and return to London.

Because I am writing this account, you obviously have proof that the plane arrived in London safely. Still, I eventually learned the reason for the delay. As the plane was about to leave London, they noticed something very seriously wrong with the engines. The defect was so complicated in fact that they had to send for special engineers to fix it. Their trips to Heathrow Airport and their work had taken the entire day!

An experience like this arouses so many questions. Was my intuition wrong? Or did I correctly intuit something which, at the time I sensed it, was really ready to happen? Why didn't I intuit correctly that the flight would have trouble and be late, but not crash? Is there some higher intelligence capable of modifying what would be the usual cause and effect? Was some higher intelligence "watching, guarding, and protecting" me and others? And why isn't everybody always protected? Could it be that it is for people who have active communication with a higher dimension, whose brains keep their *delta* brain frequencies active, as I will explain later?

It is experiences like this that require one to add a study of metaphysics to his or her training in neurology and psychiatry in order to have a more complete understanding of the mind's capabilities and how the mind interacts with a higher dimension of consciousness. Can the fact that time is not linear in a higher dimension, as described by physicists, help explain precognition such as I and many others have had? Some people receive more of their intuitive ideas from this higher consciousness than others. I have a friend who doesn't use a map when he drives long distances. He just calls on his intuition when he comes to a crossroads to learn which way to turn.

Carl Jung's concept of synchronicity arouses the same questions about time being non-linear and a higher intelligence in another dimension. Synchronicity (*syn* = together and *chronos* = time) is loosely defined as uncanny coincidences that have no apparent causal connection, but can turn out to be very influential in the lives of people experiencing them. We are all very familiar with the effects of synchronicity, even though we don't call it that, and miss a lot of evidence about it if we are not on the lookout for it. Dramatic plots in plays and novels are full of people meeting by chance in places where they would not ordinarily have been at that time, and ending up spending their lives together. The more one's perception and intuition are *alive*, the more can one be aware and make use of the synchronicity which is around us.

Intuition can exercise its protective functions for dangers that are not physical. At work there is often a competitive situation. We might have to prevent others from unfairly taking credit for our contributions. We need to see to it that our good ideas are recognized, accepted, and applied. Intuition can be very helpful in choosing the best new employee. And it can warn of any dangers regarding our own positions or jobs.

Crucial to having the help of intuition at work is to ask for it. When you go to a store or restaurant you won't get anything unless you ask for it. And you won't even be there in the first place unless you want something that they provide. So for intuition to work *at work*, or for any personal project, you need to have a goal or an achievement in mind. And you still won't get anywhere unless you have the enthusiasm and energy to go ahead with it. So here is a seven step sequence for getting and using intuitive help with planning or problem solving:

1. Feel enthusiastic and energetic about a project or problem.
2. Collect all relevant factual information.
3. Define the area of the desired understanding.
4. Assign the search to the unconscious mind and give it time to develop the insights. (This could be hours, days or even weeks.)
5. Consciously receive the insight from the unconscious mind. (See further in this essay for 15 possible ways this can happen.)
6. Interpret the intuitive message into rational under-standing.
7. Use logical analysis to turn the intuitive information into action.

Let us now look into the source of intuition in terms we are familiar with. We say it comes "out of the blue." "Out of the blue" suggests that we believe it comes out of the sky, from some power located in the universe. But some of us can't believe in anything that cannot be proven by recognized scientific techniques.

In this regard, I happen to come from a family of two generations of scientists and have studied physical chemistry with a Nobel Prize winner, which is a "purer" kind of science. Medical school is full of scientific facts you have to learn. But all of this has not convinced me, as it has some scientists, that scientifically unexplainable phenomena cannot exist. Quite the contrary, the enormous advances in scientific research in this century have convinced me that there must be natural laws which can explain these phenomena; they just haven't been discovered yet.

Before Einstein's theory we did not know about the quantum physics which elucidate our material world. Now about a thousand physicists are researching higher dimensions of energy which they call *superstrings*. Jonas Salk, who developed a polio vaccine, also wrote about the next stage of human evolution which he believed to be higher levels of consciousness rather than some physical change in human beings. We already have a preview of this in people who have advanced psychic abilities. If some humans are capable of this, all of us must have this inherent capacity, just as we were born with intuitive ability.

Very young children love fantasy, through which they make their own images and feel as if they are real. To them many toys and animals have human personalities. Just think of television programs made for children such as *Sesame Street,* as well as new movies like *Toy Story.* As they grow older, children have to adapt to reality instead of fantasy in their daily lives. In school—at least in traditional educational settings—educators train children's left brains, but children's intuitive right brains get much less attention and training.

For centuries, people have been getting accurate, needed information from a source other than their fellow humans. In looking for an explanation, the only one I can find is that some form of higher intelligence exists which we can tune into when we have the need. An example is the process of *dowsing.* For those of you who are not familiar with the word "dowser," it means someone who finds out where in the earth to dig for a supply of water. The dowser walks over the area, in his or her mind asking for that information, holding a forked stick out in front, which will move when the spot for the well has been found. People in

Germany have been doing this for centuries. For them, the stick often flips up against their chests with such force that they wear leather vests to protect themselves. With Americans the stick usually bends down instead, and it usually isn't a stick, but a plastic substitute of some kind.

Now, here are some questions without the answers. What is the route through the brain that makes the dowsers' muscles move so strongly? And what enters the brain at the exact moment they are over the water source to make it happen?

I have a dowsing friend who is a retired banker. He has been dowsing since the age of six, when a dowser came to his parents' home in Vermont to find where they should dig for a well. One day he was visiting me and said that the water in my house had too much iron in it. It came from a well 400 feet down that was dug ten years before with seven gallons a minute, but seemed to be getting less. He said, "Let me find you a much better well." He went outside, wandered around, and in ten minutes came back with the news that on the several acres that were not woods, there were only two places where water was running close to the surface. I went out with him, and we had fun confirming his dowsing. We put a stake where the well diggers should dig. We dowsed on that spot where 90 feet down two underground streams crossed that would bring 12 gallons per minute.

A few days later I arrived home at noon to find that the well diggers had already reached 90 feet and water was pouring out of the hole. They were in a state of shock that what I had told them was not only true, but so accurate—where to dig, how far down to go, and how much water they would get. Dowsers also ask about the quality of the water.

More evidence that it is the mind and not the body that receives this very specific dowsing information is that my dowser friend has found well sites in South America for companies like Coca-Cola which needed tons of water. But he did not have to be present in South America to do this. He stays home in Pennsylvania with a detailed map of the area and dowses from the map, using a pendulum as an indicator. Is there anything more amazing than that? But it is routine among advanced dowsers. Some don't need any dowsing indicator, they just "know" when they have reached the spot they need.

We don't have to depend only on the universal mind for our intuitive information, however. We create a lot of this information from memories we have put into our own unconscious minds. That is why it is the habit of very intuitive people to notice details of what is going on around them—sights and sounds of their physical surroundings, the activities, needs, and feelings of the people around them, and the overall atmosphere of a situation. You have probably often joined a group of people and noticed that there was tension "in the air" or that everyone seemed more comfortable together.

When we want our unconscious minds to put together ideas and facts in an unusual, creative way, the more memory material we have stored and integrated in our minds' warehouses, the better it will be. The information used by your intuition can also come from subtle hints that most people may not have noticed.

Levels Of Organic Brain Evolution

In the evolution on the planet of which we are now the most advanced form of life, reptiles were the first living things to have brains. The most basic part of our brains is like theirs, hence called the *reptilian* part of the brain. Reptiles do not even control their body temperature, and probably don't have any warmth of feeling either.

The next level of brain evolution added both of these—body temperature control and feelings—and that was attributed to mammals. Think how emotionally attached to their masters dogs are, and vice-versa. There was a dog who couldn't be found at the time his family moved to another state. A year and one-half later he turned up at their new home one thousand miles away, thin, tattered and exhausted. That this is can happen indicates that a dog's brain may process information from a higher source, in order for him to be guided over a long, complicated route to a specific place. In addition, this particular dog was pushed by powerful emotional memories of a family he wanted to be with again. He had added a whole area of brain to that of reptiles, which we call the *mammalian* brain, or which in human anatomy is referred to as the *limbic system*.

The dog's experience shows us which of our functions our limbic brain performs. It also demonstrates that intuitive information can be received without using the cerebral cortex, even though the latter makes up 80 percent of the weight of the brain. The human brain weighs three pounds; in these three pounds are 10 billion cells. Nature is way ahead of computer science in putting maximal function into minimal space. This three percent of a hundred pound body uses twenty percent of the oxygen we breathe and it doesn't have a muscle to move. There is still so much we don't know about the brain!

We have evidence of how important the limbic brain is because it is unusually well supplied with blood. The limbic brain directs a whole second nervous system which is outside the head. It is called the autonomic nervous system, and it regulates and balances the physiology of the body with the help of the endocrine glands.

For balance, like on a see-saw, you need two opposing weights. In our bodies, one side is the sympathetic nervous system which uses adrenaline as a fuel. It serves to maintain a sufficient level of body energy and supplies extra energy if danger is perceived, or if an interesting or exciting experience occurs. The balance on the see-saw is the parasympathetic nervous system. Its fuel is acetylcholine. Its job is to do maintenance and repair, especially when the body is at rest. The emotions, the physiology of the body, and messages from the "universal mind" are all processed in the limbic system.

You can see how emotions, as well as intuitive messages, are expressed through the body. If people get embarrassed, an extra supply of blood makes the face red. Later in this essay, I share a personal case demonstrating how intuition activated a compulsion to do something that was very needed even though there was nothing in my mind to indicate why.

The third evolutionary addition to the brain is the brain *cortex*, by far the largest part of the brain in humans. It is where we receive and process information through our five senses. The cortex processes language, as well as analyzes and integrates facts. These functions are highly localized, as has been demonstrated by brain imaging. A lot of cortex space is taken up by nerves connecting various parts of the cortex with each other and with the limbic system. The cortex stores a vast number of immediately available facts and understandings. The prefrontal cortex is the decision making area of the brain. Emotions, as well as facts, values, and conscience, collect there to contribute to decisions. There must be a dysfunction in emotions as well as in the prefrontal cortex when people cannot stop themselves from drinking, smoking, doing drugs, gambling, even when they know how harmful these activities can be.

Memory storage sites in the cortex are located close to the areas where the impressions enter the brain—for example, the visual in the occipital, and the auditory in the temporal lobes. Related bits of memory are distributed widely in the cortex and limbic system, and are so interconnected that one piece of visual information (e.g., rain outside) can light up evidence of brain memory activity on brain scans in many locations. More intuitive people tend to notice more of these stimuli, record more memories, and have a larger supply of them to put facts together in a creative way.

Receiving Intuitive Messages

Having described sources of intuitive information, the following is a list of 15 forms by which intuitive messages can be received. I am sure there are more. They come in three different ways. Note that sometimes they take a detour through the limbic system and are expressed through the body; sometimes the outside world originates them.

A. *Through the mind*—something specific or a gradual clarification of a complicated situation.

1. a "hunch"
2. a symbolic message in the form of an image, a memory, a song
3. a relevant dream
4. internal seeing or hearing
5. a significant insight that pops suddenly into one's mind
6. a new realization of how disparate ideas are connected (this is the mechanism of creativity)
7. a gradual awareness of how certain knowledge elucidates a situation or indicates how to proceed
8. awareness that events are flowing in a certain direction
9. a glimpse of the big picture

B. *Body and feeling changes*

10. a muscle contraction or a sudden upset stomach
11. an energy increase relative to an action to be taken or an energy decrease

      12. unexpected changes in one's feelings about a situation

C. *Experiences one didn't initiate*

      13. a synchronistic experience

      14. an unhappy experience (like a job loss which may lead to a better job)

      15. all options but one in a situation disappear

Some of these forms are more familiar and frequent than others. Let me give you an example of an infrequent one—Number 11, a body energy increase relative to an action to be taken.

One day I had a compulsion so strong to do something that I couldn't postpone it for even ten minutes, and couldn't understand why. I had two coffee tables with stains from glasses on them, which I wanted to take to a furniture repairer I knew. I had postponed doing it for months, because there always seemed to be something more important to do. This particular afternoon I arrived home and was unable to do anything else before I took those tables over to Mr. H. Since I had a lot of vegetables in the garden, I picked him a selection, including a red cabbage.

When I arrived at Mr. H's shop, I found him in a terrible condition emotionally. A growth over his spine, which he had ignored, had just been found to be cancer. He was very frightened, and all alone since he is Austrian and his family still lives in Austria. It was then that I realized why my intuition had come to me in such a forceful way—not an idea, not an understanding, but a compulsion to take a certain action instantly, which I didn't understand. But then I realized that I was the one person he knew who could comfort him in a variety of ways. I am a medical doctor he could ask about his cancer. I am a psychiatrist who could help him with his emotions. And there were ways in which I could help him recreate the reassuring emotional atmosphere of his childhood home. In this regard, I am the only person around who can speak to him in his native German. And, interestingly enough, I had brought him red cabbage, which he said his mother used to serve in the most delicious way.

So what caused my compulsion? It could be that Mr. H. thought he would like to see me, but he didn't telephone. The drive was so strong in me that I think there must have been some benevolent universal mind stimulating it.

Levels of Consciousness

There are ways to increase one's intuitive ability. An important factor is increasing the ease of communication between our conscious and unconscious minds. Sigmund Freud, back in the beginning of this century, defined three levels of consciousness. *Full consciousness* is what one is paying attention to at the moment. *Subconsciousness* is what one is not thinking about at the moment, but can bring to consciousness. *Unconsciousness* is that which one is not able to bring to consciousness. An additional category, in my opinion, involves memories which one can re-experience in a state of hypnosis.

To be sure, there has been a lot of research done on the broad subject of consciousness. Dr. Willis Harman, President of the Institute of Noetic Sciences (an entity that is focused in this area), has been researching consciousness for years. Dr. Maxwell Cade of London, has spent his life trying to find out in scientific terms what are the characteristics of higher levels of consciousness. Dr. Cade developed a special double electroencephalograph to help monitor electrical impulses in both hemispheres of the brain during different states of consciousness. This approach permitted him to study what was going on in the right and left brains separately and simultaneously. He called it the *Mind Mirror*.

Dr. Cade's device records brain wave frequencies from .75 Hertz (i.e., cycles per second) up to 38 Hertz. The recordings are arranged in fourteen horizontal rows of diodes, representing fourteen different brain wave frequencies. At the same time, they register at each frequency the power in microvolts being used, by how far from the center the diode is lit in each line. The zero power for each electroencephalograph is in the center where they meet. So it ends up with a line of lights in a pattern for each side of the brain (see Figure 1).

The fastest brain waves are called *beta* (more than 13 cycles per second), and are what we use during our ordinary waking consciousness. If we do mental arithmetic, for instance, we use beta only on the left side, because it is logical, unemotional thinking. When we dream, we are in *theta*, which is down to a frequency of about 4-8 cycles per second. Then there is the *alpha* state (8-13 cps), when we are quiet mentally, but not asleep.

The most interesting frequency for us is *delta*, which is on the border of no electrical brain activity at all, i.e., less than 4 cps.

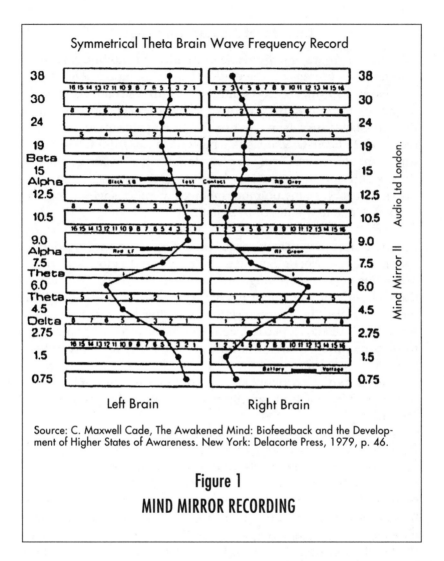

Figure 1

MIND MIRROR RECORDING

I have measured on the Mind Mirror a number of dowsers and other highly intuitive people and they have active delta waves *all* the time. Normally we have them only when we are in deep, non-dreaming sleep. You might say that intuitive people have an antenna that reaches out to receive messages from a dimension beyond the electromagnetic spectrum, and that this is facilitated when we are in deep sleep.

Dr. Cade found that people capable of advanced states of consciousness, like the yogis who visited him in London, produced *combinations* of brain wave frequencies, not just one group of frequencies at a time like most of us do. Moreover, these advanced people used all four frequencies all day while they were awake, with equal microvolt power per frequency on *both* sides of the brain. So it is possible to distinguish brain from mind, and the Mind Mirror shows how they can be separate. In this regard, when people's minds have been projected out of their bodies, their brains show no microvoltages at all on the Mind Mirror. Figure 2 diagrams a variety of adult mind state "prototypes" as seen on the Mind Mirror, including those considered to be *advanced* states of consciousness.

One day I was using the Mind Mirror with a group of interested people. There was a large man in the group who said he was often "out of body," and presumably had been earlier in the day while he was in our presence. Of course, I was very skeptical about this information; but, there he was, connected to the Mind Mirror, and there was no voltage. I whispered this to someone sitting next to me. The man evidently heard me, because he said, "You want voltage?" and the Mind Mirror exploded with voltage. Had he kept his mind in the room even though it was not using his brain? Such experiences only show us how much more we need to learn about the different and separate functions of the brain and mind. The implication is strong that we share the vibratory frequencies of a higher dimension.

Even surgeons believe in an out-of-body state. Some people who were operated on under anesthesia describe having their minds out of their bodies, but near the ceiling watching what is going on. Afterwards, they have been angry at the surgeon if— *during the operation*—he had said something uncomplimentary about them, such as that they were so fat they made the operation difficult. Surgeons especially avoid saying anything that indicates that the prognosis is poor.

Intuition At The Crossroads

As a psychiatrist, I am constantly intrigued with how idio-syncratic our subjective impressions are. It seems that we go through three "crossroads" in absorbing and processing an experience, and at each one we differ more extensively from what other people have understood from the experience. The first crossroads is that we *perceive differently.* The second is that we *interpret differently* what we have selected to perceive. The third is that we take away *different understandings* of the experience.

For example, we could all go to the same market to buy food

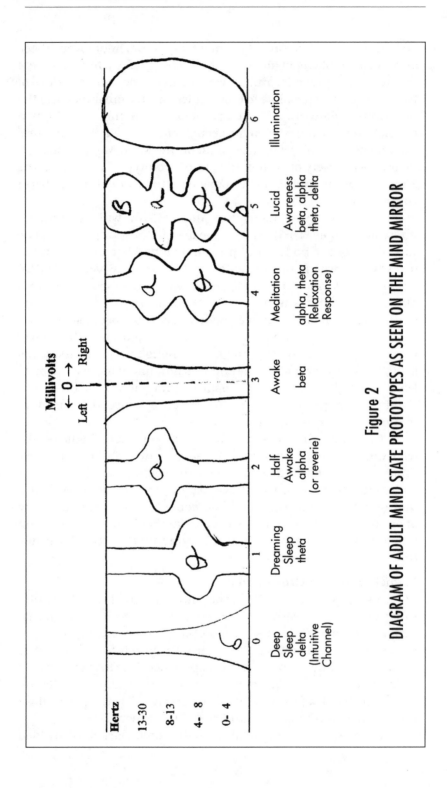

Figure 2

DIAGRAM OF ADULT MIND STATE PROTOTYPES AS SEEN ON THE MIND MIRROR

for a dinner party. We would likely buy different selections of food. Then we might cook them differently. Then, of the people who eat the meal, some would like it and others might think it was too spicy. Then there might be vegetarians who would not eat certain foods. We all started in the same place with the same intention of buying food for a meal, and ended up with different dining experiences.

When I visited India, I was looking forward to having a wonderful vegetarian diet. With the first mouthful I thought my mouth was on fire, and that was the end of my eating Indian food. What I had not realized was that in a hot climate with no refrigeration for hundreds of millions of people, food spoiled quickly, and to mask that unpleasant taste strong spices are needed.

So, on entering a situation, what we perceive varies in selection and amount. It depends on how much and in what way(s) a situation matters to us, and how much knowledge we bring to it. Think what a mechanic perceives about a machine he needs to fix, compared with someone who knows nothing about machines. It also depends upon whether a person's habit in life is to perceive much or little.

At the second crossroads of an experience we interpret what we have selected out to perceive. A prize fight may be so interesting to millions of people that they will pay $45 to watch one on television. I interpret a prize fight as an activity whose goal is to make the opponent unconscious with a knockout blow, thus damaging his brain, maybe for the rest of his life. I consider music amplified above 100 decibels to be bad because it causes deafness. But some health clubs must consider it good, because they play background music that loudly all day. This is not to mention people who go to rock band concerts.

Our emotions and values can give us idiosyncratic interpretations. Sixty years ago, many Germans saw a swastika as inspiring; most of us interpret it as horror. Once, while living abroad, I unexpectedly saw an American flag in a parade, and was surprised to find that I interpreted it with such strong positive emotions that I had tears in my eyes. Here was my limbic system at work, registering my emotions and producing a body reaction that bypassed my conscious cortical thinking.

The third crossroads is the understanding we take away from an experience. There are many reasons why people go away with different understandings of the same experience. Someone who brings a background of related knowledge to a speech likely will go away with more additional understanding than someone who does not. One's racial, ethnic, and cultural background frequently has a huge influence on this experience too.

Using the three crossroads concept, let us apply this frame of reference to a business situation. There is a manager who has a meeting to plan a new project. His personality and habit are to lead and be obeyed. He feels that he knows more than all the others about the project. So he pays very little attention to their ideas and does not solicit their feedback. He doesn't notice their feelings or their negative reactions to some of what he says. Thus, he gets no benefit from the knowledge from their different specific experiences, which he did not share. He loses their good will. He leaves the meeting with the understanding that his new project will be successful. He could be wrong. The knowledge of others at the meeting about difficulties for the project was not considered. The people whose job would be to work on the project could believe in it so little that it would fail. They could feel so unappreciated and unvalued that they could cause it to fail, even though they were not consciously trying to make that happen.

This example illustrates a manager with very little intuition compounded by an overly strong ego. Therefore, he misses information and clues that could be useful to him. In my practice, I have found that the private emotional life of such a person is restricted and not very interesting. By comparison, an intuitive person is usually comfortable with him or herself, enthusiastic, curious, interested in observing life and learning, caring and noticing how other people feel, including what they need and enjoy, and has interesting goals to work toward and fill his or her life. An intuitive person has a sense of having more ultimate control and advantages in life. Intuition and right brain functioning add creativity, humor, ability to solve problems, reach goals, and manage people more effectively. And let us not forget that the ancient meaning of intuition is that it watches, guards and protects.

Improving Your Intuition

Here is a three-step process for improving your intuition. First, we must believe that the process of intuition exists, welcome it when it comes to us, and seek it when logical available answers aren't enough. Second, it is important to be on the lookout for intuitive messages (refer back to the fifteen kinds) and expect them. Third, keep a record of your intuitive experiences to learn which of its receiving forms are more natural for you. Your written record has the advantage of adding to the evidence, and therefore to your confidence, that your intuition is improving and becoming more reliable.

How do intuitive messages reach our consciousness? The fact that dreams provide intuitive-type information and that we need to be asleep to have dreams shows us how waking consciousness thinking can act like a road block to intuitive ideas getting through. It explains why people meditate to get ideas. When we clear the mind from outside stimuli and conscious mind chatter, we open the door to our intuitive selves. That is why listening to classical music or engaging in physical activity helps to clear the mind. Techniques for increasing right brain functioning are important. The right cortex has many more connections with the limbic system and the unconscious mind than the left cortex, which is filled with language and logical thinking all day. A picture can stimulate emotions much more reflexively than words, and can contain more details and implications than a thousand words. The mode of right brain conceptualization is images, which is why symbolic images can be an intuitive message.

Being in an environment that eliminates electromagnetic waves, such as that used to protect some computers, is the ultimate way to increase connection with a higher consciousness. It eliminates background electromagnetic noise from all the radio and other waves in our surroundings which our ears don't hear, but our minds perceive. Telepathic messages are more clearly perceived in such "clean" environments (e.g., one of these is called a Faraday Cage). In any event, creating a milieu or atmosphere that facilitates the use of intuition is especially important in the contemporary world of "busy-ness." For intuition at work *to work*, the pathways to whole-brain, whole-person functioning must be open.

Intuition is a crucial factor if you wish to maximize your protection, success, and richness of life. The limbic part of the brain and its storage of emotional memories is a central path of intuition. Right cortical brain function is an integrator of concepts for new ideas and plans. There are at least fifteen forms in which intuitive information can reach conscious awareness, and by paying more detailed attention to what is going on in our minds and bodies, and in our surroundings, we can find those forms which are most natural and useful to ourselves. This will greatly increase our capabilities and our joy in life.

Joel Levey, PhD, is co-founder of Seattle-based InnerWork Technologies, Inc., a firm that specializes in building and renewing organizational cultures in which team spirit, community, creative intelligence, and authentic leadership thrive. His clients include Hewlett-Packard, AT&T, Bell Labs, Du Pont, Weyerhaeuser, Travelers Insurance, Petro-Canada, and NASA. His work was recognized by US Army West Point logisticians as "The most exquisite orchestration of human technology we have ever seen."

Joel and his wife Michelle are co-authors of *Quality of Mind: Tools for Self Mastery & Enhanced Performance* and Nightingale Conant's best-selling business audio program *The Focused Mindstate*. They are contributing authors for numerous works including *Learning Organizations: Developing Cultures for Tomorrow's Workplace; Community Building: Renewing Spirit & Learning in Business; Rediscovering the Soul of Business;* and *The New Bottom Line.*

3

Mind Treasure: Intuitive Wisdom And The Dynamics Of Mystery And Mastery At Work

Joel Levey

The more and more you listen,
The more and more you will hear.
The more you hear,
The more and more deeply you will understand.
— Kyentse Rinpoche

Visionary Research

During a visionary research process at a leading chemical manufacturing plant, a project manager commented, "I do not have much of an imagination, and I am not very intuitive, but I did smell something in that visionary exercise." This observation triggered a chain of associations and inquiries that led to identifying a waste gas from a chemical processing plant that, when captured, turned into a multi-million-dollar new business. From this we are reminded never to underestimate the power of sharing a hunch and working it through collective intuition.

Indeed, I have had many opportunities to observe the power of hunches and collective intuition in the workplace through my own work as a researcher and consultant. One of the most inspiring examples of intuition in my work was a pioneering two-year research project at Weyerhaeuser. Understanding that research methods could be dramatically accelerated by tapping intuition and developing creative intelligence, Jon Dunnington, the program leader, invited me to coach his team in the personal and team skills necessary to succeed in "visionary research." The intent of this project was to discover and demonstrate the power and potential of new ways of thinking and knowing that could help R&D teams achieve a higher level of performance and make breakthroughs that would help build a better world.

We took to heart Einstein's statement that, "The world we have made as a result of the level of the thinking we have done thus far creates problems that we cannot solve at the same level at which we have created them.... We shall require a substantially new manner of thinking if humankind is to survive."

For two years, the members of our team met every other week to search for breakthrough ideas. The results of this process were astounding. We learned that the questions we held in our minds would organize our attention. We also learned that the quality and scope of our individual and shared intention determined the questions we asked. People on the team were inspired and excited by the consistency of results and the implications for greater creativity.

"Our questions were at times like heartfelt prayers," one person said. "In the silence of our deep listening together, it was as though each of us had learned to push the pause button on the stories we keep telling ourselves about who we are. In this state of deep-shared listening, we were both many and one. We were like many islands meeting at their common roots, deep under the surface of the sea.

Another example of our visionary research process on this project involved one of the leaders of an aqua-culture project. He began by discussing his quandary over the disappointing rate of spawning of salmon in rehabilitated streams. No one knew why so few salmon were returning. In search of clues, he invited us to join him on an imaginary journey through the life cycle of a salmon. He painted a vivid picture of our life in the hatchery, being loaded into a truck, and set loose in the river. Then, as we approached the mouth of the river and encountered salt water for the first time, he set our imagination and intuition loose to explore the many forces that might shape our lives as salmon and determine if we would return to spawn or not.

Surfacing from this long, deep dive, we took time to jot or doodle our impressions and then to discuss insights that had come to mind. Some of us described the trauma of being loaded and unloaded into the truck that took us from the hatchery to the river. Others had valuable insights regarding moving from fresh water into the salt water of the open ocean. Others offered possible clues about conditions at sea that might affect our life cycle and spawning rates. Together, these many pieces formed a picture that offered an inspiring number of valuable and unexpected insights for increasing the successful release and return of the salmon. Similar intuitive approaches consistently proved fruitful on many other projects related to forest products, land management, and resource issues over the years that we worked together.

Working in this way, each person's insights offered a clue or elicited an insight from others. Our inquiry would build naturally upon itself like atoms coalescing into a complex "thought molecule." Ideas led to questions, to intuitions, explanations, and finally applications. It seemed that if we could have harnessed the power unleashed by the joy and wonder in this work, we could have lit up the world. Indeed, this *was* intuition at work!

The answers to our questions were often surprising and unexpected. As one team member reminded us, quoting the respected Benedictine sage, Brother David Steindl-Rast, "Another name for God is surprise!" At times, this notion rang so true that we were left stunned into a deeply-reverent shared silence. Often we talked about what it would be like to focus these individual and collective skills toward addressing some of the really big challenges facing humanity. At times, we sensed that our research work—this remarkable experiment in deep, shared intuitive inquiry—was creating a story that would offer inspiration, courage, and guidance for other R&D teams for decades to come. Though the challenges were great, the Ocean of Wisdom seemed intent on splashing itself into our minds as a deeply intuitive knowing. This would come through our thoughts and dreams. It would provide business solutions and personal inspirations that mere observation or logical analysis could never have yielded.

Aspiration And Inspiration

There is no inspiration,
without aspiration.
—Tagor

In our work we are often asked to help leaders and teams develop the personal and interpersonal skills necessary for breakthroughs in creativity, intuition, and performance. Our success in this work lies largely in the methods and mental models we use. Central to all of these models are the complementary themes of aspiration and inspiration, creativity and receptivity, active and quiet mind skills, mastery and mystery.

Rabbi Zalman Schachter once helped me to understand the relationship between the active and receptive dynamics of questioning, prayer, and intuition. He reminded me that our lives are filled with prayers, albeit mostly unconscious ones. When we are hungry, our prayer for food organizes our attention to look for restaurants, or fruit trees, or whiffs of dinner on the wind. When we are lonesome, our prayer for companionship organizes our attention to notice people who have partners and those who are potentially available.

Our questions—conscious or unconscious, spoken or unspoken, individual or collective—are prayers, aspirations, and yearnings that infallibly organize our attention. Our questions make us more intuitively receptive to inspiration in whatever forms it may take. As our understanding of this process deepens, we discover that we live in a responsive universe. If you drop a little stone in the pool it sends out and draws back a little wave. If you drop a big stone in the pool, it sends out and draws back a big wave. The moment there is a yearning in our hearts or a question in our minds—consciously or unconsciously—there are echoes of information intuitively available to us. The answer or clues might be revealed in the patterns of a cloud, in a bird's song, or by what a person three seats away is saying. As we learn to listen more deeply, we discover that the answers to our question are always here, though often our "circuits" are usually too jammed to hear them.

Moment to moment, the mystery reveals itself to us, and through the experiences of our lives we intuitively discern the answers to our deepest questions and most heartfelt prayers. As a great Persian poet reminds us, "When you search for the

Beloved, It is the intensity of the longing that does all the work. Look at me and you will see a slave of that intensity."

The Dual Path Of Wisdom

The Dual Path of Wisdom presented below is a powerful conceptual tool for understanding the interplay of creativity and receptivity necessary for intuitive insight at every level of human affairs. Just as our path through life is woven of the complementary paths of our left and right feet, the Dual Path of Wisdom is composed of two complementary paths (see Figure 1):

- The Path of Mystery: Insight and Discovery
- The Path of Mastery: Innovation & Development

Viewed in detail, the synergy of these paths can be applied to organizational learning by addressing the potentials for insight, intuition, and innovation across nine interrelated domains.

The Nine Domains Of Intuition And Innovation

Briefly summarized, these nine domains can be viewed in the following way. Every human being has a deep yearning for a high quality of life (Quality of Life). To realize this we rely on ourselves and others to provide quality goods and services (Quality of Products) by doing quality work (Quality of Work). In an increasingly interconnected world, doing quality work requires building and maintaining quality working relationships (Quality of Relationships). These, in turn, reflect the quality of our actions (Quality of Action) and communications, the Quality of our Personal Energy Management, the quality of our Active Mind Skills (i.e., thinking, reasoning, intention, imagination), the quality of our Quiet Mind Skills (i.e., attention, mindfulness, sensing, etc.), and the quality or depth of wisdom (Quality of Wisdom, i.e., intuitive insight, sense of whole systems, and compassion) that we bring to our life and work.

The Quality of Wisdom is the foundation of these nine domains. Our intuitive ability to tap wisdom is determined first by the quality of our Quiet Mind Skills and then, enhanced and expressed as intuitive insight, incorporates the faculties of each successive level above. To the degree that we have developed any of the fundamental skills or qualities listed in each of the nine domains, our ability to access, develop, and express intuitive insight will be strengthened.

Viewed as a whole system, the complementary Paths of

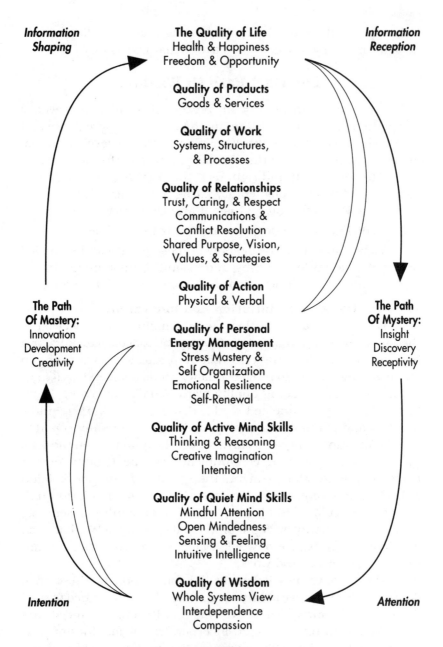

Information Shaping

Information Reception

The Quality of Life
Health & Happiness
Freedom & Opportunity

Quality of Products
Goods & Services

Quality of Work
Systems, Structures,
& Processes

Quality of Relationships
Trust, Caring, & Respect
Communications &
Conflict Resolution
Shared Purpose, Vision,
Values, & Strategies

Quality of Action
Physical & Verbal

The Path Of Mastery:
Innovation
Development
Creativity

The Path Of Mystery:
Insight
Discovery
Receptivity

Quality of Personal Energy Management
Stress Mastery &
Self Organization
Emotional Resilience
Self-Renewal

Quality of Active Mind Skills
Thinking & Reasoning
Creative Imagination
Intention

Quality of Quiet Mind Skills
Mindful Attention
Open Mindedness
Sensing & Feeling
Intuitive Intelligence

Intention

Quality of Wisdom
Whole Systems View
Interdependence
Compassion

Attention

Figure 1
THE DUAL PATH OF WISDOM: INTEGRATING THE NINE DOMAINS OF INTUITION AT WORK

Mystery and Mastery weave the nine domains into cascading interrelationships that are fractal in nature like a succession of wheels turning within wheels. Understood in this way, we glimpse the profound relationship between our inner and outer worlds and the link between the most subtle and the most fully manifest realities of human existence.

The Path Of Mastery: Innovation, Development, And Creativity

The Path of Mastery gives meaning to information by shaping it into images, ideas, communications and actions. This path spans the nine domains and unfolds along a spectrum ranging from the emergence of the most subtle idea or intention through the progressively more tangible stages of formulation, communication, and action. The primary tools of mastery are action, communication, and the Active Mind Skills of intention, imagination, and thinking, which are all accentuated by building synergy between Active and Quiet Mind Skills. The fruit of this path is the joy of accomplishment, a sense of confidence as our wisdom and skill grow, and the affirmation of seeing the fruits of our intuitive insights expressed and applied through our work. Following this path inspires us with a sense of mastery, confidence, and "control" that is complemented by the Path of Mystery's sense of insight, intuition, and discovery.

The Path Of Mystery: Insight, Intuition, And Discovery

The Path of Mystery complements the Path of Mastery. Along this path we engage in inquiry, discover insights, and awaken intuitive wisdom. This path teaches us to live with questions, listen deeply for inspirations, and engage in research or inquiry that ripens as progressively deeper and deeper intuitive insights. Through careful observation and deep receptive listening many subtle and complex patterns of relationship are revealed that might escape superficial observation. The fruits of this path are the wisdom, inspiration, joy of discovery, and sense of wonder which, as they mature, guide us through the next generation of innovation and development on the Path of Mastery.

Wisdom And The Synergy Of Mastery And Mystery

Weaving together, the Paths of Mastery and Mystery define the Dual Path of Wisdom. As our wisdom deepens, the quality of our life improves. Weaving these complementary paths together helps us to continually access, organize, and express a deeper wisdom through our work. The Path of Mystery taps the intuition necessary for continual renewal, inspiration, and innovation through our work. The Path of Mastery assures continuous improvement, adaptation, innovation, integrity, service, and responsiveness to the changing needs of our environment. In this way, we participate in the natural cycles of discovery and development, insight and innovation, wisdom and work, that serve as the in-breath and out-breath of the creative process.

From our work we have come to hear numerous statements about the synergy of mastery and mystery. For example, after learning to recognize and develop various mind skills (the "Active Mind" skills of thinking, reasoning, intention, and imagination, and the "Quiet Mind" skills of attention, mindfulness, and sensing), an R&D manager in a large financial services firm made the following observation: "I never realized how noisy and out of control my mind was until I began to observe it. Yet with practice, I noticed two interesting things. First, just by watching my mind, sometimes it would grow more quiet, sort of like how a muddy glass of water settles down and becomes clear when you stop stirring it. Second, and most exciting, I've learned to discover the clarity in the midst of confusion, the peace within turbulence, the silence here with the sounds. Though the Active Mind functions are more noticeable, the functions of the Quiet Mind are always on and attentive. When ordinary thinking, imagination, and intention subside, the lucid clarity of mindful attention remains. As this awareness grows, I am flooded by intuitive insight and am able to accomplish in hours what months of work could never provide."

A second example of this synergy comes from comments made by numerous doctors who consciously use intuitive diagnostics. One medical professional summed it up thusly: "As a medical doctor, intuition is a vital diagnostic tool. The quieter I get inside, the better I am able to feel or sense my patient's condition from the inside out. Intuitive diagnosis not only suggests the nature of their physical ailments, but the intricacies of the cause, and most optimal course of treatment. With practice, I've learned to distinguish the difference between my thoughts about my patients and direct intuitive comprehension of their actual condition. The feedback from standard medical tests helps to clarify and confirm my intuition. Interestingly, this insight can be gained just by holding a patient in mind, even if they are physically distant from me at the time. This has lead me to reconsider the many of my previously held assumptions and beliefs."

A third example is from an especially intuitive R&D project manager in the computer industry who noted, "By nature, I'm a very analytical engineer and I take pride in the precision of my work. This work has expanded my understanding of how information is generated and received. I've learned to hold a question about a design problem in mind with a high degree of coherence, and then, like a stone dropped into a deep pool, to release the question and simply listen for the reverberations. Sometimes these come as a felt sense that ripens into an image that lends clues to the answer. At other times, clues or answers may come to mind as metaphors or even in a dream. Through this work I've come to a deeper understanding of the verse in scripture that says, *"Ask and ye shall receive. Knock, and the door will be opened."*

A fourth example is from a chief researcher in a leading biotechnology firm who told us, "My genetics research is often guided by intuitive 'gut feelings.' Over the years, I've learned to listen to these subtle and deeply-felt physical sensations and ask, 'What does this mean?' If I am able to listen deeply enough, then the feeling ripens into an idea or an image that informs and inspires my research. In my profession, a single intuitive insight can be worth millions of dollars, years of work, or generations of people who live free from disease or suffering. With so much at stake, can we afford not to learn how to listen deeply to our intuitive intelligence?"

A final example here comes from a manager in the Information Systems Division of a large financial services organization who commented that: "Troubleshooting large systems computer failures can be a stressful and time consuming job. Each day the system is down costs millions of dollars. Developing mindfulness and Quiet Mind skills has helped me and my crew to more quickly quiet and focus our minds under stress and to sort through possible causes to find rapid solutions."

Creative Intelligence

At the very heart of the intuitive process is what we call "creative intelligence." Creative intelligence is a measure of the integration and synergy developed between our Active Mind Skills, Quiet Mind Skills, and Wisdom.

Wisdom weaves its way into the world from the inside out.

Emerging first as subtle, formless impressions, often ephemeral, transparent, so subtle and elusive that they could easily be ignored. If the receptive mindfulness of our Quiet Mind Skills is keen enough, even the most subtle intuitive insight will be noticed, drawn into awareness, and developed through our Active Mind Skills into thoughts, images and impressions that can then be communicated to others. In order to better understand these different modes of mental function, let's look more closely at the Active and Quiet Mind Skills.

Active Mind Skills

The Active Mind Skills (AMS) are the tools of our intellect and reasoning. They include intention or will, thinking, and creative imagination. These skills each play a role in shaping information through the power of intention. They also give form and meaning to the complexity of our inner experience through the power of thought and imagination. The AMS are vital to organizing and expressing our inner knowing, insights, feelings and intentions through tangible action.

Quiet Mind Skills

The Quiet Mind Skills (QMS) represent a domain of powerful mental functions that are complementary to and essential for the effective use of the Active Mind Skills. The QMS are primarily receptive mental functions that gather information through the faculty of mindful attention, sensing, and feeling. These involve the quality of receptivity, "being," or presence, in contrast to the creativity, or "doing" nature of the AMS. Because the mental functions and brain states associated with the QMS are more subtle and less "visible" than the AMS, they are rarely recognized, and seldom fully developed. By way of analogy, the AMS are like the forms and patterns of matter or clouds that we can see or touch, and the active forces of wind, water, or electromagnetism that shape them. By contrast, the QMS are more "transparent" mental functions that are vast in scope, clear, and open like the sheer presence of the sky.

At work, the QMS determine the coherence and power of all other mental functions. The QMS also provide access to the subtle revelations of intuitive insight so vital to breakthroughs in creativity and innovation. By allowing us to focus our attention more deeply on the work at hand, they enable us to access a deeper, more fundamental wisdom that reveals insight into the nature of our innermost being and the world in which we live. Consciously or unconsciously, all the great scientists and sages of the world have tapped the QMS as the access states necessary to discover the "universal organizing principles" that have inspired and guided the development of humanity throughout the ages. The Quiet Mind Skills also awaken within us a sensitivity to the life-giving forces that we express as universal values, such as wisdom, wonder, creativity and compassion.

Discovering Reality

As multidimensional beings, we are inseparable from our multidimensional universe. Understanding our inseparability from all creation, we realize that intuitive intelligence is as integral to our being as the water of the ocean is to the myriad of tiny waves that rise and fall upon it. We come fully equipped to discern and understand the full spectrum of reality. To develop intuition (our "eye of contemplation") is to learn to contact reality directly.

Generally speaking, as mind relates to body, mental activity, or spirit, it bifurcates itself into a dualistic subject–object mode and represents direct experience to itself symbolically in terms of abstract thought. These thoughts have a reality of their own, as merely symbolic thoughts which are different from the realities that they attempt to represent, i.e., thinking about spirit is indeed paradoxical. For this reason, all of the world's great wisdom traditions remind us that the absolute nature of reality cannot be reduced to mere concepts, names or symbols. It must be, and can be, directly intuited. As the great philosopher Sengstan said in his classic work, "The more you talk and think about the truth, the farther astray you wander from it. Stop talking and thinking and there is nothing you will not be able to know!"

Intuition is direct, unmediated knowing. This is our direct experience of our universe via the multidimensional antennae of our body. This mode of knowing is direct, continuous, unbroken, non-symbolic. Intuition functions in a realm prior to thought and is different than thinking. If we learn to "listen" deeply enough, intuition will reveal a mother-lode of profound insight in response to any question we hold in mind.

Intuition as direct, non-symbolic experience also takes place because we are multidimensional beings, endowed with an omnidimensional depth that transcends and defies description or

definition in terms of ordinary physics and biology. These dimensions of our reality are described as consciousness if we wear
psychological lenses, or as Spirit if we take a more religious or
spiritual view. Whatever we call it, our most fundamental deep
reality is as mysterious as quantum or transluminal reality is to
physicists. At the heart and core of our being, each of us is in
contact with this ground of reality out of which all things come.
Here we touch dimensions of ourselves that are non-local, trans-
temporal, unbounded, omniscient, incomprehensible, inexpress-
ible, yet intimately real. Though we may be unable to express fully
intuitive insights drawn from these levels of reality in linguistic,
mathematical, or artistic symbology, even a moment of such
direct apprehension may inspire and guide a lifetime's work or the
development of a culture.

Cultivating a mindful awareness of the interrelationships of
our various ways of knowing develops the keenness of mind
necessary to recognize the difference between our thoughts about
reality and our direct, intuitive wisdom.

Frontiers Of Intuitive Research

We live at an exciting and terrifying time when the tools of
modern science and technology provide us with more information
about our world then we can assimilate. It is said that human
knowledge doubles every eighteen months; yet as it does, we seem
to feel more out of control and lacking in wisdom.

Foremost among the leading research efforts on intuition
and the mind-matter interface is the Princeton Engineering Anomalies Research (PEAR) on the Scientific Study of Consciousness-
Related Physical Phenomena, founded by Robert G. Jahn, Dean
of the School of Engineering and Applied Science, and his colleagues in 1979. Describing the implications and applications of
thousands of experiments over sixteen years of research, they
remind us that:

Beyond its scientific impact and its technological applications, clear evidence of an active role of consciousness in the
establishment of reality holds sweeping implications for our view
of ourselves, our relationship to others, and to the cosmos in
which we exist. These in turn must inevitably impact our values,
our priorities, our sense of responsibility, and our style of life and
work. Integration of these changes across society can lead to a

substantially superior cultural ethic, wherein the long-estranged siblings of science and spirit, of analysis and aesthetics, of intellect and intuition, and many other subjective and objective aspects of human experience will be productively reunited.

There is considerable evidence from decades of rigorous research at Princeton, Stanford, Duke, SRI, Menninger Foundation, and other respected research centers around the globe to suggest that, although ordinary sense perception and logic are inoperable beyond certain thresholds, intuition can plumb and accurately discern the most subtle or distant domains of reality. Thousands of rigorously-conducted scientific studies in physics, engineering, psychophysiology, biology, and other fields have produced "anomalous," unexplainable results that impel us to expand our definition of reality and the interface between matter and consciousness. Though considerable effects are being measured, our respected colleagues are dumbfounded and unable to explain adequately their findings within existing scientific paradigms.

What is clear is that under the right circumstances we are, individually and collectively, able to access accurate information intuitively. Though the actual mechanisms are unclear, the personal and group skills necessary to enhance intuition are consistent and lie largely in the realm of the most subtle Quiet Mind Skills and in their synergy with the Active Mind Skills and the skills associated with the domains above them.

A basic outline of strategies for developing personal and team intuition in our work with business includes:

- Learn to recognize and reduce inner and outer conflicts and distress
- Develop more respectful, caring and trusting relationships with ourselves and others
- Develop the Quiet Mind Skills, including the quality of mindful attention and the capacity for sustained "deep listening"
- Learn to recognize and question assumptions
- Learn to develop greater focus and coherence of intention and aspiration
- Learn to view self-world-universe more in terms of dynamic, multidimensional and interactive flows and fields of energy-information

- Develop the Active Mind Skills, communication skills, and quality of working relationships necessary to develop, communicate, and apply intuitive insights through your work

Intuition is a fundamental and natural mode of knowing. Intuitive intelligence is rooted in both the biology and the multi-dimensionality of each human being. Though intuition has always played a key role in empirical research, technological development, and human survival, the crucible and crisis of modern times provides us with an especially high stakes set of incentives to accelerate our learning and deepen our intuitive wisdom.

> My own working assumption is that we are here
> as local Universe information gatherers. We are
> given access to the divine design principles so
> that from them we can invent the tools that
> qualify us as problem solvers in support of the
> integrity of an eternally regenerative Universe.
>
> —R. Buckminster Fuller

Each day the beauty and pain of our world calls out to and through us. Breath by breath, life passes, death approaches, and we take our world to heart. Holding Mastery in one hand, and the Mystery in the other, we are able to take a stand rooted in true wisdom. In each mindful moment we catch a glimpse of the answers to our most heartfelt questions and prayers. Will we care enough to listen deeply? And will we listen deeply enough to discover and apply the "divine design principles" necessary to bring more wisdom and compassion to life?

In this brief essay it is impossible to explain fully the mechanisms and methods necessary to develop the intuitive wisdom of individuals and teams. Yet, if you are left with inspiration, an aspiration to understand more deeply and to help others do the same, then my intentions are fulfilled.

Part Two

FROM MYSTERY TO MASTERY

Weaving The Illumined Walk Into The Ordinary Life
Elle Collier Re

Intuition: From Inspiration To Application
Sharon Franquemont

Intuition, Success And Leadership:
A Holographic Approach
Susan Collins

Elle Collier Re is a God-centered spiritual shaman and seer, and an international teacher/trainer in the principles of non-dualism and the path to soul release. She has been working with individuals and groups since 1975, and is the founder of INEI-RE—The Return Path, a center for spiritual unfoldment in Kalispell, Montana.

4

Weaving The Illumined Walk Into The Ordinary Life

Elle Collier Re

Nowhere is there safety until we
utilize all of our Nature.
Nowhere is there the bountiful
until we are not in lack inwardly.
Nowhere is there pure comfort until
there is no fear of betrayal.
There are, in fact, only walls
wherever we are until there is only
Love wherever we are.

We are all here to establish our identity, acknowledge and find support for this identity, and to pursue its expansion. For this to occur, we must become alive to our unity with everything, exploring this unity with each breath, each sighting, each feeling, each normal, physically-backed sense. Every creature, human, and circumstance we encounter bears on our existence and brings forth a response in us, even if unwittingly.

As we allow this understanding, we are learning how to trust and use the events of life instead of just fighting against them. To appropriate the greater good from each situation, there must be trust in mutuality. Without this, we cannot partner with life fully. Blessings arrive from befriending the circumstance. We cannot acquit our partnership with this world. Even if we subscribe to non-participation, we have been drawn into the result. Perhaps our greatest fulfillment lies in the seed idea that we are not here to gain for the one only, but for the whole; thus true empowerment in all aspects of our lives can begin.

We have the means to a unification of principle even with the diversity at our fingertips. There may be a thousand ways to see an image, yet our eyes try to repeat what they first saw. When that view is repeated enough, other possibilities are as if non-existent. We can alter our understanding only if we make room for other possible solutions, only if we "see" from different angles. There are many styles here, many themes. We can ignore these themes by isolating ourselves within our own "culture," creating distance from each other whenever the principles vary. Yet, because our most basic, personal requirement is to trust in our expression and its fit within this entirety, isolation is without real satisfaction.

We are partnered to a rich and ongoing theme of creative responsiveness. When there is love, honor, and obedience to the greater need, private concerns are addressed as well. We are fit to a "marriage" made in heaven that none can break asunder. If we could understand this even in a limited way, it would become obvious that we are each perfectly designed into a portion of this marriage, each according to his/her way of being an answer to the whole model.

There are gifts that belong to humanity that would see to a reinvention of our enterprise, and a better society overall. We know they are available, though we are still tantalized with the weapons of defensiveness and argument. We usually change only when a better lie is given to reprimand the old, such as when Democrats in the United States try to piece together a seemingly balanced system by pouring more ideas into it, without having weeded any out, or when the Republicans promise a balanced budget by decreasing what enriches and enlivens, supporting the gold diggers rather than the whole. Rarely do we think totally for ourselves except when the pressure mounts to a point of overshadowing our sense of safety. The lie has been heard, preached from the ignorant until it is the only "truth" we buy. We need our Inner Authority to revise the data by chewing and participating in it until we wear out the effort of conflict and begin to perceive the interrelationship. The root of our intuition is founded on this principle. Thus a means for solution begins.

There is no lasting answer, however, until we get to this viewpoint that is and always has been the riskiest of all—we are organically and indissolubly linked to each other. Within every atom of our body we have the exact treatment to cure the cancer of insanity—the atom has faith in itself. Its function within the whole is unquestioned. Our cells know how to exist within the complex of other cells, forming a society of nurturers and suppliers acting for the whole. If the mind infiltrates and takes over the cellular consciousness with its fear, the body is confused. It loses its skill to interpret and act according to the paradigm that has been built out of all genetic history—when exposed to a problem, create a solution.

We are virtually slaves to this intellect/ego whose prime objective is to keep us from insane choices, but which maintains the belief that we are separate. It is the immaturity of that belief model which inspires the paralysis of fear. It is love that re-inspires, nurtures, and fulfills. This is not a passive love. This is no longer a fixation on a love so soft and needy that rapture scorns it. The fire of pure love casts ignorance out. This love is rich with power and vitality and calls to all alike to fix the danger here. This love is not unkind nor particularly in favor of making friends. This love is just. It has the principles of the Golden Mean within it, which allows all to live and flourish together yet gives no support for the overtaking of another, nor worries about the unprofitability of that vast a loving. It is the most formidable weapon we have, for it is hungrier than the fear or the hate, and dissolves the conflict by changing everything into its own likeness.

What is it we seek? Emergence. Emergence into the Light of Being. The will to create the restoration of sanity arrives out of the love and thrill of dancing in the present breath without regarding the safety as much as the challenge to just be alive. We cannot climb on the roof without intriguing the birds, confounding the squirrels, and separating ourselves from earth enough to tear a tiny rift in unforgiveness; for here we are, on top for a moment, in control of our footfall for a tiny breath and able to laugh at the thought of being snuffed out. We exact from ourselves the means to threaten our existence, and find a win unlike any other before it.

What lies behind thought and life as we see and experience it is the exquisite totality—the presence that permeates and gives support to all things. The riddle that would be answered begins by simple acknowledgment of the expansiveness of the universe and even the atom. Being created out of a big bang that gave the impetus for all to unfold is an awe-inspiring concept. How does a universe get a start? What propels all this into motion? What is it that even endows conscious alertness to the not-yet-known and yields the clues to begin the answering besides the simple and splendid ability to wonder?

Is it "wonder," then, that began all this out of the mind of the creator source? Are we in the likeness of source? Our minds expand when they touch the significant, are enhanced when the clamoring for attention is replaced with curiosity. Without wonder, all secrets remain so. Without wonder, the human instrument is enormously debilitated. Our real career of becoming the greatest we can be, comes forth in this state of wonder and awe at life's possibilities. Human existence is born into the premise of discovery.

But if it means letting the old be torn down, will we allow it? There is a tide to our mind as there is to the ocean—an instinct to be drawn deep into the greater self when we finally feel pulled too far onto the shore of dry intellect. We are brought again to truth when we let go of our fear of it; yet there is a fear of release. It feels like we are being pulled into annihilation, all anchor points giving way. It is not easy to want what seems like denial of life. If, however, we allow ourselves to step through this veil, this false fear, we are met by a relief so broad that we are swept into the rare opinion:

I am. Beyond Me there is no thing. No outside. Only Me.

From that perspective, we win a long sought-after truth—no betrayal other than self-betrayal can occur. We know ourselves to be that which inspires and brings forth everything we perceive, from love to hatred, from the beautiful to the vulgar, and back again. If we would but focus on the energy within matter, we could see, and penetrate behind the illusion of otherness. Every opinion we have held onto for more than a day would be reframed by this most extraordinary viewing of the cause and effect behind matter. There is no alternative to this way of "seeing" if we would have the absolute transcribed into the finite. Thus begins a way back to sanity.

The final way into the clear knowing power of trustworthy intuition is neutrality. Its real name is matrix, for it is the birth point to the next breath. It is the mind of matter that beholds itself before it is born. It is the voice of stillness that reasons without judgment, yet has no different name than innocence and truth combined. It is the day to the night. It does not fit definition yet presents the key to all knowing. When neutrality and love combine, there is no doorway that does not yield. Therefore, it is the magic solvent to any glued vision.

We cannot grow without neutrality, and searching has no value without this key. It is that which evolves us, yet denies us access until all baggage is loosened. It awaits us, for we are its seed that will father a quantum and glorious leap into the truth as we have not yet perceived it. For neutrality is, you see, what gives us eyes to know the inner way, ears to hear the playful tune of cosmic humor, and feelings to sense what next can be inspired when we do not fear the outcome.

As fear totally leaves, everything can resolve itself into its magnificent, fluid, perfect state of harmony once again. When all tension leaves, we trust implicitly the signals of the world, and we find inwardly the awareness to translate those signals into usable instruction. It would be nice to issue a warning to the mind: "Stand back mind. Wait. Find neutrality." And the warning should continue to flash until the mind no longer observes the need to declare itself the primary leader—just follower of the signals. Thus is the way found into the delivery room where each answer is finally birthed.

We need to believe in this: that life is a riddle with a solution, a solution that may have nothing to do with the finite you. The marvelous truth is that when the finite is finished, you resolve into focus.

And so it is. The path again is renewed.

Namaste—I bow to the divine you are.

Sharon Franquemont, author of the forthcoming book, *You Already Know What To Do* (Tarcher/Putnam), is a coach, consultant, and educator for intuition. She is a national and international speaker and seminar leader addressing such diverse professions as business men and women, psychotherapists, and educators. She has worked in the field for twenty-five years and taught graduate students for five years at John F. Kennedy University in the School of Human Consciousness Studies and the School of Management.

5

Intuition:
From Inspiration To Application

Sharon Franquemont

The real important thing is intuition.

—Albert Einstein

Intuition And Inspiration

His voice firm and direct, Steve said, "Can we get together this week?"

Steve, a highly successful employee of a well-known San Francisco firm, had been out of touch since he and his wife bought a beautiful home in a distant county. I looked forward to our meeting, but wondered what was so urgent.

"Two weeks ago my company let thirty percent of our employees go. I am OK and none of my group were let go, but I am still shaken. We'd heard rumors for weeks, but nobody was prepared for the number of people affected. Work is really hard. My heart just isn't in it," Steve conveyed.

As Steve told more of his story, I wondered silently to myself, "How many times *today* is this type of story being told? How many times was it told yesterday or will it be told tomorrow?" I wished once again for the chance to equip today's offices and board rooms with a sign reading: Intuition Required.

The employee–employer has never needed intuition more. In

this age of rapid turmoil, corporate icons such as IBM, Sears, and Boeing, etc., are falling not to the takeover raiders of the 1980s, but to discount houses with efficient computer analysis or changing world dynamics. Many previous strategies, such as mimicking the competition's success tactics, do not work. Witness the mixed results of mimicking the Japanese by blanketing America's corporate culture with TQM.

The American culture is not a blanket. Its most effective response has always been inspiration. Inspiration brings together people or teams who are "in-spirit" or "called in" by the spirit of things. Pursuing intuition, which is the language of spirit, is pursuing a conversation with the spirit of things.

The word intuition comes from the Latin word *in-tueri* meaning "apperception" or "to look in on." Another popular definition is direct knowledge. The purest forms of intuition are always correct and reflect the highest form of logic. Often the profound wisdom of intuition's "logic" becomes clear months, or even years, after the intuitive solution is applied.

For example, in 1979 when Ford Motor Company was facing dark days, chairman Donald Peterson felt as if it was time for Ford to abandon the traditional "committee car." He acted on his hunch and empowered the intuitive–creative branch of Ford. For the first time, industrial designers were put on equal footing with the marketing, engineering, product and financial departments. His decision resulted in the highly successful Ford Taurus. Over fifteen years later, the Taurus is still America's best-selling car.

Today, in the 1990s version of dark days, Steve and thousands of others cry out for renewal and inspiration. Lacking the insights of Donald Peterson, people ask themselves "How do I go ahead?" or "What is ahead?" "When" to go ahead has already been decided for us. The time is now.

Although now is the time for intuition, intuition is not new. It is, was, and will continue to be a timeless resource reported in every culture of the world. With the dawn of the scientific age, intuition went into the background due to its lack of predictability. Intuition, however, did not disappear. In fact, many creative, scientific breakthroughs rest on the laurels of intuition's sudden "flash." The apparent randomness of these intuitive flashes permitted use of their wealth, but barred scientific research into their source.

Intuition And The Four Ps

I believe that it is time for our "inner" technologies to match outer scientific and technological accomplishments. Science can't explain intuition because the skills necessary for its development are not in the rational mind. They rest in our character development and states of awareness.

Max DePree, a great American leader and business executive, writes about a time he and a friend entered the locker room of a local tennis club. The room was a mess. A group of high school students hadn't bothered to pick up after themselves, so DePree spontaneously began gathering up their towels. His friend then remarked, "Do you pick up the towels because you are the president of a company or are you a president because you pick up the towels?"

Character development is a central theme of Stephen Covey's bestseller, *Seven Habits of High Effective People.* Covey explores conduct that contributes to lasting success. Successful intuitive development also requires human beings with strong values and rich ethics. This triangle shows the inner technologies needed to develop a full range of intuitive abilities.

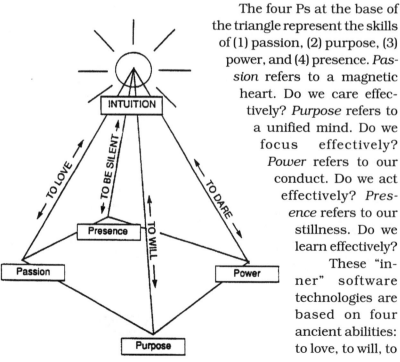

The four Ps at the base of the triangle represent the skills of (1) passion, (2) purpose, (3) power, and (4) presence. *Passion* refers to a magnetic heart. Do we care effectively? *Purpose* refers to a unified mind. Do we focus effectively? *Power* refers to our conduct. Do we act effectively? *Presence* refers to our stillness. Do we learn effectively?

These "inner" software technologies are based on four ancient abilities: to love, to will, to dare, and to be silent. Love is necessary to care effectively. Will is necessary to focus effectively. Power is necessary to act effectively. Silence is necessary to learn effectively. These four abilities form the information highways between intuition and specific inner technologies.

A sincere choice for intuition *is* the only software map required to get on the highway. You and your organization need nothing else. The blueprint for your character development and awareness skills is already inside. This is where we need to look.

Intuition And The Inspiral Method Of Intuitive Awareness

The Inspiral Method of Intuitive Awareness is based on my twenty-five years of facilitating intuition within adults. It will catalyze your blueprint. The method provides a model of intuition and a map for its development (see Figure 1). The word "inspiral" is a combination of in-spirit and spiral, which is the universal symbol for transformation. Working with the Inspiral Method transforms spirit and allows spirit to transform us. We are both inspired and inspirational.

There is nothing mysterious about this. It is the natural outcome of inner growth. The Inspiral model also suggests "You are *already* using intuition. You are *already* using phrases and words to describe your intuitive experiences at work and at home. Awareness is all you need."

Intuition, according to the Inspiral Method, is an ability to obtain knowledge without rational processes. This ability is spread over a continuum of seven steps ranging from instinc-

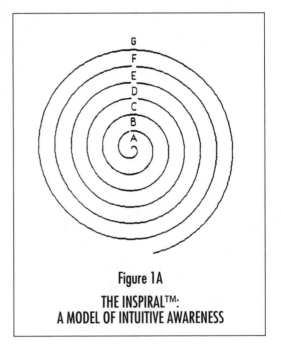

Figure 1A

THE INSPIRAL™:
A MODEL OF INTUITIVE AWARENESS

Figure 1B   THE INSPIRAL™: A MODEL OF INTUITIVE AWARENESS

Level	Type of Intuition	Intuitive Exercises	Skills Developed	Applications
A-1	Instinctive Intuition (Good)	Body/Sensory Time =Present Solidity	Full Presence Stress Management Stillness Strong Foundation	Accounting/Quality Maintenance Contractor Relations Distribution Experts
B-2	Emotional Intuition (Feelings)	Empathetic/Emotions Time = Past Fluidity	Interpersonal Skills Wealth of Past Atmosphere Expert Values/Diversity	Personnel Human Resources Sales/Brand Names Customer Relations
C-3	Creative Intuition (Create)	Abstract/Mental Time = Past, Present, Future Connections/Answers	Innovation/Risk Taking Problem Solving Transpersonal Comfort Rejuvenation	R & D Design/Engineering New Products Dev. Creative Dept.
D-4	Systems Intuition (Systems)	Pattern Recognition Time = Continuous Scanning/Linking Interdependency	Management Corporate Culture Community Positioning	Systems/Diagnostics Advertising/PR Marketing/New Products Consensus Builder
E-5	Visionary Intuition (Visionary)	Intention As Influence Time = Future Ethics In Motion Perceptual Choice	Leadership/Paradox Comfort With Unknown Sustainable Life Integration	Visionary Leadership Scenario Building Strategic Planning Chaos Control,
F-6	Inclusive Intuition (Inclusive)	Unification/Synthesis Time = Omnipresent Spaciousness Wholeness/Ease	Multiple Dimensions Ego Freedom One Pointedness Service/Stewardship	Global Leadership World as Team Work Competitor Alliances Mission Unifier
G-7	Universal Intuition (Universal)	Absolute/No Name Time = No Time Reality Emergence Perfect Ordinariness	Peace Master Timelessness Master Cosmic Humorist Effortlessness	Universal Identity Presence As Action Motionless Oneness Precision Evoker

tive intuition to universal intuition. The model names the seven steps, lists types of exercises for each, and suggests specific applications in the organizational environment.

The first three ways of intuition, Instinctive, Emotional, and Creative, are common. Phrases such as "my gut," "it 'felt' right," "a light bulb went off" are all indicative of an intuitive process. These non-rational words "gut," "felt," or "light bulb" describe instinctive, emotional, and creative intuition, respectively. You are probably familiar with one or more of these phrases and may have used them yourself.

Instinctive Intuition:
Gut Knowledge

Our spirits are *natural.* Many times our instinctive response to situations is correct. Peter Anderson, whose money management firm oversees around $105 billion dollars, said, "I trust my instincts a lot. I trust *my gut* more, not less. I've made good decisions and good money doing it the past 27 years."

What is instinct? In 1982, I stood on a hill in Kenya, Africa and watched millions of grazing wildebeests. Suddenly, and for no apparent reason, the millions began to form a line. Like a wave going across a body of water, each grazing cluster of wildebeests fell into a long, winding line and the march northward began again. Instinct provided the "knowledge" necessary to make the journey.

Instinct is a word we use to describe an intuitive process found in the body. Our body is intuitive. It knows what to do. Traditionally, Western people associate acting without thought with negative, unconscious behavior. When character development is coupled with intuitive training, however, spontaneous, effortless and *inspired* behavior follows. Like the wildebeest, our journey is natural.

Instinctive intuition lives close to the rhythms of nature and the Earth. Practice with this type of intuition provides guidance for better environmental practices, hints for innovation in the environmental arena, and restores a more natural rhythm to your daily life.

Two simple exercises for increasing your awareness of instinctive intuition are (1) Belly Breath and (2) Nature's Rhythms. People use the word "gut" to describe instinctive intuition because information *does* register in the belly. To practice the Belly

Breath Exercise: (1) simply focus your attention on your belly, the area immediately beneath your belly button. (2) Follow your breath in and out until you are calm. (3) If you have trouble concentrating, place your hands on your belly as you breathe. (4) When calm, talk to yourself about your concerns. (5) Pay attention to your belly's response and take its "opinion" into account. After practice, you will do this naturally.

Nature's Rhythms is best done outside. All you need is a patch of earth. The Earth is the oldest living thing with which we are acquainted. Using your imagination, discuss your situation with the Earth and ask for her advice. Relax. Watch what nature shows you in and around your patch of earth. Look for the lessons you can apply to your situation.

Emotional Intuition: Feeling Knowledge

Our spirits are *sensitive*. Human sensitivity is powerful enough to send and receive information without normal sensory means. We've all heard stories of people knowing when a particular person is going to call them, knowing when a beloved is in danger or has died, or knowing serene victory *before* the final score is tallied. Strong emotions, such as future victory or sadness, radiate information. Traditionally, this type of intuition has been called psychic.

Emotional intuition is found in daily activities as well as the stories of dramatic moments. Terms we *already* use to describe emotional sensitivity to non-rational information are vibing, sensing, reading, feeling, getting, scoping, using radar and scanning. A person or a team adept at emotional intuition is an excellent resource for (1) creating an atmosphere, (2) handling interpersonal relationships, (3) judging emotional appeal, (4) keeping values on target, and (5) honoring diversity.

Business analyst Bennett W. Goodspeed remarked years ago that "environmental sensitivity will be a key to strategic success." Goodspeed realized that predictions are in error not because of analysis, but because of what isn't taken into account. Emotional intuition identifies anomalies in the environment, raises questions, breaks us out of our "pattern blindness," and fosters insight.

Adeptness in emotional intuition requires sensitivity to subtle emotional currents *and* detachment from personal response. This detachment frees the information available from our personal wishes and projections. Once free, intuition's spirit releases emotions that inspire, encourage, liberate and inform. This information can then be evaluated along with logical data.

An exercise that you can use to improve your emotional intuition is: (1) Use the breath technique to relax. (2) Place your attention in the chest. (3) Imagine that your heart is like the lens of a camera and open your heart up at a pace that is comfortable for you. (4) Once open, allow love to flow out on the exhale and to flow in on the inhale. (5) Focus all your attention on the chest and love. (6) Be alert to how your heart guides you following this exercise.

Creative Intuition:
Innovative Knowledge

Our spirits are *creative.* Creative intuition produces innovation, genius, or artistry in all walks of life. When something is creative, we are struck by its "spirit." Intuition's spirit inspires, creativity follows, and an innovation or beauty is born. Intuition is the silent partner of creativity.

Philosophers and shamans describe two levels of the world. In Western philosophy, a term used to describe the world we consciously relate to as *explicit.* The silent world where intuition dwells is called *tacit.* Carlos Castenada's shaman, Don Juan, refers to these worlds as the *tonal* and *naugal,* respectively. Things we call creative—an invention, a song, an idea, a superlative performance, etc.—are all part of the tonal or explicit world.

We are also in continuous, often unconscious relationship, with the tacit or naugal worlds. We have terms that describe this world and our relationship to it such as, "The problem is on the back burner" and "I want to sleep on it." Intuition lives in the "back burner" and in our "sleep." Innovation is born there.

Intuition travels on love or caring. People who love their work create a "field" of knowledge to which intuition responds. Next time you are challenged by a problem, love what is behind the problem *even if* you don't know what it is. Then relax. Keep a record of when and how you access intuition. Once you know your favorite techniques (for example, Einstein was famous for his "cat naps"), use them consciously in the future.

An exercise you can use to enhance your creative intuition

is: (1) Identify your problem vividly with your imagination. (2) Follow the breath to relax. (3) Imagine a room divided by a curtain separating creativity from intuition. (4) See yourself seated in the creativity side of the room. (5) Imagine an assistant coming out from behind the curtain and inviting you in. (6) Enter intuition's side and observe everything without evaluating it. (7) When it feels appropriate, leave your problem behind the curtain. (8) Bring back everything you learned. (9) Thank intuition as you leave.

Most people are acquainted with and remember these first three types of intuition. The intuitive awareness staircase is based on the Inspiral Method and is designed to help you remember the next four. The words on top of each stair create "sentences" going up and down. The top sentence going UP the staircase is *"Good feelings create systems (which are) visionary, inclusive, and universal."* Those same words are used to create another sentence going DOWN. *"Universal, inclusive, visionary systems create feeling good."* These sentences show the importance of going up and down the spiral without assuming one state is more important than another. The words below each stair name the types of intuition.

Systems Intuition:
Pattern Knowledge

Our spirits are *collaborative.* Systems intuition links us to each other and large scale patterns or trends. Individuals sensitive to these intuitive skills are attracted to marketing, public relations, investments and globalization. A key feature of systems intuition is the ability to experience intuition as "surround sound"— Intuition is embedded in patterns everywhere.

Gary Markoff, VP for Investments at Smith, Barney and Shearson, describes his art as "riding the waves and watching the currents." Markoff appears to surf the investment ocean using intuition for a surfboard. His job is to identify the wave pattern that will take him and his clients successfully to an enhanced financial shore.

We can, of course, miss intuition's message. The loan officer of a bank had a large loan outstanding to a prominent department store. One day his wife returned agitated from a shopping trip to the store. When the officer asked her what was bothering her, she

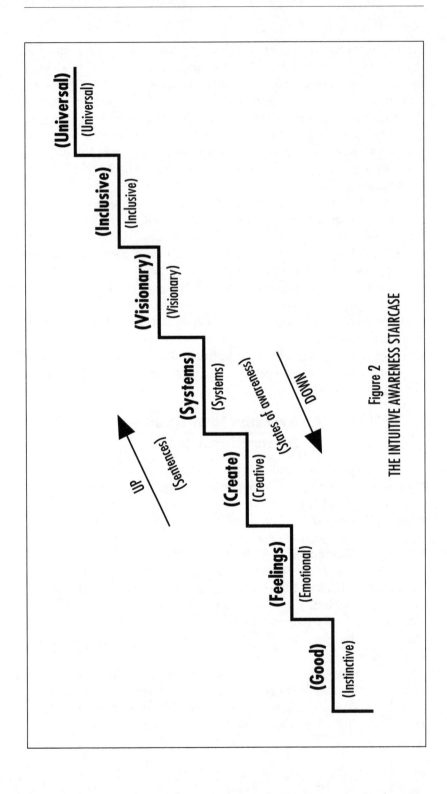

Figure 2
THE INTUITIVE AWARENESS STAIRCASE

shared that everyone was following her around and seemed bored. Alarmed by his wife's impression, the loan officer requested an immediate analysis and was relieved to learn all appeared well. Within the year, however, the department store folded.

System intuition encourages us to receive information from our whole system. Vital input can come to us from anywhere in the system. Intuition chooses the easiest conduit rather than a linear path. If the loan officer listened to his wife's agitation and his own alarm, the spreadsheet information would not be valued above his wife's and his own intuition.

A smooth functioning system honors every participant, keeps the objective in sight, is aware of itself as a whole, and monitors its interactions with other relevant systems. In our organizations, shared tasks define the boundaries of the whole. We are together to work. Intuition thrives in the work setting where goals are clear, collective integrity is established, and passion for the task is central.

An exercise that will help you develop your systems intuition is: (1) Follow the breath exercise to relax. (2) Place your full attention on a pattern you'd like to know more about. (3) Imagine yourself loving what is "beneath" the pattern. (4) Imagine visiting a complex ecosystem like the woods or beach. Let your imagination be vivid and sensory. (5) Turn your attention to your body. Remember and re-create the body sensations you've had when struck by a profound insight. (6) Focus completely on the sensations without interpretation. (7) Now really go to the woods, beach or another site in nature to explore and learn. Notice complex interactions at your site. Let one or more systems provide insight and understanding about your chosen pattern.

Visionary Intuition:
Precognitive Knowledge

Our spirits are *visionary*. Visionary intuition is like a two-way mirror. We can look outward toward a vision of our desired future and sometimes our *actual* future looks back. We call these latter experiences precognitions. We see or know the future before it occurs. Our vision either guides the future reality or the future reality reveals a vision.

The word "visionary" is not meant to imply that the only valid information is visual. Visionary intuition can provide information through body sensations, auditory sounds, spontaneous activities of the body, clarity in the heart, sudden spoken comments, etc. Often these multisensory experiences surprise us. We can treat them like unbidden guests from the future or welcome them and assess their informational wealth. Do not hesitate to assess your unbidden visions of the future. True intuitions suffer from lack of acknowledgment, not caution and assessment.

Traditional, strategic visions of a desired future provide individual or organizational infrastructures for intuition. The created vision is a snapshot, a picture of an intention that intuition can "ride in on." Think of your vision as a template for future possibilities. The template filters out irrelevant data and guides in experiences relevant to the vision. Relevant experiences might reveal dysfunctional habits, suggest "course" alternations, require personal transformation, as well as provide inspiration and next steps for fulfilling the vision. In this sense, intuition is neutral. Its assistance reveals the relevant and irrelevant equally.

Collaborative intuition is powerful. A shared vision of the future mobilizes us. The power inherent in shared visions is also neutral. The results depend on the ethics of the people wielding that power. It has been used both to land on the moon and to eradicate human beings. The ethical spirit within us loves to collaborate with others to achieve goals that benefit all life. Our unconscious wounding wants to achieve victory over others and provide comfort for ourselves.

Fortunately, as intuitive abilities expand, there is a natural ethical boundary. Some types of intuitive experiences are available only with psychological and ethical maturity. They are a by-product of inner growth and cannot be conjured up by curiosity or desire. Visionary intuition, whether spontaneous or developed, is a sacred covenant between yourself and the future.

An exercise that will assist the development of your visionary intuition is: (1) Assemble a sheet of paper, old magazines or other pictures, scissors and paste. (2) Follow the breath exercise to relax. (3) Keep your mind as blank as possible. (4) Spontaneously select whatever pictures attract you. (5) Create a collage pasting the pictures relevant to the present on the bottom third of your paper. (6) Use the middle third to depict immediate next steps. (7) Use the top to reflect the unknown future. (6) Place the collage where it will be seen daily.

Inclusive Intuition:
Unitive Knowledge

Our spirits are *unifying*. Native American tribes share a prayer whose meaning is the same in every Native language. The words, said to begin and end every important event, meeting, and ceremony, mean "For all my relations."

These words are based on the cultural and spiritual belief that all life is related. Nothing is done without honoring and assessing the impact of that fact. Although we are many, we are also One. Our actions effect each other deeply because spirit is always working to unify life not foster competition.

Ironically, the etymology of the word "competition" comes from the Greek word meaning "running together on foot." Let us remember the "together" part of the translation because honorable men and women working together as equals adds a new dimension to life. It sets the stage for community. A Tiwa Indian friend of mine explained that your heart comes from your community or tribe. Without a tribe, people have no heart. Without a heart, knowledge is empty and of no lasting value. Inclusive intuition reveals the knowledge that exists *only* because people have come together with heart. The insights and creativity achieved go far beyond the sum of each individual's contribution; they literally belong to the tribal community.

John Sealy Brown of Xerox PARC talks about "communities of practice." He defines these as the social fabric that emerges from sharing a task over a period of time. Core competencies live in these communities and surround them. When such communities add intuition to their required skill base, they are guided by the heart behind their task, inspired by a continuous stream of supportive stories, and surprised to discover how their individual visions have united.

Inclusive intuition is directly related to our spiritual unity. Practice with inclusive intuition creates a boomerang effect. If you wander into strictly self-serving acts, you and your associates will *gently* and *automatically* be called back to inclusive acts. Although meetings may never begin by acknowledging Oneness, inclusive intuition changes priorities. Full environmental responsibility, genuine community participation and the desire to cooperate with the competition all spring from its roots.

An exercise that catalyzes your inclusive intuition is: (1) Draw a circle on a piece of paper and place a dot in the center.

(2) Inside the circle write the names of everything you'd like to be One with (include anyone or thing you are struggling with, too). (3) Relax with the breath exercise. (4) When you are ready, take a deep breath in and imagine yourself as the dot inside the circle. (5) On the exhale, imagine yourself going out to the edge of your circle becoming One with everything in the circle as you go. (6) Repeat inhaling to the dot; exhaling to the All. (7) Complete your exercise with the dot.

Universal Intuition: Beyond Knowledge

Our spirits are *universal.* The Lakota language, which emphasizes verbs rather than nouns, describes a sacred person as "going beyond knowledge he or she." The description emphasizes an evolving activity sharing a personal field rather than a person who has attained a state of being.

Inclusive intuition supports people becoming One. Universal intuition is without separation, so there is nothing to bring together. In this awareness, the known, the knowable, and the knower are indistinguishable from each other. Lama Anagarika Govinda, in *The Way of the White Clouds,* tells of watching a human being run effortlessly across a field of boulders moving from one boulder to the next as if they were continuous solid ground. He describes the ability to do this as "The movement is pure, for the mover does not trouble it in going by being different from it."

This is an example of universal intuition at work. The field, the boulders, and the runner are a seamless web. The simple presence of a person acquainted with universal intuition stimulates dreams, transformation and activity. He or she radiates clarity, compassion, and wisdom within the context of ordinary existence. Such human beings are not one with love, purpose, power, and silence; they *are* love, purpose, power and silence. Or in Lama Anagarika Govinda's terms, they do not trouble these qualities by being different from them.

Leadership from this domain is provided by an encounter with pure spirit. Leadership doesn't act on you or even inspire you. Leadership becomes you. You know what to do. The splits between body and spirit, mind and heart, and ordinary and extraordinary dissolve. The universe lives inside you as you.

In many ways we have come full circle to instinctive intuition. Universal intuition is a natural state. Like the acorn whose teleology assures an oak tree, we are engaged spontaneously in what Franz Kunkel calls theosynthesis. Plants know what sunlight means and how to use it. We, too, automatically turn toward the inner light for nourishment as we deepen our relationship to spirit. And, like plants, our evolving consciousness has the power to change the atmosphere on Earth.

An exercise to develop universal intuition is: (1) Use the breath exercise to relax. (2) Choose a quality (love, peace, joy, wisdom) you'd like to be. (3) Focus on something or someone that symbolizes that quality to you. (4) Open your heart. (5) Invite the quality in. (6) Focus on the quality in your heart. (7) Expand the quality outward to the universe. (8) Focus on the universe and let the quality go.

Conclusions

The seven ways of intuition in the Inspiral Method are different expressions of intuition's wisdom. They all have equal value. Students of the Inspiral Method experience it like a staircase you go up and down. All judgments disappear and your personal and professional life are alive as this poem depicts:

> And the illumined soul
> Goes up and down
> These worlds, eating any
> Food it likes, assuming any
> Shape it desires
> Chanting...Oh, wonderful!
> Oh, wonderful! Oh, wonderful!
> —Unknown

Our spirits need intuition. Intuition is integral to spirit's activity in the world. A spirit-filled person, community, or organization radiates a connection to the source of life and leads us to remember our own.

Practice with the Inspiral Method of Intuitive Development will enhance your ability to love, be present, live your purpose, know profound silence and restore your connection. Experiment with intuition. Evaluate your results. Look for pragmatic outcomes as well as improved truthfulness, clarity, joy, meaning, and love. Don't settle for less.

The full spectrum of intuition is a way of life, not a series of techniques, so your skill base will eventually have an impact on many facets of your existence. Unlike traditional science, take your measurements from the inside out. Results will begin with changes in perception, lead to insights, and culminate in an enhanced *quality* of life. Daily applications of intuition soon become inspired conversations with your own spirit and the spirit of all life. You will be an inspired and inspirational human being.

Susan Collins is the author of *Our Children Are Watching: Ten Skills for Leading the Next Generation to Success.* She began her career as a research psychologist at the National Institute of Mental Health and next spent fifteen years observing highly successful people—corporate heads, artists, musicians, sports and entertainment professionals, innovators, and inventors. From her observations, she was able to identify ten success and leadership skills which she teaches in her Technology of Success seminars across the country.

Since 1983, she has taught these skills in corporations—American Express, Digital Equipment, Kimberly-Clark, Florida Power and Light, Ryder System, IBM—schools, universities, and governments, as well as in public seminars. *Our Children Are Watching* brings the Technology of Success—in print—to parents, teachers, individuals in business and government. A nationally-known speaker and gifted storyteller, Susan is a frequent guest on TV and radio.

6

Intuition, Success, And Leadership: A Holographic Approach

Susan Collins

Intuition is a natural part of the learning process, first appearing as curiosities and questions, possibilities and suggestions. Intuitions are the seeds of the future, but the development of these seeds will depend on the way they are viewed by leaders—parents and educators, managers and executives, legislators and presidents. Our intuitions can either be viewed as the seeds of weeds or of flowers—as threats to authority and harbingers of disloyalty, or fruitful opportunities and signs of creativity.

Our leaders are responsible for our safety and effectiveness as we begin to learn. They decide, based on their own experience, what we should and shouldn't do—what is safe and dangerous for us, right and wrong, good and bad. They teach us how and when to use the methods and limits they know, and they hold the power to—for our own sake, or theirs—prevent us from taking action.

But in this time of accelerating change and ever-expanding databases, of proliferating products and services, frustrations and stresses, violence and abuse, we must begin to recognize intuition as our best hope. Together, as leaders, we can rethink the familiar methods of leadership—the methods of parenting, educating, managing, and governing.

We must begin to see that the naive questions and uninformed answers, the "yeah buts" and "that doesn't make senses" may be the very clues we will need to discover the faults and cracks in our crumbling foundation, the clues we will need to solve the problems that face us. And together as leaders we must hothouse and cultivate this emerging crop.

The Big Picture Of Success And Leadership

Let us look at success and leadership in more detail. The process of success has three phases that we shift up and down in. The phases of success, like gears of a car, each have their own purpose, timing and use.

To drive, we start in first gear, overcoming inertia and moving our car forward. Shifting into second gear, we continue to accelerate and gain momentum. Shifting to higher gears, we move toward the destinations we have in mind.

To succeed, we start off in the first phase, succeeding at overcoming internal inertia—old fears and limits, old doubts and habits. When we can consistently perform the new skill safely and correctly, we shift into the second phase and begin to accelerate, doing more-better-faster so we'll be able to compete. Reaching the uppermost limits of the methods our leaders have taught us, we shift into the third phase by intuiting our own methods—creating new products, services, and systems. Then we gear back to teach others to use them.

The First Phase:
Succeeding At Following

Think back over something you recently learned—how to do a new job, how to use a new tool or program, how to live in a new city. The first phase is a scary phase. We know we don't know and we are dependent on leaders to teach us "their programs." We try and fail; we try and succeed. But how do we know when we're successful in the first phase? We know we're successful when our leaders tell us we are, when they acknowledge that we are doing what they want us to do, we are correctly using their "software for success." Early successes in any skill are the successes of trying—overcoming fears, doubts and uncertainties, learning to put our confidence in leaders until we develop self-confidence.

How do we know when we're in the first phase of success, or when someone we work with is? Here are some clues: we/they find trying hard, feel scared or nervous, concerned about right/wrong, good/bad, what they can and can't do, what they should and they shouldn't do, what's possible and impossible. We/they ask a million questions, urgently demand attention, wait for permission and need immediate feedback. "Is this right? Are you sure? What should I do next?"

The Second Phase:
Succeeding At Competing

Once we can perform the new skill safely and correctly consistently, our leader shifts us into second, giving us our independence, and then the meaning of success changes. Trying no longer counts, we have to produce. Instead of immediate feedback, leaders provide periodic grades, charts, and graphs so we can begin to assess success for ourselves.

To succeed in the second phase, we must do more-better-faster, constantly increasing quantity and quality to remain competitive, working longer hours, assuming additional responsibilities, putting more effort in but getting less satisfaction out. Until nearing the shifting point—stressed and exhausted, frustrated and pressured, disappointed and disillusioned—we find ourselves wondering, "Is there something wrong with the world—or with me?"

Compelled by competition and ever-expanding lifestyles, we let go of anything that seems to get in the way of productivity—time spent with friends and family, recreation and relaxation, old familiar values, even integrity. We push harder and harder until there isn't any more, any better, any faster we can do with the methods we've been taught, and we either break down into disappointment and disease, or we break through into third.

The second phase is easy to recognize by the words that are used: win/lose/beat, more-better-faster, longer, harder, secrets, strategies, campaigns, improvements, grades, scores and graphs, lean and mean, more with less, quantity and quality, cutthroat competition, stress and exhaustion, production schedules, no time, time management, no energy, workouts, no money, borrowed and leveraged, credit card indebtedness, physical and emotional imbalances. These descriptors sketch the personality of the stressful second phase.

The Third Phase:
Succeeding At Creating And Leading

Now we must choose—we can continue to live lives of breakdowns and recoveries, energizing on adrenalizing foods and high adventure, filling ourselves up on tantalizing shopping sprees, prizes and perks, evermore sensational workouts, vacations and drugs. Or, we can shift into the third phase harnessing our intuition, creativity, and leadership.

Outcome-oriented and no longer method-bound, we dream about what we want—methods and products, innovations and inventions, new ways of living happy healthy lives here on Earth—communicating our dreams in detail so others can share them, finding others who will contribute expertise and data base. In the third phase, instead of struggling to outdo, we join together to create, finally realizing that "your success is my success too." Our notion of team expands beyond family, beyond community, beyond corporation and country, to include the global marketplace, the universe as a whole.

No longer satisfied with "haves and have nots," winners and losers, we commit to providing information and support systems, technologies and delivery systems, products and services to meet the needs and wants of every one of us.

The essence of the third phase is: interacting and networking, horizontal instead of vertical, aligning and empowering, respecting Mother Earth and all of her creatures, creating shared dreams and enjoying shared realities, appreciating each person's value, living in ease, honesty and integrity, confident together we can create the future we want.

In the third phase we succeed by leading others to success—our children, our students, employees and fellow citizens, and the shift into leadership lets us discover the most powerful successes of all—not just the successes produced by our own efforts, but the successes produced by everyone we create with and lead. By succeeding at leading, our successes are multiplied, and finally in the third phase we experience not just satisfaction, but fulfillment.

But leaders, like drivers, can't always "drive in third gear." It is essential that we be able to gear back appropriately to meet the needs of individuals who are in the first and second phases. We must be able to use their fresh points of view, their naive recognitions of the myriad possibilities we've overlooked. With the Big Picture of Success in mind, we can nurture future success.

When Is Intuition Born?
And How Is It Developed?

The seeds of intuition are sown in the first phase, nurtured by our leaders' carefully considered responses to questions and curiosities, by their sincere desire to see us grow and succeed, by their willingness to share what they have learned and intuited. In the beginning we are expected to follow their methods and intuitions exactly.

Then freed from control, we are gradually given our independence. No longer having to wait for leader input, we learn to make decisions for ourselves. In the second phase we can test the efficiency of our intuitions by monitoring the scores, charts and graphs that our leaders regularly provide for us. As our self-confidence increases, our confidence in leaders simultaneously decreases. Our urge to compete drives us to shortcut, collapse, and consolidate the methods they've taught us, forcing us to risk their disapproval.

As we press harder and harder against second-phase limits, the birth pains of intuition continue to increase. To keep up appearances, we learn to tell others what they want to hear, misrepresenting the truth and compromising our integrity. Unauthorized and unapproved changes force us to become secretive— asking fewer questions, providing fewer answers, and living with the constant fear of being found out or fired.

Our vocabulary and demeanor become warlike as we fight our way toward the top, mounting campaigns, camouflaging and sniping as we battle corporate enemies. Buoyed by wins, reeling from losses, we skew our lives toward work more and more.

Depending on how much of The Big Picture of Success our leaders can see, they will either view our developing intuition as a magnificent butterfly emerging, or see it as a harmful bug to be slapped at or exterminated—a threat to power and authority, an act of disobedience and disloyalty. The punishments for using intuition are publicly proclaimed and rebroadcast by the rumor mill to deter anyone else from following in our footsteps. Then, strategically blocked from the third phase, we are barricaded in second by ever-increasing lifestyles, mortgages, and credit card debts.

Some leaders employ even more elegant tactics to prevent our shift into third, enticing us to stay back by offering perks, raises, and positions These rewards retard our development temporarily, making us believe second-phase success is the greatest success of all, making us feel individuals who keep methods secret, who hoard power and information, who are intent on outdoing are the most successful people of all, caging us in a world where no one is a teammate and everyone is a competitor.

But today we are seeing the consequences of overusing "second gear." Those "most successful ones" are falling prey to high blood pressure and heart attacks, stomach ulcers and malignancies, diseases and disillusionment. Our communities are fraught with violence and abuse, broken homes and "lost" children. Second-phase heroes like O.J. Simpson continue to do more-better-faster until their worlds fall apart and they careen—at high speed—beyond the limits of society.

The Three Phases Of Leadership

Leadership, like success, shifts through three phases. Having experienced the first phase ourselves, we can sense the unique needs of first-phase learners. We can appreciate their desire for black-and-white rules, for constant feedback and encouragement to help allay fears and anxieties. And knowing what it takes to succeed in the first phase, we can give them the phase of leadership they need.

Having succeeded in second phase ourselves, having at times bought into the notion that competitive success is all there is, having struggled to beat and win, having fallen prey to disease and illness and having gotten our balance, we can teach those who follow us how and when to shift to third. We can nourish their developing intuition, responding to signs that they are ready to create and lead.

As leaders we must recognize that the naive questions and curiosities of first-phase learners can be the "childish" eyes that see the "Emperor has no clothes," that reveal cracks in all-too-familiar facades, lurches in our logic, flawed assumptions, or unchallenged absurdities. Often "childish" questions lead us to create solutions and streamline systems.

As leaders we must be flexible, shifting up and down appropriately, operating in whichever phase team members need us to join them in. But we each have a tendency to get stuck in one "gear," forgetting what it was like to be in the others, not realizing we may have been "rewarded into first," "barricaded in second" or "attached to the creative third."

Here's a suggestion for keeping "success gears" greased. Set aside a few minutes to create a Most-Dreaded-Fears List. Think of areas in your life you avoid like the plague—hobbies or skills you sense you're not good at, projects you've tried and failed at in the past, things you sense you have no aptitude for at all. Then, once a year, choose one item from your list and learn how to succeed at it.

Here are some items you might want to put on your list: scuba or sky diving; aerobics or weight lifting; ballroom dancing or learning how to play the trumpet, violin or piano; beginning a new relationship; giving up smoking, coffee, or sugar; losing or gaining weight—or anything else you are embarrassed to try, anything you fear you won't be able to do as well as others can, anything you are afraid you won't be able to create. And as you succeed through the three phases, think about the people you know, the phases they're in, the needs you can now recognize.

Leaders act as the "automatic transmission" for new learners, shifting for them until they learn when and how to shift for themselves. We must hothouse and protect them in the first phase, but in the second phase we must accelerate their freedom, remaining nearby, measuring and monitoring, easing up on rules and limits as they begin to improve and intuit. We must be able to appreciate their need to break rules, their desire to shortcut and improve our methods, their deep-seated mission to make the world a better place.

Instead of feeling hurt and angry, instead of seeing them as disrespectful, we can begin to celebrate these shifts, acknowledging their willingness to try new things, acknowledging their productivity, incorporating their suggestions for improving our products, services and systems, and cheer them on to making next-generation changes.

Why Is Change So Difficult?

In the first phase of success, we have to overcome inertia. It takes a blast of energy to move us ahead, and that blast must be generated by a new vision—a new holographic image.

Dr. Karl Pribram, neurosurgeon and physiologist, "the Einstein of brain research," has discovered that the human brain stores, retrieves and recalls information holographically. We have all seen holographic images on credit cards, at Disney World or in science exhibits. Holograms are generated by two or more laser beams; similarly holographic thoughts are generated by two or more laser-like sensory inputs.

Dr. Pribram says thoughts actually generate an electromagnetic force field that attracts what we think. The more detailed thoughts are, the more power they have. If we want to change what we do at work or at home, then we must change our minds, the holograms we use. We must train ourselves to think about what we want in great detail—instead of what we don't want, what we fear or dread.

If we want to lead others to make changes in the workplace, at school and at home, then we must learn how to make these desired changes attractive to them—showing them details of the ways these changes will make their jobs easier, telling them specifically how the changes will make their lives easier, giving them a feel for why these new behaviors are worth doing, worth investing energy in.

Yes, changing takes energy. We have to update the holographic data we have stored in our brains about that method or person. We have to see, hear, feel, taste, and smell what we want in our mind. Our language speaks the truth: We have to want something so much "we can even taste it."

But holograms of new behavior are sketchy and nonspecific initially. Their sound tracks are unfamiliar; their voices, hard to recognize. Incomplete holograms produce anxious feelings, feelings of unclarity and uncertainty. Indeed, it is this very lack of holographic detail that makes the first phase of success so difficult; that makes changing behaviors so challenging; that makes the need for skillful leadership so essential as we start.

Past history is pulled back in mind as we venture into new territory. Our brain sorts through past holograms, making sensory comparisons—"this looks like the time when..." "This sounds the same as..." "This feels just like..." and based on past comparisons we decide about now.

To change, we must learn to make new comparisons, comparing current input—not with the past—but with the future we want, with the holographic outcomes we have in mind. We must learn to throw a "dreamer's hook" up onto our dream so—like mountain climbers—we can pull ourselves up to them, so we can let our intuition and intention guide us all the way there.

Sensory Fill-In

Our brain naturally strives to complete holograms, so we must realize that when our brain lacks future detail, it will fill in from the past, or from other people's holograms. In the first and second phases we want someone to assist us in building our holograms, someone to show us what to see, hear and feel. But when we use details others have in mind, we may not get what we want.

Yes, what we think is what we get...like it or not. So if we want to get exactly what we want, then we have to think about that in great multisensory detail. Thinking is programming. And we must choose leaders who also have what we want in mind.

What Has Held Back Intuition And Creativity?

In the first phase of success, we didn't have enough detail. We were dependent on someone else to provide details from their holograms. In the second phase, we begin to elaborate on the holograms we've been given, developing our intuition—adding and changing details, discovering our own ways of improving and shortcutting, of doing things more efficiently. In the third phase of success we trust our own intuition. No longer simply adding to or adjusting other's holograms, we build holograms of our own, selecting parts from other holograms, cutting and pasting, adding and subtracting until our hologram looks, sounds, feels, smells, and tastes like what we want. In the third phase we finally have the wisdom and power it takes to intuit and create.

As leaders—whether parents or teachers or managers or those in government—we are responsible for developing the intuition of those who follow us, for reinforcing their ideas, their more efficient methods, their innovative theories and systems, instead of forcing them, through our authority and position, to follow our rules and do what we tell them.

The Pressing Need For Intuition Today

In our rapidly changing world, we must learn to shift phases appropriately so the dreams of everyone on Earth can be realized. So parents will notice and reward their children's early creativity—their new ideas and inventions; pictures and sculptures; their creative songs and tunes; new ways of dressing and playing, eating, and speaking. These ways may be the very ways we will need in the future.

Yes, our children will be tomorrow's leaders. But will we have prepared them to live in a world where the information we have taught them will be long out of date? Where our products, services, systems, and technologies will be outmoded and long forgotten?

Will we as parents and educators recognize when obedience is actually necessary, when sticking to recipes and rules really matters, when dependence should be expected, when fears are only natural? Will we be able to break skills down into "easily-succeed-able" pieces, lay out surefire courses for success, devise more subtle and precise measures? And will we have the self-confidence it will take to let the next generation change what we have spent our lives intuiting and creating?

Will we as owners, supervisors, and managers have The Big Picture of Success and Leadership so clearly in mind that we shift them from first into second into third appropriately, and then help them gear back to continue learning new skills? Will we be able to recognize the corresponding loss of self-confidence, sudden bouts of dependence, rash of what we might call—in other phases—inane questions and uninformed answers? We must learn to sense who needs more freedom and who will be slowed down by it, who is ready for responsibility and who would be demotivated by it, whose intuition and creativity is effective and productive and whose "half-baked ideas" indicate they need more information and detailed explanations.

Will we be able to update our reward systems so the creative and innovative will be encouraged, so our new crop of leaders will grow and thrive, so they will be able to rapidly assume leadership. So the "William Gateses" can emerge to create industries in their twenties and thirties? So the teenage "computer whizzes" and "Doogie Howsers" will be able to practice their chosen profession as soon as they are ready?

Will we, as those who are governing, have the knowledge it will take to structure society's rules and regulations to provide not just for the first phase needs of our society, for safety and effectiveness, but for our second- and third-phase success needs as well—for efficiency and productivity, for creativity and leadership? Can we fashion our laws so that when citizens are healthy and effective consistently, they will be given more freedom, given a second set of rules tailored to second-phase success? And when those citizens are productive and competitive, can we shift our laws a third time so we can provide support for new businesses and technologies, new aesthetics and philosophies, new ways of living happy healthy lives here on Earth? Will we be flexible enough to provide not just "one way" but as many ways as are needed by everyone on Earth? And, all the while, we must remember that the most fulfilling successes of all are the successes of those we lead. The real goal of every leader is to create the leaders of the next generation.

In Summary

Intuition is the unconscious product of accumulated knowledge—myriad questions asked and answered, hundreds of methods workable and unworkable, thousands of improvisations and "make-dos," billions of information bits—computed in "a moment of need" and experienced as a hunch. The light coming on.

Intuition is what success and leadership are all about. Intuitions provide solutions to the problems we face, as-yet unimagined methods for whatever we want—whether it's putting a man on the moon or creating healthy, productive lives for everyone on Earth.

The intuition of a beginner is undeveloped. The intuition of a competitor is kept secret. But the intuition of an individual in the third phase of success is useful and available. That individual is open to others' input, is committed to outcomes and flexible about methods, operating beyond the concerns of ego and ownership. That individual has the intention of creating and contributing. That person's success is no longer just their own. That persons' success is the success of everyone involved. That person's success is not just satisfying but also fulfilling.

Part Three

ASSESSING VALUE AND VALUE-ADDED

Gary Zukav is the author of *The Dancing Wu Li Masters; An Overview of the New Physics,* winner of the American Book Award for Science, and *The Seat of the Soul,* a national bestseller. His books have sold over a million copies and have been translated into sixteen languages. He is on the Council of Elders, Native American Earth Ambassadors, and is on the board of advisors of EarthSave, Intuition Network, Humanity Federation, and Learnscience.

He is a Fellow of the World Business Academy and recipient of its Pathfinder Award. He has served on the editorial board of *East-West Review: Business News for the Perestroika Era;* the Literary Advisory Board, Earth Day 1990; and as chair of the Government and Politics Strategy Group, Campaign for the Earth. Zukav graduated from Harvard with a degree in international relations, and was a Special Forces officer in the United States Army with Vietnam service. He lectures internationally on consciousness, evolution, and the soul.

7

Economics, Intuition, And Spiritual Growth

Gary Zukav

The use of intuition in the workplace marks and manifests a radical transformation in the domain of commerce. This transformation is far deeper than the displacement of the intellect as the prime decision-making faculty. It is the reorientation of business away from the exploitation of physical and human circumstances toward its utilization as a tool of human development and contribution to Life.

Intuition cannot be accessed without attunement to inner dynamics, and inner dynamics cannot be brought into consciousness apart from feelings. The language of intuition and the language of emotions are closely related interior experiences.

As this reorientation emerges, therefore, feelings—now the anathema of the workplace—will become central to it. This will not result in decreased efficiency, as is now feared, but in an explosion of creativity that is beyond the capability of current businessmen and women to conceive. As the concept of work shifts from mutual exploitation of employer and employed to co-creativity in the context of souls assisting one another in the process of spiritual development, the orientation of all involved in business activities will shift from fear-driven competition to fulfilling and exciting cooperation.

Intuition, now a curiosity to the business community, will

become its central decision-making faculty. Like feelings, the signals that come from intuition are interior. They often contradict the analyses of five-sensory circumstances that underlie the imperatives of the intellect. Developing the ability to listen to them will be fundamental to all human endeavors, including economic.

In other words, the emerging interest in intuition in the business community is part of a major and unprecedented shift in human evolution that is currently underway. Recognition of intuition as an aide to business is part of that transformation, and cannot be separated from it. The desire to utilize intuition is characteristic of an emerging humanity that is different in fundamental ways from the current humanity.

Humankind has crossed an evolutionary threshold that irrevocably separates all that preceded it from all that is now occurring. Said another way, the changes that are occurring in the human species have no precedent, and, therefore, our future can no longer be extrapolated from our past.

Since its origin, humankind has been limited to the perception of the five senses. It has evolved through the exploration of what can be seen, tasted, touched, smelled, and heard. This evolutionary modality is the same as evolution through the acquisition of the ability to manipulate and control external circumstances. This is external power.

External power is the ability to grow food, build fires—such as those that propel missiles—and clean teeth. It is the capability to create computers, automobiles, and tractors. Everything that does not occur naturally in the world is built with external power—shelter, clothing, telephones, and sidewalks. In other words, the evolutionary modality of humankind, until recently, has been the pursuit of external power—the ability to manipulate and control.

Humanity is now leaving this modality behind, and the limitations of the five senses that accompany it. It is becoming a multisensory species—one that is not limited to the five senses. The emerging multisensory human has the ability to obtain data that are not available to the five senses. That is intuition.

Intuition is a curiosity to five-sensory humans. Five-sensory humans are focused on the physical world. Multisensory humans participate in a much larger arena. They understand that the Universe is far more than the physical reality that is the entirety of existence to five-sensory humans. They see themselves as immortal souls that are evolving in a loving, wise, and compassionate Universe.

Nonphysical reality—which is invisible to five-sensory perception—is as much a part of the experience of multisensory humans as trees, birds, and mountains. It is the home from which they come, to which they return when they die, and which surrounds them continually as their experiences in the domain of the five senses unfold.

Intuition is the voice of this reality. It is direct access to sources of information that the five senses cannot detect. Multisensory humans depend upon intuition in the same way that five-sensory humans depend upon the five senses: They do not make decisions without taking into consideration the data that they obtain from it.

Intuition is the inner knowing that often contradicts physical facts. It is the feeling that a circumstance is not what it appears to be. It is the knowledge that a transaction will lead to trouble, even though all indicators show otherwise. It is the insight that a troublesome colleague is somehow a friend.

The development of intuition in the business community does not occur in the old context of pursuing external power, but in one that is entirely new. This is critical to understand: The development and utilization of intuition is part of a new way of being human. If this reality is not appreciated, the utilization of intuition will produce startling results.

Multisensory humans are also startled by intuition, but the context in which they utilize intuition makes the content of intuitive understanding comprehensible. That context is this: Intuition accesses sources of wisdom and compassion whose interests lie wholly in the development of the immortal soul.

The desires of the personality and the needs of the soul are not always the same. The goal of a multisensory human is to align his or her personality with his or her soul. This is the goal that has replaced the pursuit of external power as the evolutionary goal of humankind: alignment of the personality with the soul. It is in this context that interest in intuition is awakening species-wide.

The personality is that part of an individual that is born into time, develops in time, and dies in time. It consists of psychological, emotional, physical, and intuitive components. The soul is that part of an individual that is immortal. It exists before the personality is born, and it remains after the personality dies.

The personality is an energy tool that the soul adapts in order to interact in the domain of the five senses—in the Earth school. For each learning experience of the soul in the Earth school—each lifetime of a personality—the soul adapts a personality that is perfectly suited to its needs.

The soul is the real, powerful, and purposeful essence at the center of each human. It is that part of an individual that strives for harmony, cooperation, sharing, and reverence for Life. The personality has its own agendas. Confusion concerning the utilization of intuition enters here: Data obtained through intuition is provided for the purpose of assisting the soul in its development. Intuition does not serve the desires of the personality except when they coincide with the needs of the soul.

For example, a five-sensory investor in pursuit of external power strives to maximize return on his investment. He pursues the ability to manipulate and control. The larger his portfolio becomes, the more he is able to shape his physical circumstances: to buy larger houses, bigger boats, newer wardrobes, and the admiration of colleagues who are oriented in the same way.

He hopes that intuition will increase his profits. This may or may not happen.

The sources of wisdom and compassion that intuition accesses are in advance of your own. Among these sources are nonphysical Teachers. Nonphysical Teachers are impersonal energy dynamics that we personalize—that we treat as though they were personalities like ourselves. We call them "Angels" or "Teachers" or other names that make ourselves comfortable. Intuition permits consciousness of their continual assistance to us.

Nonphysical Teachers comprehend more than we comprehend, know more than we know, are wiser than we, and have more compassion than we have. They see the nonphysical dynamics that lie behind the physical circumstances of the Earth school. They perceive the interactions of personalities as interactions between souls in the domain of the five senses. They see the consequences of each action. They live in the beauty of the perfection of a compassionate Universe that provides at each moment for the needs of each soul.

Nonphysical Teachers do not, and cannot, make decisions for others. They are perfect expressions of the living Universe that supports each soul at all times with love and wisdom and that responds to the action of every individual in the way that is most appropriate for his or her spiritual growth.

Nonphysical Teachers, in other words, are not interested in your bank account. They are interested in your soul. If the experience of an increasing bank account benefits your soul's development, they will assist you in creating one. If otherwise, they will assist you in diminishing what you have.

For example, if a soul needs to experience abundance in the concrete terms of the Earth school, the bank account of that personality, and all other physical aspects of her or his life, will begin to reflect it. This matter is complex. Abundance is not translatable into amount of stock owned, but in certain circumstances, it is expressed in that way. The issue is whether the soul is expanded through particular experiences of its personality. If it is, the personality is assisted by the Universe in every way to create those experiences.

The experience of material abundance may serve one soul, while the experience of ever-returning grass in the spring fulfills the needs of another. In other words, one personality may need to experience the luxury of physical abundance that comes with ease to attain an understanding of the endlessly abundant nature of the Universe, while another may need the experience of loosing everything material in order to understand himself or herself as the source of eternal abundance.

The question is not whether material wealth has value in itself. From a spiritually aware perspective, no physical circumstance has value apart from the benefit that a soul obtains through experiencing it, and every physical circumstance maximally benefits the soul that experiences it.

The language of the Universe is not one of right and wrong, but of limitation and opportunity. At each moment, you are prompted by the Universe to move into freedom, but the choice is yours. Eventually, you will. Whether that happens in this lifetime or another is unimportant to your nonphysical Teachers. Their goal is to assist you in your learning, not to determine how it shall occur. That is for you to decide.

What you have chosen in your past shapes your present. What you choose in your present shapes your future. As you make the choices that continually confront you, you create your future in the process of responding to what you have created in your past. Said another way, the present experience of each personality is always what it needs to be given the wisdom of the choices that have been made.

With each choice, a new doorway opens, and a new set of possibilities appear. Within those possibilities, there is a new optimal choice, and so on. Nonphysical guidance always prompts you toward that optimal choice.

For example, you are rudely treated, and anger engulfs you. How shall you respond? Shall you act in anger? Do you determine that you shall not act in anger, no matter how much anger you are feeling? With your choice you choose the experiences that you yourself will encounter. If you desire to be struck in anger, strike in anger. If you seek to experience the wrath of others, give others your wrath. Do you choose the company of those who challenge their anger, or those who act it out? Choose wisely, because it is your own future that you are choosing.

The most important choices that you make are not those that are usually considered the most important, such as your career, your mate, and where you live. More fundamental choices that you make at each moment about what you are, and how you relate to the Universe and others continually create your experiences of yourself, the Universe, and others.

In each moment of choice, intuition—the loving, wise, and compassionate voice of the living Universe—is there to assist you, to illuminate your circumstances, to cast your challenges into new Light.

To all of this is added the factor of karma. The creative power of choice is not limited to a single lifetime. From the five-sensory perspective, life begins at biological birth and ends at death. From a multisensory perspective, personalities in the Earth school are aspects of immortal souls that have chosen to interact in the domain of the five senses in order to heal.

A five-sensory personality thinks that it is a body and a mind, and that its existence is accidental. A multisensory personality knows that it is an immortal soul and that nothing is random. A five-sensory personality strives to manipulate and control a world of matter. A multisensory personality strives to align itself with its soul in an eternal Universe of spirit.

Nonphysical guidance always prompts you toward your highest goals, the goals of your soul. That is intuition.

Intuition is what makes multisensory humans multisensory. Your awakening interest in intuition is part of the magnificent transformation that is occurring throughout humankind, individual by individual. This is what you must remember if you are to use intuition the way that it was designed to be used.

The Universe will not choose for you, nor overshadow the choices that you make. If you choose to strive for domination of others, your choice will not be ignored or rejected. You will experience all that your choice creates in the lives of others. That will happen in this lifetime or another, but it will happen. The compassionate Universe does not fail to insure that you encounter—in the intimacy of your own experience—all that you create so that you can learn to create wisely.

Intuition is the tool that will bring you to the conference where you will meet the colleague that you need to meet in order to create new vistas of cooperation, sharing, harmony, and reverence for Life, or the colleague that you need to meet to assist you in your choice toward competition, hoarding, discord, and exploitation. It is the dynamic that will further your growth through whatever channel you choose it to flow.

If you use your intuition to find and implement ways to align your personality with your soul, you create authentic power—experiences of joy, fulfillment, meaning, and purpose. You become vital without fear. Eager anticipation of cooperation replaces pre-combat anxiety. The joy of contributing replaces the temporary thrill of winning. Your life becomes meaningful. You become valuable unto yourself.

The emergence of intuition is fundamental to the evolutionary shift that is now occurring in the human species, and cannot be separated from it.

You are part of that shift. You have an important role to play, and you were born to play it. To find that role, use your intuition moment by moment, choice by choice. Go within. Listen with your heart. Take the path that leads toward meaning.

Your intuition is a gift.

Use it wisely.

Joanne Badeaux is a transactional attorney. Her law firm specializes in corporate and real estate law, and wills and trusts. Her clients include computer companies, manufacturing companies, nonprofit corporations, schools, and individuals. She received her law degree from Texas Tech University in 1982 and her undergraduate degree from Texas A & M University in 1979.

She is on the board of directors of Sisters in Spirit, an organization dedicated to increasing spiritual awareness among women, and she is a volunteer for Children of the World, both nonprofit corporations. She founded, and led for two years, a Houston Noetic Science discussion group that met monthly to discuss transformation in business and health.

The other consciousness-shifting organizations of which she has been a member are the World Business Academy, Renaissance Business Associates and the Isthmus Institute. Her favorite newsletter is *The New Leaders*. She has studied numerous courses through Unity Church of Christianity and Landmark Education. She lives in Houston, Texas with her 14-year-old son.

8

The Value Of Intuition

Joanne Badeaux

Joanne's Longing

Oh intuition come to me.
Come to me in the night as I sleep.
Come to me as a lover.
Come to me in the day as a cloud,
    a ray of sun, a spark of knowing.
Come to me as a calling...
    a listening.
Come to me always
    as you are the part of me
    that stayed behind to be my intuition.
Speak to me now.
Do not let me be in silence.
Oh intuition come to me
    for you are my soul's voice.

Has listening to your intuition added value to your life? What happened in your professional life when you listened to your intuition as opposed to when you ignored your intuition?

Intuition is traditionally defined as a subconscious thought process that emerges without a rational basis. I define intuition as a higher voice guiding each of us on our life's path. Further, I suggest that the value of intuition in our careers is in using it to discover meaningful work regardless of income.

This essay begins with an outline of phrases that are

intended to prompt your own reflection about your reasons for listening to intuition, how you experience and implement intuitive ideas, and whether you have quit following your intuitive directions.

Second, it describes common business problems that entrepreneurs encounter, and compares superficial and intuitive solutions. This section also includes case studies of entrepreneurs who made dramatic life changes based on intuition. They each said that they made their most valuable career decisions by following their intuition.

At the end of this essay, you have the opportunity to discover the role that intuition has played in your professional and personal life by participating in a graphing exercise. Even if you do not read this essay, I encourage you to try the graphing exercise to see if you can find a direct relationship between your use of intuition, the direction of your career, and your fulfillment.

Intuition On A Business Level

Intuition is usually a spark or trace of an idea rather than a fully realized concept. In keeping with that thought, I have written this section in the Confucian tradition, which will give you only one piece of an idea at a time. As you read this outline, please contemplate your own understanding and use or rejection of intuition. The phrases that follow are my ideas that I suggest you compare to your ideas.

Definition Of Intuition
- Gut instinct
- The "ah ha"
- The light that goes on in your head.

Results From Listening To Intuition
- Synergy (when people are decisive in who they are and what they are doing, they attract others who can help them accomplish their goals)
- Power
- Ability to relate better to customers and employees

Business Direction From Intuition
Can decide:
- With whom to be in business
- Which opportunities to accept or reject
- Which products to promote
- Which employees to hire and fire
- Which career path to choose and when

Feelings Associated With Listening To Intuition
- Excitement and anticipation
- Sense of moving forward
- Dread knowing something is not working

Experiences Of Intuition
That subtle nagging or bolt we feel:
- When we walk into a room of people
- When we listen to others speak
- When we are exerting authority
- When we are sitting quietly at our desks

Implementation Of Intuition
- Stop current activity, get un-tangled (do not cling to the

familiar solely because it is familiar)
- Plan, stay focused on intuitive thought
- Be as practical as possible in the implementation
- Use expertise if applicable
- Accumulate resources (finances and people)
- Enroll others in our idea
- Follow through, do not lose your vision

Intuition On A Spiritual Level

Definition Of Intuition
- Our inner guidance
- God's presence in us
- A gentle nudging, a whisper

How We Know Intuition
- When we feel the world is in harmony
- When we feel we belong where we are
- When we know love is real

Reasons To Listen To Intuition
- It takes each of us on our soul's path, it is our soul's map
- Regardless, and in spite of the material world, our life will unfold more meaning-fully when we listen to intuition
- It is the guide to the life for which we were born

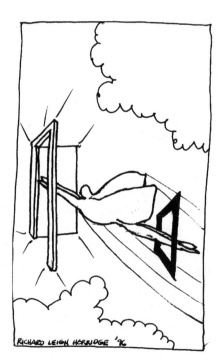

RICHARD LEIGH HORNIDGE '96

How Intuition Comes To Us
- In our dreams
- In conversation with others when we hear things that:

- Make us pause because they touch a place we had forgotten about
- Take us aback
- When we feel inspired

Have You Lost Your Intuition Or Quit Listening To It?

After you read this essay, it is my hope that you continue applying or begin to apply intuition in your life. Intuition is an eternal guide for each of us. Indeed, you may have once had an intuitive nature, but quit following it for one reason or another. If that is the case, consider why you are refusing to listen, then work through those reasons, and begin to again pay attention to your intuition.

One common reason we block intuition is fear. We block our intuition when we initially believe something is the right thing to do, but we don't allow ourselves to do it. This could be due to prior negative experiences such as:

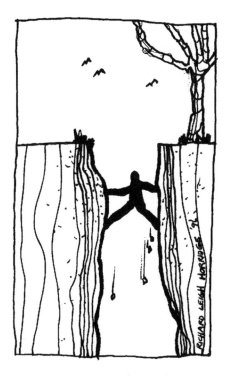

(1) Acting impulsively on an intuitive idea and failing

(2) Verbalizing an intuitive idea and being criticized

(3) Fearing loss of credibility

(4) Fearing loss of money.

(5) Receiving little support from close friends and family who perceive intuition as impractical

(6) Disregarding intuition as irrational due to its subtlety

Open to your intuition, welcome it, and confidently act upon your intuition.

Entrepreneurs' Use Of Intuition

Entrepreneurs succeed or fail for many reasons unrelated to intuition; but, the degree of failure can be amplified when intuition is ignored. Success can be enhanced when entrepreneurs heed their intuition. External characteristics of successful entrepreneurs that are unrelated to intuition include competency, skill, sufficient working capital, knowledge of the marketplace, and listening to customers. Internal characteristics of successful entrepreneurs include not fearing fear, not fearing risk, commitment to goals, and vision.

Intuition is a guide, a key, a direction for a solution when there is a problem. Ignoring intuition can result in hesitating to make a decision, which results in a loss of money. Business people routinely ignore problems because they hope they will go away, or because they think that if they confront the problem, they will incur a loss. When clients encounter legal problems and ask me for advice, they do not directly refer to listening to intuition, but they say, "I knew," "I felt," "I should have listened to..."

Common Business Problems

As an attorney for thirteen years representing entrepreneurs from all walks of life, I offer these observations about what I interpret are the differences between "superficial" and "intuitive" approaches to solutions. I use the superficial category to mean typical, reactionary, quick-fix solutions. I use the intuitive category to mean thought-out, deeply contemplated solutions. In each observation, entrepreneurs complicate their business by not listening to their intuition.

1. Employer ignores problem employee.

Superficial solution. Become more familiar with human resource information.

Intuitive solution. Employer can remember her initial impression of the employee who is now creating the problem. Most employers who are sued by employees say that they knew or sensed from the beginning that the employment would not work out, but that they lacked a tangible reason not to hire the employee, and it seemed easier to take a chance than to continue the recruiting process.

Regardless of whether the employer or employee is right,

both parties put themselves in a tenuous position by not heeding their intuition that the job is not working. The employer is putting herself at greater risk by building a dependence on the employee, and by allowing an unhappy employee to divert the other employees' focus from the common goals of the company. The employee who ignores intuition puts herself at greater risk by possibly, consciously or unconsciously, declining in job performance, thereby increasing the possibility of an unfavorable job reference after her termination.

2. Founders, shareholders, partners become disgruntled, but do not acknowledge their dissatisfaction to each other.

After founders create a business, they may begin to hear or see the other founders say or do things that make them uncomfortable. They begin to question or lose confidence in the long-term future of the company.

Superficial solution. Founders could meet among themselves or with a third person (mediator) to question whether they share common goals. If the goals are too divergent, some founders could leave the company before the company is destroyed due to internal tensions.

Intuitive solution. Founders could really listen to each other express their views about the company. They could feel the effect the conversation is having on them, not from a rational view, but from a gut view. If a founder feels apprehension, knowing in his heart that the venture is not going to work, then he could stop the venture, get out, or stay at the core of the discontent to determine a method by which the founders can realistically continue the company.

3. Founders, shareholders, partners do not agree on how to spend profits.

Superficial solution. Founders can objectively discuss long-term and short-term profits with their CPA.

Intuitive solution. Founders can look at why they created the company, what they initially expected to get out of the company, and what they are in fact getting out of the company. How founders want to spend the company's profits is an outward sign of their inner feelings. If a founder is fulfilled, she will generally want to reinvest the profits in the company since the company is an extensions of herself. She is not motivated to take money out of the company for personal material objects because her company is a source of joy. Conversely, when a founder is not fulfilled by the company, she will want higher salaries, perks, and bonuses from the company to substitute for her lack of joy. Ultimately, founders who lack fulfillment in their company will want to leave or will deplete the corporate assets for their own personal gain.

4. Business owners allow accounts receivable to become seriously delinquent.

Superficial solution. Call a collection agency.

Intuition solution. Listen to why the customers are not paying their accounts. While listening, the business owner will get a sense of when a customer is using the company and does not intend to pay for the service or product. By heeding this intuitive thought, instead of relying on hope of payment, the owner can stop providing services or products to slow-paying customers before the company's cash flow is jeopardized.

5. Business owners or employees refuse to acknowledge or accept their instinct that the market no longer needs, wants, or is willing to pay a profitable price for their product or service.

Superficial solution. Try to continue to create a demand. Business owners can hire consultants to analyze the company. Employees can contact personnel agencies to find another job.

Intuitive solution. Owners and employees can listen to their intuition telling them that their existing service or product is outdated, and can immediately begin to retrain, re-educate, or produce a product that is in demand. By listening to their intuition that it is time to move on, individuals can muster the courage to let go of the known security, power, and esteem. Even though moving to something new may be painful, it may be closer to the individual's true career path.

6. Business owners assume a victim position saying that the company's decline or failure is due to other companies, customers, employees, or the government.

Superficial solution. Sue the company or government agency that the owner believes is responsible for their own company's decline.

Intuitive solution. When a company's profits or morale begin to decline, change needs to be considered. A business owner who is in the victim mode looking for someone else to blame will continue to drain the company. Instead of looking outward to blame others, the owner can focus his energy inward and follow the direction that intuition is leading him. Then he can focus his energy on implementing his new plan derived from his intuition. The business person can reemerge stronger with a new perspective and a new business or career.

Four Case Studies Of People Who Added Significant Value To Their Lives After Listening To Intuition

These entrepreneurs said they made their most important life decisions by listening to their intuition, then choosing career paths that led to their greatest and deepest success, regardless of financial rewards.

The examples that follow show (a) how each person received their intuition, (b) what they thought about it, (c) how they implemented their intuition, (d) how others responded, and (e) where they felt they would have been had they ignored their intuition.

John Renesch—Publisher

John Renesch is editor and publisher of *The New Leaders* business newsletter and founder of Sterling & Stone, Inc., which publishes books on transformations in business. Before becoming a publisher, he was the managing director of the World Business Academy, an investment broker in commercial real estate, and an event promoter. In 1990, he received the Academy's Willis Harman Award for his volunteer efforts. Renesch says "I do not stay in a career unless I feel challenged."

Renesch says he began publishing the books and newsletter, for which he had no experience, because "I thought it was needed, not because I saw it as a business opportunity." He decided to "do something nice for the world now rather than later." Renesch says, "I am as clear as anyone can possibly be" that publishing books and newsletters on transformations in business "are exactly what I am supposed to be doing. This is my job in life."

"The core of my dedication came from anguish and personal growth," he says.

His vision—according to practical tests—was highly unlikely to succeed. While attending his first seminar on publishing a newsletter, after he had published four of his own, he learned that of the eleven mistakes a person could make in publishing a newsletter, he had made all eleven.

Renesch said that if he had done the market research for publishing his newsletters, he would not have started the newsletter. I "felt led to do this," that "I should be doing this," he says. This is "my assignment on earth." He said he did not know if he would make a killing, but that he hoped that he would make a living.

Initially, Renesch's friends supported him psychologically, but were pragmatically skeptical. Now people in his life say he is doing important work.

"Among the living dead," is where Renesch says he would be without following his intuition. He would be, he says, living life without really being alive, without contributing to others.

Garrett Robinson—Humanitarian

Garrett Robinson is the founder of Bridges Foundation, Inc., a nonprofit corporation that provides transportation of quality humanitarian goods to Third World countries. In 1974, Robinson began his career as a congressional aide in Washington, D.C., where he worked for eight years. Subsequent to that, he began his own lobbying firm, later became the head of an international oil and gas exploration company, and finally was involved in industrial real estate development in California for seven years. Throughout his life he was interested in helping Third World countries, especially Haiti. His nonprofit corporation has had eight successful shipments to Third World countries, carrying seven million dollars worth of food, medicine, clothes, and other humanitarian goods.

Robinson defines intuition as "a maturity from making decisions on a daily basis under pressure; rather having the ability to discern a situation and decide whether it is the right thing to do. If not the right thing to do, move out quickly and get out." He also states that we are "subconsciously being bombarded by facts all of the time, the facts accumulate, and something brings intuition to the forefront."

In 1993, a friend pointed out to Robinson that his influence in Washington, D.C. and talks with "big shots and wealthy people over the last twenty years have not produced improvements for Haiti. And, in fact, Haiti is worse off than before." Robinson says the comment triggered a decision. "I finally wanted to do the right thing for myself and for Haiti." He says "I wanted to cleanse myself of my maniac life." He says he took a "dramatic step, walked out on faith, gave up my lifestyle and put all of my energy and resources into Bridges." He says he felt "relieved" and "as if a big rock had been lifted."

Robinson's family, long-standing friends, and business associates viewed him with "suspicion and doubt" and condemned his idea and new direction in life. Many of these people continue to refuse to give him support (emotional or financial).

If he had ignored his intuition to found Bridges, he says he would have been unsuccessful in getting back into the commercial world now because "I would be working against my own body."

Sue Cobb-Mertz—Educator

Sue Cobb-Mertz founded Armand Bayou Montessori school in 1981. The school is American Montessori Society affiliated, has 130 children, 25 teachers, and a continuous waiting list. In 1993 the school received a grant through a group called Initiatives for Children. This group, comprised of large corporations, recognizes schools for their work with children.

Cobb-Mertz described receiving her intuition as a "spiritual inspiration while sitting on the floor of a Montessori classroom for the first time." In one instant, she says, "I knew that Montessori would be a part of the rest of my life." She had been a housewife for fifteen years and had never held a job. Cobb-Mertz was deeply drawn to Montessori because "it validated my beliefs about respecting children's needs, then meeting those needs."

Her friends and family supported her idea to first work part-time at a Montessori school and later to become a partner of one. With their continued support, she ultimately started her own school, beginning with only thirteen students. To implement her intuition to have her own school, Cobb-Mertz had to meet the state regulations, negotiate a lease, and obtain loans from family members and MasterCard—all first time events for the former housewife.

Cobb-Mertz says "I am happier owning the school than anything else I have ever done in my life outside of the home." She said that by listening to her intuition, she became "one of the lucky ones that found out my life's job without having to live a life of misery."

Kathy Whitmire—Public Official

Kathy Whitmire was elected the first woman mayor of Houston, Texas, serving from 1983-1991. She is now a fellow at Harvard University's Kennedy School of Government. Before going to Harvard she served as the first woman chief executive officer of the national Junior Achievement organization. She is also on the Board of Directors of the New York Stock Exchange and an advisor to Kellogg Foundation's National Fellowship Program.

When a friend suggested that she run for city controller, her first public office, she says "I knew immediately that was what I would do. I knew political office would be a large part of my life." Even though her husband had died two months previously, Whitmire quit her job at the University of Houston and closed her CPA practice to run for city controller. She says "I had no fear and never looked back at my decision to leave the private sector" even with the consequences of losing the election and having no job or income.

"I put everything I had into winning the election," she says. Whitmire hired an experienced campaign manager and sought the assistance of experienced political activists. Her campaign worked well, but her friends and associates said that in her circumstances, running for office was "outlandish."

Whitmire says that "self-confidence is the key point to intuition," and that "having a vision and enlisting others in your idea" are the ways to implement your intuitive ideas.

Politics was Whitmire's lifelong interest. If she had not used her intuition to know when to enter politics, she might not have become an elected official and realized her lifelong dream.

Graphing The Value Of Your Intuition

Let's try something experiential. By doing the following exercise, you may see a direct correlation between listening to your intuition and being fulfilled. Your results may answer what role intuition should play in your future.

Instructions: You will have three lines on one chart, representing "income," "intuition," and "fulfillment." Take each one of these personal scenarios, one at a time.

1. Starting at the left margin, with a solid line, chart the amounts of *income* you have made in your life at the various ages shown along the bottom axis.

2. Draw a line to show the times in your life you relied on (high score) and ignored (low score) your *intuition.* (Overlay this line in a different color in the chart below.)

3. In a third color, chart your soul's path, i.e., the times you felt closest to (high score) and furthest from (low score) fulfillment, love, or God. (Overlay in the chart that follows.)

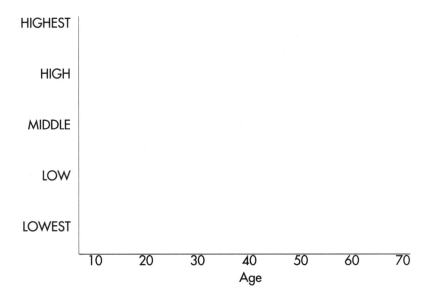

Results—Value Of Intuition

1. Did you have more income in your life when you listened to your intuition?

   (a) If so, were you fulfilled in your job or career?

   (b) If not, did you have the material things you needed in your life, and were you fulfilled?

2. Did following your intuition give your life value?

   (a) Do you define "value" as profit?

   (b) Can you include fulfillment and inner peace as value?

Send me a copy of your results. I will poll the number of people who made more or less money when they listened to intuition. I will also poll the number of people who felt furthest from and closest to fulfillment when they listened to their intuition. Send results to Joanne Badeaux, 18333 Egret Bay Blvd., Suite 110, Houston, TX 77058; (713) 486-4737.

WILL YOU FOLLOW YOUR INTUITION?

Gary D. Markoff is first vice president of Smith Barney, Inc. *Money* magazine named him "One of the Best Stockbrokers in America" in their fifteenth anniversary issue. He is also an advisory board member of the Intuition Network Business Consultants Group.

Markoff holds a B.A. in economics and lives in Boston. He is listed in *Who's Who in the East, Who's Who in Industry and Finance,* and *Who's Who in Emerging Leaders.* In 1986, he ran the marathon at the Moscow Goodwill Games.

9

Intuition At Work In The Financial Markets

Gary D. Markoff

Introduction

To invest successfully in the financial markets over a long time frame and in many environments, one must be skilled and versatile in all aspects of the investment arena. These include fundamental and technical analysis, as well as the more subtle realms of intuition and psychology, both one's own and that of crowd.

Only after years of experience in all these areas, is it possible to evolve from a beginner to an expert, with consistency of results the by-product. One of the masters in my business is George Soros. In 1995, the *New Yorker* magazine described Soros' legendary trading style: "It depended on information, but also to a great degree on a certain mind-set (powered by both intuition and a superlative analytical capacity) and on a process of trial and error—a continuous playing out of his preoccupation with the relationship between participant and observer."

I will discuss in this essay what it means to me to operate from such a "mind-set," exploring this "relationship between participant and observer," distinguishing fundamental from technical analysis, examining the role of intuition and psychology, and sharing examples generated from my seventeen years of experience as a professional investor.

Spontaneous intuition has led me to many profit-making opportunities in the stock and bond markets, domestically and globally. Intuition alone, however, is not enough to generate consistent results. There are other important building blocks that go into the decision-making process. This process consists of an operating platform which revolves around sets of distinctions from the diagnostic tools of fundamental and technical analysis interwoven with intuition and an understanding of where we are in the "cycle of psychology." By examining these areas I hope to help you perceive the financial markets more fully, in a holistic "whole-brain" way.

The ability to perceive and distinguish the conditions of the market environment as a whole is essential. By way of an analogy, winters in Alaska get about as severe as anywhere on this planet. The Eskimos, in order to survive as a race, have developed over twenty-seven distinctions for the word "snow." Those of us who aren't Eskimos don't possess these same distinctions and, if left in similar circumstances, would die fast.

For the Eskimos, these distinctions enable them to perceive their environment in such a way that to survive they simply build igloos with snow, in order to get out of the snow. Their protection is made up of the very same elements that threaten their survival and existence.

So, too, must an investor generate multiple levels of distinctions. In order to survive in the harsh mental, psychological, and emotional environment of the markets, the more distinctions that one develops for reading the financial landscape, the keener the instincts and observational skills. In this way, one can not only survive, but thrive.

The conditions that affect the price of a stock or bond may change rapidly, and at any one point in time depend solely upon the interaction of the supply of and demand for that financial instrument. Affected by this ever-changing balance between supply and demand, prices swim in a sea of endless possibilities. Different participants emerge at varying price levels to buy and sell based on their methodologies, market outlook, and degree of fear and greed. As prices move up and down in what appears to the uninitiated as random action, there is revealed an underlying order to the expert-intuitive eye. Chaos theory explains this and nature illustrates it. Witness the food chain in motion in the Serenghetti and in the oceans, where all the indigenous animals go for their piece of the action in a divinely orchestrated and natural dance. We will examine the flow of market action in the section called the "Cycle of Psychology."

Deepening the discussion, the broader categories that will be explored and distinguished are the financial markets themselves, styles of analysis, human nature (including how the brain functions), individual and crowd psychology, economic history, and some exotic indicators that I have found to be effective. My desire is to leave you with enough that you will begin to perceive the markets with an expert's eye, approaching the markets more confidently, and hopefully having fun.

The Human Brain And Crowd Psychology

In the early 1960s, Dr. Roger Sperry produced breakthroughs in understanding how the brain operates by severing the corpus callosum (the membrane which separates the left and right hemispheres) and observing that the two hemispheres actually control separate functions.

He discovered that the left portion of the neocortex has evolved in humans so as to process things that are logical, mechanical, rational, intellectual, analytical, mathematical, and linear in nature.

The right side, which does not understand spoken language, performs our nonverbal artistic, symbolic, feeling, visual, sensing, assimilating and intuitive functions. The left and right hemispheres communicate in an elaborate dance that may resemble the dynamism of a pinball machine. An example of this is how Albert Einstein came upon his discovery of the theory of relativity by first dreaming that he was riding a rocket on a beam of light, and then creating the mathematical equation ($E = Mc^2$) that would explain his intuitive insight in an analytical, rational way.

For his work, Dr. Sperry was awarded a Nobel Prize in Medicine. Now, in the last thirty years, with the advent of CAT Scans and MRI machines, doctors and scientists have been able to watch and assess how the brain operates. This technological capability is fostering a deeper understanding of our human evolutionary path, and the vast yet untapped potential for both analytical and intuitive/creative thinking.

Scientists have developed a model that suggests that the brain may be composed of even more than just two hemispheres, but may be part of a development in our species that has raised mankind from simple reptilian-like functioning (where we act instinctively, repeating routine patterns), to emotional intelligence in the limbic system, and now up to the two halves of the neocortex for conscious processing. Even in our ancient limbic system, however, there is an innate built-in intuitive sense originally designed for survival.

Understanding this process and how it affects the marketplace is a very valuable distinction when it comes to observing the recurring patterns in stock and bond prices as they display themselves on the charts. The markets consist of millions of people in pursuit of personal power (represented through money) and satisfaction, motivated by greed or fear. I see it all simply as our basic fears—the fear of not having enough, the fear of missing out, the fear of losing, and the fear of being wrong. These fears all tend to stem from a basic survival instinct, and an underlying feeling of insecurity. Rarely is the pursuit just for the thrill of playing the game itself.

When humans don't feel safe and experience fear, we lose touch with our natural intuition. When we lose touch with our intuition, we lose our sense of feeling and sense of balance. Even for professionals, the moment we choose to enter (or exit) the markets and commit, we become vulnerable to being swept up in the emotions of the moment. It requires discipline, patience, non-attachment to the outcome, and a plan of action, to stay in a place of self-trust. Long-term investment success, therefore, ultimately comes from understanding and developing an internal, not external, sense of control. For me, this is the ultimate game.

Styles Of Investing And Analysis

Several basic styles of investing have developed over the years. These include value investing, i.e., looking for where the earnings prospects and asset values aren't fully reflected in the stock price; contrarian investing, which is the idea of going counter to whatever is the prevailing wisdom in the media or on Wall Street; growth investing, looking for the innovative and rapidly expanding companies establishing new markets or trends; and momentum investing, which is the art of identifying a prevailing trend, jumping on to ride hard on the trend for as long as possible, and then attempting to jump off before everyone else does.

John Templeton, the founder of the Templeton funds, calls his style "MDP" or buying at the maximum degree of pessimism.

Over the years, he has developed a keen ability to identify when market participants have reached an extreme degree of fear (fear of being wrong and the fear of losing money), and steps in to buy. With the benefit of a forty-year track record generating an annualized 17% rate-of-return (this is nearly 50% greater than the market averages during the same time frame), it pays to heed Sir John's advice. He has developed a sixth sense for "feeling" and "sensing" fear, and has the guts to act on it.

Jimmy Rogers, author of *Investment Biker,* CNBC commentator, and former partner of George Soros, is a consummate contrarian investor. His natural instincts are always to go against the crowd's prevailing belief system, even if he needs to put money into a third world country's market in order to escape conventional thinking. Rogers is another one not to buckle to pressure from the crowd. The essence of being contrarian, as my dad taught me, is to "zig when others zag."

The style of the day as I write this essay is momentum investing. It is an extension of growth investing, but kicks in after caution has given way to conviction. This is partly due to "hot" money pushing into mutual funds chasing performance (the fear of missing out and the fear of not getting enough), and partly due to where we are now in the cycle of psychology, midyear in 1996. This methodology is akin to driving forward while looking in the rearview mirror. This is fine as long as the road ahead is straight. Imagine though what happens when a bend appears!

Generally, there are two basic styles of analysis applied in the study of the financial markets. One is called fundamental analysis, the other technical analysis. Fundamental analysis is an effective tool when attempting to dissect the underlying numerical aspects of a company, such as its earnings per share, book value, cash flows, dividend yield, sales per employee, debt/capital ratio, return on equity, etc. However, in its simplest form, fundamental analysis can be very intuitive. It may be no more complicated than going to a store in search of a particular item you desire and finding out that what was shipped to the store yesterday is already sold out today. This is a reflection of strong consumer demand and undoubtedly will show up in the company's revenue and earnings.

Technical analysis is an effective tool when attempting to get a visual sense of the trading patterns in a stock, interest rates, currencies, commodities, or anything, really, that has an underlying database. This form of analysis uses tools like 50- and 200-

day moving averages, relative strength, trend lines, angles of ascent and descent, overbought and sold oscillators, volume-at-a-price measurements, standard deviation bands, moving average convergence-divergence (MACD), Fibonacci ratios, point and figure, candlesticks, etc. Like an EKG (electrocardiogram) is a graphical depiction of the electrical functioning of the heart, so too is a chart an expression of the underlying direction of energy and potential of a company's stock.

There is an art to both forms of analysis. Each tends to resonate to people based on their natural brain hemisphere orientation. Left-brain fundamental, right-brain technical. The debate that rages over which is the more effective tool reminds me of many of the either/or conflicts we are drawn into in life. Conservative vs. liberal, masculine vs. feminine, traditional vs. holistic medicine. My approach is to engage both disciplines from a more yin/yang, balanced perspective, i.e., taking the best as I see it from each so as to end up with "both/and" rather than "either/or" viewpoints.

The Cycle Of Psychology

Now that we have touched upon technical analysis, investment styles, brain functioning and fear, let's proceed to the chart entitled "The Cycle of Psychology." Observe the sense of symmetry in the chart. This symmetry reveals a recurring pattern which expresses itself over and over again if one studies charts long enough. My professional experience validates the cycle, because it accurately reflects most people's investing behavior and experience. Knowing and understanding this flow of energy provides a powerful observation tool.

It doesn't matter whether you examine price action for a week, a year, ten years or longer, the basic underlying structure repeats. The cycle repeats like waves in the ocean, and the art of successful investing is to be able to identify a strong wave, where you are "psychologically" on the wave, and ride it for all it's worth.

At the lower left and beginning of the cycle is where value investors like Sir John Templeton arrive on the scene. This is where *Deep Pessimism* is evident—where the economic news is rapidly getting worse and rumors of business and banking failures are present. The rally cry in *Deep Pessimism* is "sell before a further sharp market decline occurs." The buyers are taking sellers out of their pain, but demand is only equal to supply and

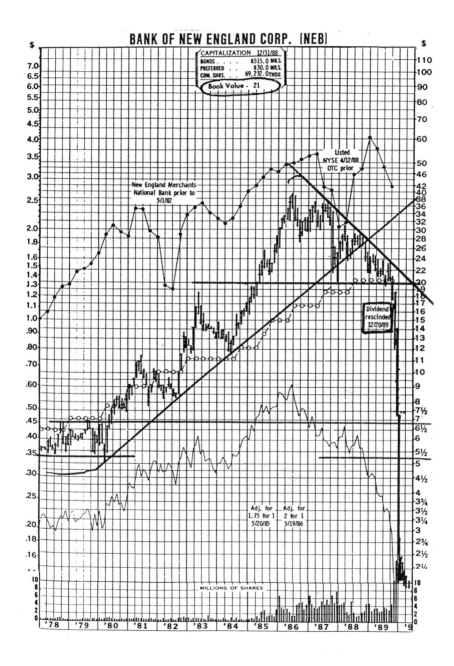

BANK OF NEW ENGLAND CORP. (NEB)

prices are in equilibrium for now, visually expressing itself in a bottoming pattern.

Followed by...*Disbelief.* The economic news is still getting worse, the rally must be based on technical factors only. The rally cry is "last chance to sell before a decline resumes." This is music to a contrarian's ear and an indication to move in. At this point, demand is starting to pick up relative to supply and prices start to rise. A right-brain, technically oriented investor at this point would notice a change in the shape of the chart pattern and know intuitively that something is afoot, price is headed higher and it's time to do some more basic fundamental research.

In the next phase, there is an *Awakening.* Now the economic news is starting to improve, but the market is perceived by the majority to probably be ahead of itself. The rally cry is "wait for reactions to buy." As you can visually observe, the "sweet spot" of the move is about to happen. It is at this phase that evidence can begin to be collected for growth investors to support the move, but the crowd psychology is still stuck in the fear of being wrong or the fear of losing money.

Next stop, *Belief.* Now the economic news is improving rapidly, stocks are going much higher. There is lots of evidence to support the thesis and the rally cry is "don't wait for reactions, just BUY!" It is here that lots of articles appear in the media. Wall Street fundamental analysts have had plenty of time to meet with management and methodically build earnings forecast models, and demand is now dwarfing supply. Prices are moving briskly as momentum players come surging in. The psychology now shifts to the fear of missing out and the fear of not getting enough. People are now spreading word of their success at cocktail parties and on the bulletin boards of the Internet and America Online, which leads us to...

Extreme Optimism. The economic news is good and getting better. Some stocks are advancing very sharply. CNBC and the television media are probably giving an unusual amount of attention and coverage, and maybe even *Time* magazine runs a cover story. As you can observe, a top may now be forming. As contrarian and value players sell to the hot-handed momentum players, short-selling supply expands and the natural cycle eventually swings in reverse.

As a long side "participant," it can be very difficult to leave the game at this point. Very little factual evidence affirms that a topping process is at hand and greed can cloud one's judgment.

But as a seasoned intuitive "observer" it can become abundantly clear that the time for a turn in the cycle has arrived and appropriate action is to cash in (or sell short). Reconciling the competing internal voices at this time comes from experience and practice. It is more important to watch the spin of the ball here (market action) than the scoreboard (share price and one's net worth), or you'll get trapped in...

Disbelief, and the cycle rolls on down. Not being willing or able to let go here can be very harmful to one's financial and psychological well-being, as will be experienced at the "oh my" of awakening and "oh no" of panic.

The Investment Strategy Of A Kinesthetic And Visually Intuitive Individual

At some point in life, we all need to ask the questions "What am I designed for?" "What am I best at?" "What am I most interested in?" What is it that will keep us coming back for more. To discover which inherent brain skill tendencies you may have (strengths and weaknesses) I strongly recommend taking either the Myers-Briggs test or the Hermann indicator test. *I have discovered that my natural strength is toward the sensing/visually intuitive side of things, in addition to being very analytical.* For this reason I spend a great deal of time scanning market trading patterns (time frames of days to months to ten years and longer) looking for a "feel" not only of what to buy, but when to buy it.

It's often the visual, nonverbal clues that lead me in a particular direction. Once I land on an idea, I immediately check out a number of factors. These include the traditional approaches of fundamental analysis, as mentioned above, to measure valuation, but going beyond that to scanning for insider buying or selling activity, examining the complexion of the institutional holders list looking for who's moving in and out and in what quantities, trying to gain a picture of what those in the know are doing, not what they may be saying, and the size of their footprint as it will relate to supply and demand and, therefore, price.

My ideas come from spending a great deal of time reading newspapers, magazines, industry trade rags of all kinds, annual reports and Wall Street research, talking to people in industry, noticing which companies catch my attention. I honor demographic trends, watching what Baby Boomers as a whole are doing, as their collective impact on the economy is enormous. I pay attention to signs and synchronicities by observing every-thing that's happening around me wherever I go, keeping my eyes and ears open. I look to see which companies are innovating and delivering consistently. And which ones have a consciousness about them, either in their corporate name (Intuit comes to mind), or in the way they handle employees or the environment. All day long I am interacting with customers, both institutional and individual, sharing thoughts and comparing notes. Lastly, I look at thousands of charts per week scanning for opportunities.

This constant interaction with my total environment allows me to generate a "feel" for where the collective mind of the market-place is, where it isn't, and where it may be headed. The idea here is to observe, infer and then boldly take appropriate action.

I use market-information programs suited to my intuitive style. I use the database of Bridge Information Systems out of St. Louis, which is predominantly for professional investors. I ask "what if" questions to the database and get answers in seconds. In the summer of 1995, I got an intuitive flash that maybe a shift in the currency markets was occurring, asked my system to graph an overlay of the U.S. Dollar trading in Yen against the Nikkei average over a ten-year time frame, and, *voila!* I had a graphical response in a matter of seconds. A buy signal was registered. By creating a graph overlaying short-term Treasurys versus long-term Treasurys over a ten-year period, I observed a pattern in November of 1994 that matched almost exactly another major buying opportunity in 1989. Yet most data-driven economists were caught leaning in the wrong direction by projecting an extension of higher rates, missing the visual clues suggesting the opposite.

Bridge also enables me to query the system screening for specific sets of criteria. This data mining process is an efficient and swift way to cull out potential candidates based on fundamental or technical information. The speed with which the screening process occurs allows for more time to blend the thought process beyond data and visual analysis and into theme synthesis.

Slowing Down While The World
Is Speeding Up

Since the turn of the century, markets have moved from "Who you know" in the 1920s to "What you know" in the 1950s-1960s to "How fast you know it" in the 1980s to "How quickly can you anticipate, recognize, understand and act on change" in the 1990s. This trend of acceleration in the rate of change is being imbedded permanently in our society and in our psyche due to the technological revolution. In 1983, Intel Corporation introduced the 286 microprocessor chip which could run at 1 MIPS (1 million instructions per second). In 1993 the Pentium chip performed at 100 MIPS. If you have any sense that life is speeding up around you and that it is harder to keep up with information flow and new technology breakthroughs, just watch as the Pentium Pro gets introduced in 1996 at 250 times the original speed, and the P7 in 1997 at 500 times. Now imagine what happens with everybody being simultaneously wired up, communicating and conducting commerce over the WorldWideWeb through the Internet! We are tapping into the "global brain" and it is overwhelming.

In order to cope with the high speed and associated stress that has come from using all the relevant information from a global interrelated economy and its never-ending impact on stocks, bonds, mutual funds and the like, it is essential to get aligned with one's own inner balance and innate talents. One must learn how to "let go." I do this through a combination of sports and meditation.

The chakra system was once taught in the Ancient Mystery Schools in Greece, and known in the Hindu tradition. It is a subtle anatomy, that interacts with our physical anatomy. The word "chakra" literally means "spinning wheel of energy." There are seven chakras that align themselves from the base of the spine up to the top of the head. Each of these chakras resonates to one of the seven colors in the rainbow and the seven notes in the musical octave. By focusing our breathing on the seven chakras, we can alter our internal energy and make our bodies more like antennas available to receive intuitive information. A "gut" instinct, a lighting up of the third (emotional) chakra, is just one of them. A chill down the back of the spine, a lighting up of the fifth (or communication) chakra is another.

To manage stress, I strongly recommend focusing awareness on these energy centers. While meditating on the chakras, a nice breathing exercise is to imagine inhaling energy up through the base of the spine, along the torso, up though the throat to the forehead, and then exhale through the top of the head. Repeat this process until a peaceful, calming sense appears. You may then notice that you have created a greater connection between heart and mind. By releasing tension, and creating a greater sense of inner ease, the intuitive self will emerge.

Intuition In Action

By bringing a conscious awareness to all that I do, I am in a place to construct knowledge out of little bits of seemingly unrelated information. This is the artwork of an intuitive player. For example, in 1988, when Massachusetts was in the middle of its self-proclaimed "miracle" and our governor was running for election to this country's highest elected office, bank stocks were heading towards what was about to become a decline of major proportions.

Individuals were still stuck in the psychology of extreme optimism, after a bull market in real estate that had lasted so long that conventional wisdom stated that real estate could only go up, and probably at least ten percent per year. Banks were making construction loans to developers in the amount of 120 percent of construction costs, and not even requiring collateral or signatures on loan documents. Respectable left-brain quantitative-only players were buying the bank stocks because of high and rising dividend yields, and buying more because, as the prices declined, the yields were perceived to only be getting better. However, I had an eerie feeling looking out the window of our 38th-floor office. All I could see were construction cranes— everywhere—building new office towers. This reminded me of being in Houston in 1980 and Denver in 1981 at the top of the oil market. People that I knew as plumbers and contractors were now calling themselves condominium developers.

When Comstock Partners wrote a major piece in *Barron's* on the coming decline in real estate prices, they were scorned for it. I knew that the psychology had turned to disbelief. In checking the long-term chart patterns of New England bank stocks, I saw the same thing over and over again. Big topping patterns, shaping up like the right side of a giant "M" (see Figure 2). The intuitive lights were flashing "crises directly ahead." Attorneys were about to start doing bankruptcy workouts instead of loans.

With the tax law changes in place from 1986 and depreciation tax benefits running out, with banks lending on balance sheets now leveraged 20:1, with the Federal Reserve tightening up on rates again, with everyone in denial, the big downturn was

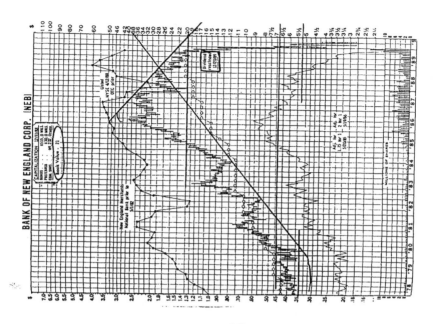

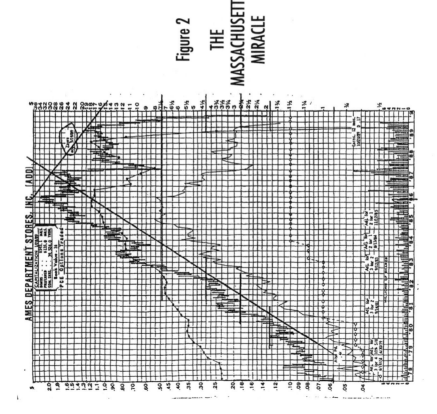

Figure 2

THE
MASSACHUSETTS
MIRACLE

about to hit. Is there any wonder the Chinese use the same character in their language for crisis as they do for opportunity? For me, the opportunity was to sell short the shares of New England bank stocks. Bank of New England, once the fifteenth largest bank in the country, fell from a 1986 peak of $40, to $20 in 1989, and was worthless within a year.

Just by knowing that Japanese investors bought a 50 percent ownership in my office building for 100 percent of the construction cost only three years earlier, sensing the bubbling enthusiasm inside Japan from their sizzling stock market and psychology of fear by others that Japan was going to take over the world economically, and seeing the parabolic nature of the Nikkei Average having gone from 1,000 in the 1960s to 8,000 by 1985 and 39,000 by 1989 lead me to buying put warrants on the Nikkei, a very successful bet to the downside. Between January of 1990 and August of 1992, the Nikkei Average fell from 39,000 to 14,000 for a decline of over 65%! And an appreciation on the put warrants of over 500%!

An opportunity of a different kind then became apparent. With both the U.S. banks and the Japanese banks in trouble, the economy in a stranglehold from no lending capabilities as bank regulators were forcing the cleaning up of balance sheets, the Federal Reserve was easing aggressively and nothing was happening positive to the economy. The media were still following the residual shock of the value of home prices declining and the constant layoffs being generated by corporate America adopting a downsizing and reengineering mentality. This constant feeding of negative information was a tip-off to look for something positive about the economy. I found it while walking through the redwood forests in northern California.

What I discovered was a giant thousand-year-old redwood tree fallen over in the forest with its roots now exposed. A sign was posted next to the tree requesting visitors not to touch the roots of the tree as they are essential to the full functioning of the ecosystem of the forest. When a thousand-year-old redwood goes over, the exposed roots become nutrients to be spread throughout the forest by the insects and animals that live there. A hole in the sky now becomes available for sunlight to reach the forest floor again, as well as creating an opportunity for a new tree to grow up and take its rightful place according to the laws of nature (Microsoft and Intel come to mind here).

Standing there, I had a sudden flash of insight as to what

was going to happen with the economy. What I saw that day in 1991 was an economy on the verge of a major growth period, led by all the entrepreneurs who were being unleashed from corporate layoffs. These layoffs were providing fertilizer to the economy (especially in technology) from places like IBM and DEC, our corporate dying redwoods. This is a story that took three to four years to be taken up by the media, and still isn't fully understood widely. As the information highway gets fully constructed with the Internet at its core, the surge of creativity and productivity will be breathtaking. The gold rush is on with intuitive entrepreneurs emerging as our new pioneers. Companies like Sun Microsystems, Cisco, Oracle, Netscape, U.S. Robotics, and Iomega, come to mind here. The list of others to come will be enormous.

Conclusion

A few tips for the road. Breathe. Still your mind. Pay attention to synchronicities; they tend to appear in bunches at turning points. Honor your intuition, dreams, impulses and hunches. When you are open to them, they will reveal important messages and signs to you. Let nature be your teacher. Pay attention to the enduring natural cycles and rhythms of life, like seasonal changes, waves, tides, the pull of gravity. They are reminders of what endures as truth. Identify trends and ride them. Don't chase fads. When you are participating, watch that you don't get caught up emotionally. Your emotions will be your enemy until you become expert at managing them.

It is the sense of unraveling a never ending mystery that makes participating in the markets such a challenge and so rewarding on many levels. Observing what's happening around the world and inside of ourselves and trying to put all the pieces together into a workable scenario can provide amazing growth in both self-worth and net-worth. When you get that sense of "aha!", the flash of insight that speaks "Yes, this is right," go for it. Track the success rate of your intuition, learn how to use and trust it. In the process, you will learn how to trust yourself more.

On January 16, 1995, Sir John Templeton was quoted in *Forbes* magazine as saying, "A person is more likely to be successful managing money if he uses spiritual principles, and the more you practice spirituality the more you learn." Good luck on your path of learning and discovery.

Roger Frantz, PhD, (left) is a professor of economics at San Diego State University. He is the director of Intuition 2000, a conference on intuition held annually at San Diego State University. He teaches intuition training classes and provides intuitive-based consulting through his company, Profits and Sense. He is also a "coach" for the Self Expression and Leadership Program offered by Landmark Education.

Alex N. Pattakos, PhD, (right) is a pracademic, avid martial artist, and cybernaut. He is also a former president of Renaissance Business Associates, an international nonprofit networking association "committed to demonstrating the power and effectiveness of integrity through elevating the human spirit at work," is on the advisory board of the Innovation Network, and chairs a national working group on technology for the American Society for Public Administration.

Pattakos is a contributing author to *Managing in Organizations that Learn* and *Rediscovering the Soul of Business: A Renaissance of Values*.

10

Economic Growth And Evolution: The Intuitive Connection

Roger Frantz and Alex N. Pattakos

Lifetime Growth And A New Economic Paradigm

It has been observed that the lifetime growth pattern of many things approximates an *S-Curve*. An S-Curve, such as the one shown in Figure 1, can be divided into three distinct parts. The first part—the bottom left segment—shows that the total quantity of activity grows at an *increasing* or accelerating rate. The second part—the middle segment—shows that the total quantity of activity continues to grow but at a *decreasing* or decelerating rate. The third part—the upper right segment— shows that the total quantity of activity moves into a phase in which it *ceases* to grow. This later phase is commonly called "death."

There are many illustrations of the S-Curve phenomenon in real life. For instance, the S-Curve represents: the lifetime growth in the number of Nobel Prizes won by Americans through 1988; the production of Gothic Cathedrals, supertankers, and miles of railways in the U.S.; the number of concerts given over a pianist's career; the growth in the height of sunflowers or humans; the birthrates of American mothers through age 50; the growth in the population of fruit flies; the output of many products (industries)

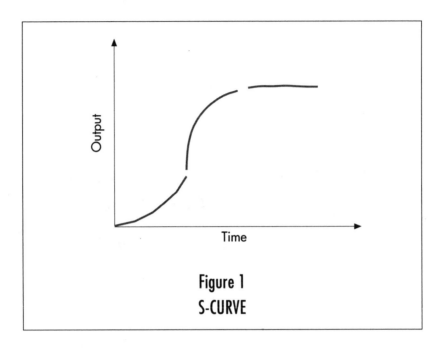

Figure 1
S-CURVE

over their life cycle; the incidence of AIDS victims as a percentage of all deaths in the U.S.; and the growth of vocabulary through the first six years of life, to mention only a few.

There are also studies of the lifetime output of artists and scientists who are considered creative by society-at-large, and whose output can be reasonably said to consist of their books, inventions, and songs. These studies show that many people die after completing 90 percent of their "creative potential." Mozart died after completing 91 percent of his creative potential. Creative potential, in this context, is neither a psychological nor a transcendental concept. Rather, it is simply a *statistical* artifact of the phenomenon being observed. Given Mozart's record of compositions, a statistical program for generating an S-Curve shows that he "should have" produced 644 compositions; he died after producing 587, or 91 percent of his creative potential. Even though he was only 35 years old, Mozart died of "old age." Brahms died at age 64 after completing 93 percent of his potential. Brahms produced 126 compositions. A statistically-generated S-Curve for his output of compositions shows a maximum of 135. These patterns are shown in Figures 2A and 2B, respectively.

There are exceptions to this "90 percent rule." Albert Einstein,

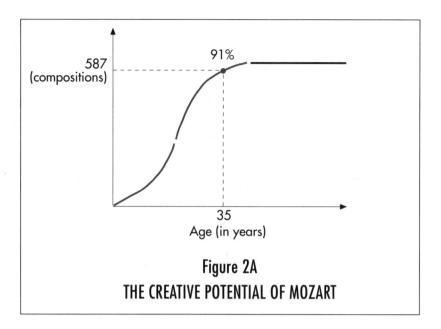

Figure 2A
THE CREATIVE POTENTIAL OF MOZART

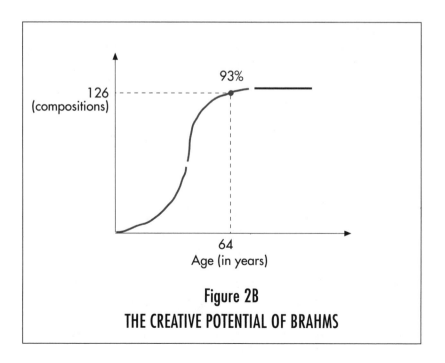

Figure 2B
THE CREATIVE POTENTIAL OF BRAHMS

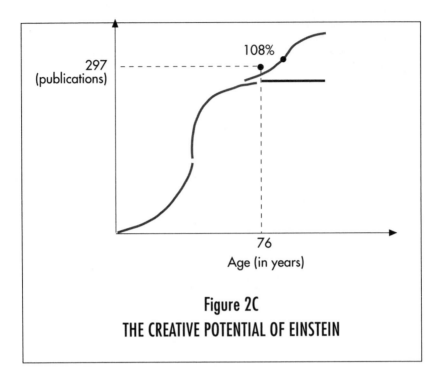

Figure 2C
THE CREATIVE POTENTIAL OF EINSTEIN

for instance, died at age 76 after completing 108 percent of his potential! Einstein had produced 297 publications at the time of his death, 18 more than he "should have." It is almost as if Einstein "got off his S" and started another path towards the end of his life. Einstein's creative output of 108 percent shows that it is possible to "get off your S" while there is still time and start another one. Had Einstein lived to age 96 rather than 76 we may have seen that Einstein's life consisted of two S-Curves, as shown in Figure 2C.

On the other hand, the poet Percy Shelley died at age 30 after completing approximately 50 percent of his creative potential of 290 poems. So we can say that Shelley died as he was entering maturity. Given some exceptions, the "90 percent rule" strongly suggests that people die when they have exhausted approximately 90 percent of their creativity. Exhaustion may set in because there is nothing more to say or because the individual is not able to express it. In either case, *when creativity stops, life stops.* The S-Curve, however, does not imply that life is predetermined. The S-Curve simply shows that lifetime creativity or

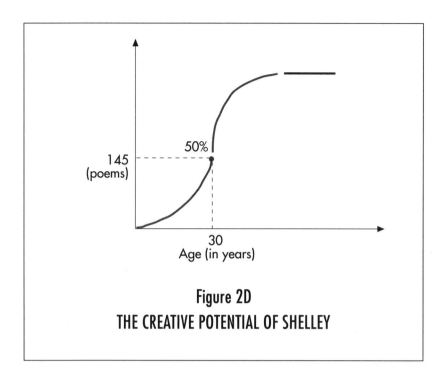

Figure 2D
THE CREATIVE POTENTIAL OF SHELLEY

output follows a pattern over time. It is up to us to decide whether or not our creative life on earth is going to be represented by one, two, three, or more S-Curves. Defining creative potential by a statistical artifact is certainly incomplete. It is also obvious that the creative "output" of most people is difficult to measure. At the same time, one can not fail to be impressed by the way in which the output of so many people and things conforms naturally to an S-Curve over a life cycle.

The S-Curve also approximates the growth of employment in various human undertakings. In this regard, the evolutionary history of employment in most industrialized economies follows a similar path. Employment tends to concentrate first in agriculture, then industry, followed by information, and then, according to the latest trend, by intuition or consciousness. In terms of employment by economic sector, the percent growth of employment in agriculture as shown in Figure 3 declined long ago and is now falling in absolute numbers. Employment in industry equaled that of agriculture in approximately the year 1900. It followed its own S-Curve and reached its maximum employment growth

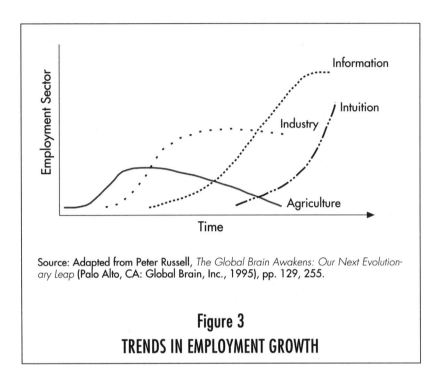

Source: Adapted from Peter Russell, *The Global Brain Awakens: Our Next Evolutionary Leap* (Palo Alto, CA: Global Brain, Inc., 1995), pp. 129, 255.

Figure 3
TRENDS IN EMPLOYMENT GROWTH

around 1950. It is significant to note that employment in information processing was just beginning in 1950. By 1975, however, the number of people employed in information processing equaled that in industry. We are now witnessing the rise of the "intuition (or consciousness) industry." It was just beginning in 1975. If the current interest in intuition and consciousness continues to follow its current "life cycle," then sometime in the next twenty-five years or so, the number of people employed in this "industry" will equal that in information processing.

A recent study by Paul Ray of American LIVES consumer research shows the rising interest in intuition in the general U.S. population. His survey of 100,000 Americans reveals that an increasing percentage of citizens identifies themselves as "cultural creatives." These adults—forty million of them—have an active interest in intuition, meditation, and the like. According to this study, moreover, Cultural Creatives surfaced only after World War II as a new cultural category. These data also show that those interested primarily in status and wealth, and those concerned with preserving traditional values, such as the need to climb the ladder of "success" or the requirement that one must "retire" at a certain age, are on the (relative) decline. Peter Russell, referring to the same survey results in *The Global Brain Awakens,* notes that this trend is not limited to any one sector of American society.

In economics, the second stage of the S-Curve is known as "diminishing returns" (or, more accurately, is referred to as the *beginning* of such a state). Diminishing returns, in this context, represents the beginning of a slowdown in growth and productivity. Even though the firm still adds economic inputs, the *growth* in output decreases. The problem is not that there are insufficient economic inputs. The problem is that the increase in inputs begins to coexist with a reduction in the growth of output. Basically, more comes in but less goes out. The notion of diminishing returns thus represents an environment in which the old tried-and-true formula for converting inputs into outputs no longer applies. This signals that new ways of doing things and new knowledge are needed. The presence of diminishing returns, in effect, creates frustration for producers and raises prices for consumers.

Diminishing returns also means that relationships (i.e., both physical and human) are breaking down. It is generally associated with a sense of discontent and uneasiness, and a breakup of the old order. Diminishing returns is about the end of the dominant paradigm as much as it is about a reduction in the productivity of traditional industries, such as steel making. The old answers and the conventional wisdom no longer seem to apply as readily as they once did. Paul Ray's survey of Americans clearly bears this out.

It is our contention that the U.S. economic system (note: we might as well add its political and social counterparts) has entered into an era of diminishing returns. We are seeing diminishing returns in the increased politicizing of life and the tension it creates for everyone. We are seeing manifestations of diminishing returns in the fact that, as a people, we are shouting more, listening less, overreacting more, interacting less. This situation gives the impression that people are losing the capability—at an alarming rate—to express themselves clearly, to understand others, or to reach peaceful settlements in their various domestic and foreign affairs.

The beginning of diminishing returns in the U.S. is due, in part, to the end of the Cold War. The end of this 50-year episode in human history has ushered in a rapid expansion of markets and economic competition. Many of the old habits and rules of organizing work are no longer appropriate. In short, we require more creativity and vision, more mental flexibility, and more *intuition*, in order to be competitive in a fast-changing global "marketspace" (a term used today to refer to the evolving business arena in cyberspace). The old paradigm—hierarchies, top-down management, treating others as if they are nothing more than machine parts, and a "cost" of production to be avoided whenever possible (authoritarianism), assuming that the environment is inexhaustible, and an overreliance on analytical thinking (materialistic)—is no longer adequate either as a tool for understanding or accommodating an increasingly chaotic and complex world.

The newly emerging paradigm contains the understanding that intuition is valuable in its own right, and that it complements and augments the presumed rigors of analytical thinking. The new paradigm, moreover, recognizes that every person has an inner personal source of *knowing* which can be brought to bear on the organization only through meaningful participation. The new paradigm is thus more democratic, less authoritarian, and less materialistic. *It is, indeed, ironic that the collapse of central planning is leading us to realize that the old paradigm no longer works, because the old paradigm is almost identical to central planning—hierarchical, authoritarian, and materialistic!* The collapse of central planning, then, represents the collapse of forced communitarian ethics, and a transition to a more intuitive-based, inner-inspired "community" of humans. Naturally resonating at deeper levels of connection, communitarianism takes on a much more profound meaning as a way of collective life (i.e., balanced, integrative, and holistic).

Intuition And Economic Evolution

The key to modern economic growth is our knowledge about how to organize and produce goods and services. In the past, economic growth was more reliant—first upon physical strength, then machine power. The past to which we are referring here could also be described as the "age of matter." As George Gilder remarks in his book, *Microcosm: The Quantum Revolution in Economics and Technology*, one of the key events of the 20th Century is the replacement of mind over matter and brute strength as the primary economic resource. So it is. Today, the key to economic well-being is *knowledge* (broadly-defined). This is true for most, if not all, of the world's industrialized economies. In this regard, a recent report by the U.S. Department of Labor included a list of desirable skills or core competencies for American workers in order to enhance the nation's economic productivity and relative economic position internationally. It is significant to note that one of the skills recommended in this report pertained to "seeing with the mind's eye." This particular kind of core competency has been echoed by the visionary architect R. Buckminster Fuller, who wrote that "reading" into the laws of nature is the key to technological progress. This is because nature "wrote all the rules" and all that humans can do, relatively-speaking, is "find out what Nature permits." More recently, Michael J. Cohen, chair of the Department of Integrated Ecology, University of Global Education (a United Nations non-governmental organization), has underscored the importance of "reconnecting with nature" in order to rejuvenate our natural intelligence and spark rewarding relationships with self, society, and the environment. Cohen is a pioneer in the integration of ecology and psychology as a way to promote health and wellness on multiple levels, and founder/coordinator of UGE's Project NatureConnect.

Knowledge is the obvious source of all technological progress. Conversely, technology is knowledge embodied or is part of any productive input. The most valuable productive input of all, in our view, is a human being. The most recent computer software may reflect the latest knowledge about software design and computer architecture and, hence, can be said to represent the latest in computer "technology." Economic systems make use of all kinds of knowledge. In addition to the knowledge embodied in machines, economic systems make extensive use of the knowledge embodied in people. For example, the knowledge of how to motivate individuals, how to create synergy among individuals, how to pour wine from a bottle to the satisfaction of a customer, how to make the best grilled-cheese sandwich, all relate directly to the human dimension. Again, *the most important knowledge is that which is embodied in people.* This knowledge accumulates through a willingness to learn from experiences, as well as through intuition. Such knowledge may be called "personal knowledge." One of the most important reasons why capitalism has bested centrally-planned communism is because capitalism makes much better use of personal knowledge.

The effective use of knowledge tends to shift the S-Curve upward. That is, all things being equal, more or new knowledge allows us to "produce" more over time. The replacement of muscles by machines altered dramatically the S-Curve associated with the production of most goods and services and, in effect, allowed us to start a new curve at a higher level of output. Moreover, few would question the fact that the "information revolution" has again lifted our S-Curve to new heights. The *complementary* use of intuitive and analytical thinking, which basically ushers in an entirely new dimension of information, undoubtedly will shift it upward again. We propose further that the S-Curve for a group of highly analytical and intuitive people lays above that for a group who are analytically sophisticated but intuitively dense. This is because knowledge of all kinds—both in absolute and relative terms—shifts the S-Curve upward. Our reference to the "complementary" use of both kinds of thinking should be underscored; it suggests that there is an *interaction effect* that also influences the shift in the S-Curve, even greater than either an increase in analytical or intuitive thinking alone would offer.

Delegated or identified by Western culture as a "female characteristic," and acknowledged but not taken very seriously for some four hundred years under the old paradigm, intuition is now taking its place alongside analytical thinking as fundamentally important. The effect of the new paradigm is a realization that intuition is a source of knowledge and a way of knowing as surely as is analytical thinking. Intuition is essentially a non-analytical way of thinking and knowing. Conventional analytical thinking proceeds logically and step-by-step. These steps—develop the model, collect empirical data, group these data into finite categories, use rigorous statistical routines to analyze all categories simultaneously, discard the data if the statistical results warrant, re-analyze all remaining categories, write-up and disseminate the results—are well known to and accepted by the scientifically-inclined thinker and can be verbalized to others (i.e., "replicated"). The thinker can also verbalize how she arrived at her conclusion(s) and, more importantly, "defend" her results if necessary. Indeed, the results of an analytical thinking process are expected to be (and, ideally, can be) *replicated* by others. If I conduct an experiment, you should be able to replicate my results if you have my data and follow my procedures. Last, but not least, analytical thinking, by its very nature, is devoid of emotions or feelings. Empirical data and information, but neither emotions nor feelings, are considered valid and reliable sources of evidence.

In contrast, intuitions are gained through a *gut feeling* or a *sixth sense*. A hallmark of intuition is its internal and subjective nature. Being an internal process, the steps to gaining an intuition are not generally known. What *is* experienced is the gut feeling or the nonlinear, "out of the blue" sensation. Neither the steps nor how you arrived at the intuition can be verbalized very easily because they are not known. Intuition is thus "knowing without knowing how you know." Being an internal and subjective experience, intuitions *cannot* (and, consequently, *will not*) be replicated like scientific experiments.

Intuition or intuitive thinking is very different from analytical thinking in other respects. In order to convey this difference, let us consider the case of many traditionally-trained academics, including economists and other social "scientists." Academic economists, for instance, are overly concerned with analytical thinking. Listen to them—they are concerned with logic and, presumably, the rigors of the scientific method. If an argument or position is logical, or, if a conclusion or result can be logically derived, then it must be "true." Indeed, logic to these traditional academics is the only criterion for what is true. Furthermore, these same scientists often base their "truths" and their "productive output" on empirical—and preferably, quantitative—methods. The cultural more, "if you can't count it, it doesn't count," has been both a blessing and a curse for creative academicians, especially in terms of providing a value-based benchmark for measuring productive output. Minus a significant paradigm shift like that described in this essay, *knowing without knowing how you know* is unlikely going to be considered a criterion for promotion and tenure decisions in traditional academic settings. Until then, many academics will continue to stay "in the closet" rather than openly admit to their intuitive yearnings.

The Two Faces Of Intuition

Intuition as both a source and a way of knowing is experienced through its two "faces": the face of the "expert" and the face of the "mystic." Intuition's "expert face" is the instantaneous voice of past experiences being brought to bear upon a particular challenge in the present. Intuition's expert face makes use of the almost unlimited amount of information stored in human memory. Because this process occurs beneath your threshold of aware- ness, it is not "known" to your conscious mind. Intuition's expert face in the world of business shows up in studies of MBA students and experienced CEOs. When asked to solve a business problem, for instance, both groups typically arrive at the same answer. However, the CEOs solve the problem in a much shorter time period. The reason for this difference appears to be that their intuition spontaneously builds a picture of the current situation based upon all their past experiences, and then arrives induc- tively at an answer. Intuition is so efficient because it does all of these "calculations" in the subconscious while leaving the con- scious mind free to engage in other activities. *Intuition's expert face is the expert within us.*

Intuition's "mystic face" is the voice of your spirit or soul and your connection to the *collective unconscious.* The mystic face of intuition brings you in contact with the collective unconscious, or humanity's "morphogenic field." This yields information to us which transcends our own personal experiences and memories. It allows us to "read" the unspoken and know the "unknowable." In many respects, this dimension of intuition refers to the meta- physical nature of living entities and therefore takes us even farther away from the perceived comfort of structured, logical thought. Because it transcends for many the acceptable bounds of rationality, linking intuition with familiar concepts like memory and personal experience, the mystic face of intuition depends as much—if not more—upon faith as it does reason. Accepting, if not entirely understanding, this aspect of intuition is a *sine qua non* of manifesting our spirituality at work and elsewhere. *The mystic face of intuition is the mystic within us.*

In both ways, intuition enhances your knowledge and hence your ability to produce. Your intuition may tell you to stop negotiating real estate deals and begin providing education for the poor. Regardless of what you produce, intuition is more than a productivity booster. In this connection, intuition is also a source of ethical and moral judgments, which is the subject of the next section. Intuition is exceptionally valuable today because it complements and augments the dominant mode of gaining knowl- edge over the past 400 years—analytical thinking. Intuition adds value because it draws upon a source of knowledge which analyti- cal thinking is not privy to; it extends our available supply of knowledge by going where logic alone can not. Intuition, as noted ife. If the "invisible hand" seems metaphysical in nature, it is. However, one must look to Smith's earlier work, *The Theory of Moral Sentiments,* to see more clearly how this is so.

It was in his first book that Adam Smith explained how an individual, behaving according to his own perceived self-interests, can rise above them to form moral and ethical judgments. His answer was simple. Self-interest and ethical judgments are compatible with each other when persons find a way to balance their day-to-day instincts for economic and biological survival (i.e., prudence) with being responsive to the feelings of others (i.e., benevolence). According to Smith, prudence is the strongest human motive, but benevolence is the "highest" and constitutes the perfection of human nature.

How do we know the feelings of others in order to respond to them? Within each of us is an "impartial spectator," according to Smith. It is the part of us which can transcend our own instinct for survival. In doing so, it enables us to "walk in another's shoes," or "have sympathy with another" (in Smith's terms). According to Smith, the impartial spectator can be relied upon when our mind is composed and tranquil, free of anger and hatred. Under these conditions, our impartial spectator serves as a guide to action that is surer than reason. Therefore, individual and social harmony are created not so much through reasoning, planning, or analytical thinking, as they are through our use of intuition.

Smith's "impartial spectator," in essence, is our intuition. Our precious intuition is the ethical basis of capitalism. Our intuition is the part of us which allows us to "connect" with another person and know, in a non-analytical fashion, what that person needs and wants to achieve their highest good. Our intuition also allows us to distinguish our own needs and desires from those of another. In other words, intuition, again, is a part of us which helps form moral and ethical judgments. It is through our impartial spectator that we are led as if by an "invisible hand" to carry out the will of our intuition. This is the more encompassing meaning of the invisible hand—that internal guiding mechanism which allows us to serve our own interests while serving a *higher purpose* at the same time.

The Search For Camelot

The importance of intuition as an "economic" resource perhaps has never been as great as it is today. In an environment

above, takes us into the unseen, the unheard, an
physical realms. This is why some of the world's grea
tists and artists recognize its value and openly ackn
influence on them and their work/deeds. Jonas Sa
stance, wrote that, "Only by cultivating and refining the
of intuition and reason complementarily can we a
wisdom we seek." Intuition is also valuable because it
the subconscious, leaving your conscious mind fre
tasks and activities. Intuition is thus a resource whic
require any "energy" *per se* to acquire and use. Intuiti
fact, be the elusive "free lunch." It is up to us, indivi
collectively, to open our hearts and minds to thi
resource.

An Intuitive And Ethical Basis For Capitalism

Intuition is a very important resource for overc
latest bout with diminishing returns. First, it is a va
available source of knowing. Second, it complements
thinking and thus adds to the available pool of basel
edge. On both grounds, intuition offers a (re)source o
growth. Third, it can be a basis for making ethical
decisions. This is important because ethical and mora
lie at the very heart of capitalism. Capitalism as an
system is based on the belief that we can be dyna
interested, and prosperous while simultaneously bei
and moral. At least, this was a belief of the founder o
economics—Adam Smith. It should be noted that Sn
moral philosopher first, an economist second. His 1776
Wealth of Nations, contains the elements of Smith's e
His moral philosophy was explained seventeen years be
Theory of Moral Sentiments.

Self-interest is a central issue for Smith. Self-in
been a much-debated topic in Western Europe since th
tion of Thomas Hobbes' *Leviathan* in 1651. Hobbes bel
self-interest was destructive to both the individual ar
The publication of *The Wealth of Nations* represented th
of the belief in the goodness of self-interest. In this sem
Smith declares that self-interest can be a means to pro
both the individual and society as a whole. Self-intere
the "invisible hand" guiding individuals and society t

that seems to be increasingly chaotic and complex, the pressures on individuals and organizations—to say nothing about communities, nation-states and other forms of *collective* endeavor—to "perform" on a higher plane are increasing at a rate perhaps never experienced before. Dissatisfied with conventional thinking about ways to approach and benchmark "success," people in greater numbers appear to be interested more in their quest for the *holy grail*—that is, knowledge about inner truth—than in the tangible rewards typically associated with progress along one's career track.

We can point to at least two factors that seem to be influencing, if not driving, this direction towards both personal and organizational transformation. One has to do with the increasing *awareness* or "shift in consciousness," if you will. In their book, *Magic at Work*, Carol S. Pearson and Sharon Seivert remind us that the journey of creating "Camelot" in our lives is "primarily an evolution of consciousness." Futurist Peter Russell, moreover, proposes that a "high-synergy" society, which perhaps is simply another way of describing Camelot, is supported by *a new mode of consciousness* that is based upon a new order of *connectivity* and *whole-systems thinking* [emphasis added]. This brings us to the second factor that seems to be behind the scenes influencing the transformational process—*integration.*

As we ready ourselves to enter the 21st Century, it is important to recognize that we live on a "small planet." Indeed, the degree to which all living things effect each other in some way is becoming increasingly apparent and more widely accepted. A large part of the shift in consciousness referred to earlier is focused on the interdependency and connectivity that exist. We now live, as described so eloquently by Jessica Lipnack and Jeffrey Stamps, in the *Age of the Network,* which suggests an entirely new way of organizing and doing business. In their words, "In the Age of the Network, the trend to integration with independence will lead to a more holistic view of all parts of life working together."

To return to the Camelot metaphor, it is through "magic" that we will be able to manifest the changes that we want to see in our lives. According to Pearson and Seivert, "magic is the art of releasing the highest and best potential in any situation." More importantly, magic is *expansive*—it seeks to increase the options that one has at his or her disposal. Viewed in this way, the journey to Camelot can only begin when we engage in activities that free intuition and increase our creative receptivity. To do this means that we must get off our "S."

Part Four

TOOLS FOR CAPACITY-BUILDING

Looking Within—The New Frontier
Joanne Black and Christine Roess

Intuitive Education
Jan Newman-Seligman

M. I. Intuitive?
Linda A. Garrett

Intuition At Work: A Question Of Balance
Gigi Van Deckter

Creative Imagery
Harnessing The Power Of The Intuitive Mind
John Pehrson

Joanne Black (left) is a partner in Business Dynamics. She was the first woman to serve as a vice president of marketing at American Express Co., and also served as senior vice president of marketing at MasterCard International and Showtime Networks, Inc. She is co-developer of *Sphericles: The Business Oracle*, a tool for gaining access to intuition at work.

Christine Roess (right) is founder of SDI Communications, a management consulting firm committed to the transformation of business through conscious communication. In 1984, she founded a women's organization in New York City devoted to the development of leadership from the feminine intuitive sphere. With her co-author, Joanne Black, she developed *Sphericles: The Business Oracle*.

11

Looking Within—The New Frontier

Joanne Black and Christine Roess

Intuition has always been a powerful force in the background of our lives. Our language is peppered with the evidence of its impact. "I have an idea"..."It feels right"..."It speaks to me"..."It came to me"..."Something told me"..., and on and on. Yet, its contribution to our lives goes largely unacknowledged and its potential uncultivated.

With the advent of modern science and its "rules of evidence," inward-looking was stripped of all validity as a source of practical value and creativity. This attitude has been particularly pronounced in business. The scientific method, with its reliance on analytical thinking, has been so effective in fueling the material production growth phase of the economy that it has come to be regarded as the only legitimate way to approach business issues. Conventional business wisdom has held that the greatest advantage accrues to the company with the best information, long-range plans, and organizational controls. For the most part, until the mid-1980s, this formula for success was sufficient to meet the prevailing business challenges, which were seen as:

- Analyze the market and identify the greatest opportunity among a vast array of lucrative possibilities
- Plan the most effective execution

• Control the organization's activities so that the plan is implemented efficiently

However, now we are moving out of the material production growth phase, with its emphasis on analysis, planning, and control. Executives are being charged with revitalizing companies faced with mature markets, global competition, and dramatic economic, social and technological upheaval. Concurrently, employees who may have thought their jobs were uninspiring but at least secure, find themselves on their own, challenged to think well outside of the box in which they were trained to think, and under increasing pressure to create new career directions.

These awesome challenges are happening to many individuals in middle age or beyond and are occurring in an environment characterized by fast, complex change and information overload. There has been more information produced in the last thirty years than during the previous five thousand and the information supply doubles every five years.

Shifting Paradigms

No one has any way of keeping track of and processing all of the useful information being generated in the world. And even if they could, statistics typically represent only information from the past—yesterday's trends, not tomorrow's possibilities. Things are changing so quickly that examples from the past are no longer dependable guideposts or models for the future. Already, an estimated two thirds of U.S. employees work in the services sector and "knowledge" is becoming our most important product. Growth, in other words, must now come from ideas. Idea production requires creativity, the ability to act in the face of ambiguity and the freedom to move quickly.

Conventional logical/analytical thinking, by itself, can actually hinder our ability to function effectively in the emerging global marketplace. McGill University Professor of Management, Henry Mintzberg, disparages strictly analytical approaches to the planning process in his book, *The Rise and Fall of Strategic Planning.* "Confounding analysis with rationality—calling it systematic, objective, logical and other good things has narrowed our view of the world, sometimes with disastrous consequences," Professor Mintzberg tells us. In this regard, the demise of organizations, entire industries, and even nations, can not always be predicted and averted through the mechanical application of strategic planning principles. Icons of American business, such as IBM, American Express, and Sears, have been outperformed by innovative entrepreneurs who are not bound by the ties of their past success. Indeed, during the decade of the 1980s, a total of 230 Fortune 500 companies (46 percent) disappeared from the list.

Such dramatic shifts in the competitive landscape are prompting big corporations and business schools from Harvard to the University of Southern California to reconsider the role of intuition in decision making. Using words like transformation, paradigm shift, creativity, and introspection, they are seeing more and more the need to make decisions based as much on "inner knowing" as on empirical analysis.

Proof of this blossoming new regard for drawing on intangible energy sources is showing up in the bastions of traditional business. IBM, for example, made a significant commitment of resources to create a tool called The Learner Within which provides a "map" of cards with suggestions for practice and development in such areas as "Accessing Energy" and "Accessing Intuition." A major advertising agency in New York City gave a unique holiday gift to its one thousand prime customers—Sphericles, a product developed by the authors to encourage and facilitate the use of intuition in business decision making. There is a growing array of innovative tools and processes designed primarily, if not exclusively, to assist individual workers (and, in some cases, teams) tap and tune into this largely unexplored terrain of consciousness and human capacity. Moreover, the use of these "technologies" facilitates the inherent ability of people to:

- see possibilities unrelated to historical trends
- identify the essential pattern(s) underlying complex situations
- create synthesis from conflict
- adjust quickly to the constant stream of new game plans
- stay in a dynamic state of production

In the words of Albert Einstein, who has acknowledged that intuition was the most important element behind his paradigm-shattering insights, "the world that we have made as a result of the level of thinking we have done thus far creates problems that we cannot solve at the same level at which we created them." Our relative success with the Newtonian scientific model has brought us to a point we must now go beyond if we are to meet the challenges and realize the promise of the emerging age. Successful business decision making in the 21st Century will require a *whole*-brain, *whole*-person approach. Intuition is not only a key element of this approach, it is the linchpin that creates the "whole."

Chaos Made To Order

Leading edge work being done by scientific think tanks, such as the Santa Fe Institute, on chaos theory and the spontaneous adaptability of self-organizing systems is breaking new ground regarding ways to operate in today's complex and fast-changing environment. This field has attracted experts from multiple and diverse disciplines, including physics, economics, ecology, artificial intelligence, chaos theory, neural networks, linguistics, and psychology and other social sciences. They all recognize that there is an underlying unity inherent in all living systems which gives them the dynamic ability to self-organize spontaneously at the edge of chaos. This is where the components of a system never quite lock into place and yet never quite dissolve into turbulence. It is where new ideas and innovation are forever nibbling away at the status quo. Margaret J. Wheatley, consultant, author, and original thinker in this dazzling new arena, sees chaos as a powerful environment for real growth. She sees corporations as trustworthy, self-organizing systems, dynamically alive like Nature herself. Using analogies of natural systems, such as rivers and clouds, Wheatley writes in her book, *Leadership and the New Science:*

> Structures emerge, but only as temporary solutions that facilitate rather than interfere. There is none of the rigid reliance on single forms, on true answers, on past practices that I have learned in business....Streams have more than one response to rocks, otherwise there'd be no Grand Canyon.

Like time-lapse photography speeding up the unfolding of a flower before our eyes, we are watching the shape of the corporation visibly alter. The continual corporate re-organizations of the 1980s have become the steep down sizing and re-engineering of the 1990s as people stream out of corporate headquarters to telecommute or start their own small businesses.

We are beginning to realize the futility of waiting for things to settle down and the organization to take a fixed form. There is no reason to believe that when this phase of the process is complete, business life will ever freeze into a permanent shape again. Quite the contrary, every indication is that the rate of change will continue to escalate. Like the organs of our bodies, which quantum science tells us are continually renewing themselves, healthy *organ*—izations are alive and in dynamic motion.

Since organizations are made up of human beings, this means that we are dynamic, "alive," spontaneously-adapting creatures. However, perhaps with the exception we make for artists, this is generally not our prevailing view of ourselves. In order to stay in creative action amidst ever-changing climates, we need to shift our self-identification from one of information bearers who learn a function and then repeat it, to an appreciation of ourselves as inherently creative beings trusting our own instincts as much as we trust data, the past, and the reputed "experts."

Co-author Joanne Black built a successful career as the first woman senior executive in several major corporations without a college degree, primarily by relying on her highly-developed intuition. In her experience, the process of intuitive decision making requires a high degree of trust—in oneself and in the process itself. Reflecting on these personal experiences, she describes the intuitive process in the following way:

> I take in as much information as I can and let it simmer. I can actually feel the idea bubbling up inside...my sense of excitement grows. I know enough not to "try" to push it. I just keep "sleeping on it" and having conversations about the issue. Sometimes I will be having a conversation and the idea comes out of my mouth, like someone else was saying it. But I know when it is right...everything falls into place and I feel a childlike joy that fills me with energy. I also know when something is wrong with an idea because I get anxious, even angry for no reason. It's a mysterious, but reliable process and *the most important part is trusting yourself.*

Increasingly, people are discovering that there is a part of themselves that does know; indeed, that can see beyond the circumstances. That part is the voice of our underlying unity and it speaks to us through our senses, in pictures, metaphors and sudden flashes. Our challenge, both individually and collectively, is to tap into this powerful way of knowing.

Developing The Intuitive Voice

We develop our muscles with physical exercise, but how do we develop our intuition? The words we use for creative ideas point to the source of this mysterious human ability—insight, innovation, invention, inspiration,...in...in...in! Like intuition, these qualities or attributes are all within us, available for the asking.

While intuitive wisdom is always available to us, we must be willing to "listen" to it. Moreover, although intuition is as close to us as our next breath, we must be willing to remove the barriers that prevent us from receiving its insights. Given that we have been trained to fight unconsciously against or distrust ourselves, the first step is *to become aware of our automatic habit of dismissing or denying our own inner guidance.*

Years of inner space exploration and study have taught us some simple, but still essential, guidelines for tuning into this fertile kingdom. They are:

- **Be Clear**—about your request for guidance. This is different from asking for what you want. In fact, it's important to be open to the precise form the answer may take. We often get fixated on a *symbol* for what we want rather than the experience itself. For example, sometimes we ask for more money when what we really want is a sense of prosperity and well-being. The stories are legendary of people loaded with money and still feeling insecure.
- **Quiet The Mind**—Relax and let go. We all have a running internal dialogue that vies for our attention and blocks intuition. It is often hard to distinguish between the voice of our ego and intuitive wisdom. The voice that tells us we're hopeless, we've blown it too many times, we might as well jump off the nearest high-rise is the same one that says, the moment after we've jumped, "but on the other hand..."
- **Focused Awareness**—Focus your attention on all of your

senses, including your sixth sense, and just be present "in the moment." This takes practice. Don't expect the voice that keeps reminding you of past guilts and future fears to evaporate. Your habitual doubting thoughts don't have to disappear. They almost assuredly will be there, often quite loudly, especially in the beginning. Just keep taking your attention away from them and trust that your intuition will find a way to speak to you if you are open and willing.

- **Suspend Beliefs**—All beliefs preclude intuitive leaps. If you hold on to what you have always thought, you will continue to get old answers to new questions. You can't receive an innovative idea if you have strong prejudices. The need to be right mutes your inner wisdom. Even in Total Quality Management circles, it has been observed that it is better to do things right than it is to do the right thing. This suggests, among other things, that one must be ready to let go of preconceived notions, including attachments to outcome.

- **Open To Radical Ideas**—Listen for intuitive insights and receive them with respect. The ego protects existing belief structures with its life. It will tend to rush in with all the reasons why an intuitive idea won't work. Our intuition often speaks in metaphors, which Harvard Business School Professor, Garald Zaltman, calls the most fundamental units of thought and communication. It is easy to get caught up in the power of words, but many of us think in visual images, not in words. Be alert to receive your inner direction in whatever form it appears, e.g., a song that comes to mind, a pattern of light that evokes a strong feeling or the impulse to take an unfamiliar action.

- **Explore Channels Of Intuitive Communication**—Find the channels that are most powerful for you. Just as each of us finds ways that suit our individual body's health and well-being, there are various channels through which our intuition communicates to us. Identify your strongest channels and support the process with tools and techniques to enhance this point of access. For instance, one advertising executive, who develops award-wining campaigns year after year, gets his best ideas while painting; a colleague listens to classical music for intuitive inspiration. Some of the most prolific executives find being *in nature* to be their greatest intuitive catalyst. Others use tools like The Runes, Sphericles, The Whack Pack, or The Learner Within to unlock the key to their inner wisdom. Now, there are even software programs, such as IdeaFisher™, Inspiration™, and MindSaver™, to name a few, and hardware systems, such as the NEST™, that are designed to enable users to tap into their intuition more easily and effectively.

- **Practice Consistently**—Include intuitive exercises in your life. One senior executive officer of a large communications company, who is known for coming up with revolutionary ideas, regularly takes two-minute breaks in his day for a brief meditation on the problem or issue he is addressing. Invariably, the solution comes during or soon after his "break." Another case in point involves a successful entrepreneur who is a strong advocate of "automatic writing" as a way of giving free rein to her inner wisdom. She says that she tries to start everyday spending twenty minutes just writing whatever is "there"; or if she has a particularly knotty issue for which she wants guidance, she will start by posing that question and then just observe what the pen in her hand wants to say. It has also been suggested that writing with one's *nondominant* hand serves as a catalyst for increasing intuitive awareness.

- **Notice Synchronicities**—These occurrences often reflect the subtle voice of intuition. Synchronicity is a term that was chosen by the eminent Swiss psychologist, Carl Jung. As he explains in his Foreword to the *I Ching* (an ancient Chinese Oracle), "...synchronicity takes the co-incidence of events in space and time as meaning something more than mere chance, namely, a peculiar interdependence of objective events among themselves as well as with the subjective states of the observer." The "coincidences" are one of the richest sources for new perspectives but we are often too busy listening to our skeptical, habitual thinking to be aware of these messages which, in fact, are really all around us.

- **Humor And Play**—All creative acts are forms of play. Humor and play are powerful tools for teaching and cultivating intuitive thinking. They are perhaps the most important and least consciously practiced in the work environment—often thought of as "wasting time." What a pity! The very thing that heightens morale, relieves tension, and spurs creativity is condemned as a threat to productivity. To illustrate, there is the case of a particularly somber senior manager who saw in a coaching session that his staff meetings were too tense and anxiety-producing and, as a result, there was little group participation and creativity. In order to remedy the situation, he committed, among other things, to being more playful. At the next meeting, he hid outside the door and rolled oranges across the floor to the table where the group was waiting. When he peered around the door grinning impishly, the staff broke up laughing and they had one of the most effective meetings they had ever had. There is no doubt that those who have the courage and inclination to make playfulness a part of their everyday routine are more likely to keep people with whom they associate "happy," more relaxed, and in a high creative flow.

• **Breath**—Probably because it's so close to us, the immense *centering* power of conscious breathing—full, relaxed inhales and slow, elongated exhales—is often overlooked. In the middle of a busy day, it is surprisingly simple yet effective to stop, take several deep inhales, each followed by a complete exhale. It's fascinating, moreover, to notice the subtle but significant impact this effortless practice has on your level of inner clarity and outer calm. If you start to pay attention to your breathing, you will notice that there are moments, like in the middle of an important presentation, when you have almost stopped breathing. This usually means that you are out of touch with your natural intuitive self. Pausing to smile and take a couple of good breaths actually conveys confidence and ease to the audience while you are spontaneously returned to the present moment and connected to your own natural wisdom.

Intuiting The Next Millennium

In the 20th Century, business and technology, guided primarily by the rational intellect, has seen its mission as the intensive development of natural resources for infinite human utilization and consumption. This unchecked drive for techno-logical progress has created possibilities for both good *and* ill beyond our wildest dreams. As successful as this level of produc-tivity has been, it now begs to be balanced with the full develop-ment of the truly infinite natural resource of our inner wisdom.

It may seem ironic that one of the greatest achievements of the age of technology, the computer, will likely be the greatest boon to intuitive thinking. The unregulated Internet operates like a self-organizing system, connecting people around the world instantaneously at any moment of the day or night, forming new "communities" (i.e., "cyberhoods") that go beyond the boundaries of government, language or geography. By the end of 1995, one hundred million people will have been on the Internet. This dynamic, spontaneous ability to connect with others promises to produce more new ideas than any managed organization ever could. We have created a whole new domain called "cyberspace" where millions of people "meet" in all kinds of combinations, totally free to create together virtually without restriction. This "externalized mind," where we all can play in whatever way most intrigues and delights us, must be the most powerful ever coming together of the intuitive and logical minds. Technology now provides a platform that supports the exploration and develop-ment of our intuition and creativity. The possibility of creating in balance—the logical, analytical left brain with the intuitive, cre-ative right brain—is a reality.

In their insightful discussion that penetrates deeply into the complex issues of organizational development, Fred Kofman and Peter Senge tell us:

> We have gained control of our environment but
> have lost our connection to it...[we are] living in
> bureaucratic organizations with no place for the
> wonder and joy of learning. Thus we have lost
> the spaces to create new meanings, to dance
> with the ever-changing patterns of life. We have
> lost ourselves as fields of dreams...to regain our
> balance we must create alternate ways of work-
> ing and living together. We need to invent a new,
> more learning oriented model for business,
> education, health care, government and family.
> The invention will come from the patient con-

certed efforts of communities of commitment,
groups of people invoking aspirations and wonder.

—Fred Kofman and Peter Senge
"Communities of Commitment: The
Heart of Learning Organizations"
Organizational Dynamics, Autumn, 1993

The rational mind will never, by itself, lead us to these
realms of wonder because rationality exists as a function of data
from the past which it must have in order to "think" at all. The
inner voice has no such limitation. It is the medium of true
creativity. The full value that will come from a conscious development of our intuition at work is still largely unknown, but benefits
that we can already see include:

• Access to *possibilities* beyond the limitations of existing
  belief systems

• *Shortcuts* seen by the intuitive mind that immensely
  expedite problem solving

• New *ability to cope* with rapidly changing environments
  replacing anxiety with excitement and skepticism with
  personal responsibility for innovative action

We are heartened that there is a large and growing network
of like-minded people who are not starry-eyed, inexperienced and
irrational thinkers. Far from it, like Peter Senge, Tom Peters, and
many others, we are well-educated, highly-experienced, *critical*
thinkers who see that the lopsided commitment to analytical
thinking is simply insufficient to whole and healthy creation.

Our intuitive voice is now asserting itself and we are eager to
hear its wisdom. This voice is not counseling a take-over. It's
pointing to a partnership, a co-creative relationship of inner
wisdom and rational analysis that can allow for an implosion of
life-giving sanity in our creative choices that will nourish ourselves and our planet and allow us to offer a quality of life for the
future we will be proud to leave our children.

Jan Newman-Seligman holds a Masters in Psychology and is the founder and director of Circus Earth Foundation, a not-for-profit educational organization dedicated to facilitating healthy collaboration, communication, conflict resolution, and creativity. She has been an educational counselor in San Diego since 1987.

She is a volunteer trainer for The Alternatives to Violence Project, a program focused in prisons and the community offering conflict resolution skills to change lives.

She teaches extension courses in the field of Interpersonal Relations, The Methodology of Interactive Learning in the Classroom and Conflict Resolution at San Diego State University and National University in San Diego. She has recently begun a book entitled, *The Technology for Collaboration: Peace-ing It All Together.*

12

Intuitive Education

Jan Newman-Seligman

The citizens of Folkstown were very pleased with their new bridge and waited anxiously for the ceremony which would officially open it for public use, thus making their long-detoured commutes into a quick crossing. Imagine their alarm when a sign posted at either end of the bridge read, "Bridge access denied until further notice." What public official would do such a thing?

Intuition is a bridge between the inner realms of energy, images, feelings and thoughts, and the outer existence of matter, form, and action. It has a natural place in life, and therefore, in education. Omitting it from the curriculum would be like closing the Folkstown Bridge; we'd still get there but the way would be more arduous. Intuition already imbedded in the curriculum would provide the bridge, the shortest distance between inner and outer awareness. However, intuition is often feared, denied, and berated because it is unscientific. It has been categorized as magic because it cannot be analyzed or understood with the normal senses. There are no tangible parts. Intuition is used to explore the unknown, but since we commonly fear the unknown, intuition has come to be feared, also.

Knowing, yet not knowing how we know, is an innate, unexplainable kind of knowledge. The idea of using intuition as a major source for decision making and pathfinding, evokes different points of view. Religious fundamentalists may view it with great suspicion. Scientists are often reluctant to validate such nebulous tools. For parents, intuition might threaten to disrupt discipline and control over the child. In the world of psychiatry, it could be diagnosed as a pathology, possibly warranting medication. Open use of intuition in politics risks public opinion. For educators, it appears to snatch time away from academics and creates autonomy.

On the other hand, some people are beginning to recognize that intuition is a profoundly useful tool. Many scientific discoveries were the result of people trusting their "hunches." Psychology is having great success in healing by accessing the patient's internal perceptions and dialogues. Politicians following their "gut" feelings and trusting their personal insight might break through to an unprecedented win. Amongst educators, introducing instinctive knowledge is being suggested as a cure for many societal ills symptomatic in our children.

As founder and director of Circus Earth Foundation, a non-profit innovative educational organization, I support the statement made by Shelly Kessler, director of the Institute for Social and Emotional Learning in Boulder, Colorado. She states, "Growing numbers of educators are recognizing that the pursuit of an exclusively academic education leaves students ill-prepared for future challenges. Academic performance, as well as self-esteem, character, and human relationships suffer." We are beginning to realize our educational model may not be capable of guiding us safely and wisely into the 21st Century.

What would our focus need to be if we were to replace the existing traditional model of education? What if we educated for balance? This would foster a growing need in education to include the spectrum of the "whole person"—joining heart and head, uniting intuition with intellect. Education of the whole person does not dismiss the academic focus already securely in place. Our error has not been in focusing on the outer-directed mind, but in overemphasizing it. Involving both the head and the heart means using aspects of human life traditionally ignored by education. Some of these are listed in the Table 1.

In order to restore balance to the educational day, it is vital that we link our traditional focus with the intangible bigger picture. As our reliance on technologies and outer resources increases, it is also important to allow time for the student to

Table 1
Educational Polarities

Traditional Focus	Additional Focus
Factual	Intuitive
Mind	Body/Spirit
Knowledge	Imagination
Thought	Feeling
Indoor	Outdoor
Speaking	Listening
Busy	Still
Working	Playing
Tension	Relaxation
Outer-directed	Inner-directed
Teacher wisdom	Student wisdom
Action (learning)	Non-action (reflection)

begin relying upon natural internal resources. Learning to trust again this felt sense of wisdom is the key to restoring balance and unlocking the richness of the whole person. With the marriage of intuition and intellect, we are carried over the threshold into the house of the whole person, into the life of a new relationship of balance.

Watching our people and our planet slowly deteriorate in the face of the technological revolution has given birth to a new revolution—the "Intuitive Revolution." Why is the use of our intuition bursting forth simultaneously in many different arenas right now? Because we are out of sync with our natural rhythms. It is the universe's way of finding a cooperative solution to keeping the balance. It is like the pendulum, the metronome, the seesaw, and a planet's orbit—for every movement there is an equal and opposite effect. It is, also, an admission of something missing; and when something shows up as missing, that missing piece will invent a way to push even stronger for recognition, so balance (cooperation) can be restored.

Can we step gracefully into the 21st Century without accessing, trusting, and utilizing our inner life as much as we do our outer life? Will we ever know what it is like to be fully human without consciously managing the full potential of the whole being? Each person has the solution to every problem deep inside, and trusting the intuitive voice of the expert in each one of us can provide guidance, knowledge and answers to solve the inevitable coming challenges. It is difficult to always express in words the complex thoughts, memories, and images that enter daily awareness and have been stored throughout a lifetime. Adding intuitive education to the daily curriculum will allow children to explore alternative techniques which can easily and effortlessly help them to heal the powerful issues on which they build their lives and guide them to appropriate decision making. To round out the academic day, intuitive curricula should include:

- The Arts
- Emotional Intelligence
- Stress Management Techniques
- Communication Skills and Conflict Resolution
- Group Problem Solving and Team Building
- Spiritual Development

The Arts

President John F. Kennedy said, "The processes of creativity are the catalyst through which some of America's most crucial issues can be solved." Creativity is necessary and pivotal in the educational process. The arts have always held a sacred place in our lives for they are inherent in all civilizations. The experience gained through art is so rich that by removing it from our educational system, we are impoverishing our children and our culture.

Herbert Read in his book, *Education Through Arts,* writes, "Education is the fostering of growth, but apart from physical maturation, growth is only made apparent in expression—audible or visible signs and symbols. Education may therefore be defined as the cultivation of modes of expression." The arts offer a variety of mediums so each student can process learning in his or her own way. Using the arts (drama, movement, dance, music, painting, sculpting, sand play, etc.) as the core of education facilitates experiences which awaken, encourage and support the creative spirit.

Each of these modes is non-linear or intuitive. The arts foster intuitive education because the arts are a medium for intuition. Through art we draw out fresh material from the unconscious in a non-linear or intuitive way leading to inexplicable insights and enhance our thinking. All information can be relayed as either fact or through metaphor. Through the arts we learn to convey through metaphor. Ironically, many great scientists and mathematicians explain through fact what their own mind could convey to themselves only as metaphor. Their creative process required that they bridge their inner metaphor with outer reality.

There is a very distinct process that takes place in which we see, hear, and feel very complex images, before we actually speak in words. We all speak this internal image language and it is the arts which allow people to tap into their unique uncensored, intuitive expression. The arts allow us a way to verbally and non-verbally express what is deeply held inside. The arts are an essential tool for children whose dominant way of being is non-verbal, children who are scared to speak, children who do not speak the primary language well, and children 'at risk.' To do away with words is not only important for non-verbal learners, but for highly verbal people who are good at hiding their feelings with thoughts.

Intuitive education fosters heightened creativity so the unconscious (holder and disseminator of unending thoughts, feelings, and patterns of ideas we might not be aware of) can be positively channeled and expressed. Otherwise, we are controlled by our unconscious patterns. Ideas we don't know we have, have us. Through intuitive arts, we become conscious of what was formally unknown.

According to Bruce Kantner in his program description for the Gaia Education Outreach Institute, "The past three hundred years of cultivating empirical, analytical, and mechanical ways of perception have left our senses atrophied, our imaginative powers dulled, and our inner modes of knowing and connecting with the natural and spiritual worlds diminished." Education through the arts is an expedient reconnection with the more fragile aspects of ourselves. It gives each student personal choices in finding his or her pathway to a sane and healthy life. My friend Diane Loomans, national speaker and author of *The Laughing Classroom* and *Full Esteem Ahead*, states that "In creative play, there are no wrong answers; there are only possibilities."

Emotional Intelligence

On the cover of *Time* magazine, August, 1995, the "EQ Factor" (emotional intelligence) was premiered. The article's first sentence is, "New brain research suggests that emotions, not IQ, may be the true measure of human intelligence." The cover exclaimed: "It's not your IQ. It's not even a number. But emotional intelligence may be the best predictor of success in life, redefining what it means to be smart."

The term "emotional intelligence" was created by Yale psychologist Peter Salovey, and John Mayer at the University of New Hampshire. EQ includes understanding one's own feelings, empathy for the feelings of others and the regulation of emotion in a way that enhances living. Learning to identify, acknowledge, appreciate and control emotions transforms people who experience themselves as victims into people who experience themselves as powerful. Learning how to manage emotions creates the most potent tool we have, self-awareness. Self-awareness is easily developed through intuitive/feeling exercises.

Intuition has been described in similar terms. Intuition is called a gut feeling because it is experienced in the gut or emotional center. Intuition is a "sixth sense," a "holistic perception," and the "poetic part of the intellect." These metaphors are conveying something other than IQ, something resembling EQ.

Seeking a broader measure of intelligence, it was reported that children in the new "emotional literacy" programs improve their ability for self-direction, are better able to carry out a self-appointed task, engage in appropriate and cooperative behavior leading to conflict resolution. The added bonus is that achievement test scores rise an average of 250 points.

EQ is not IQ's opposite. Just as linear and intuitive thinking complement each other, so do EQ and IQ. Together, they can produce wholeness. Health means to make whole, the integrated caring for all sides of our human nature and our planet. We need guidance and coaching in the exploration of all aspects of life—body, mind, emotions and spirit. Knowledge and competent articulation of feelings or EQ—strengths (our essence) and weaknesses (our shadows)—are crucial building blocks for positive self-development, for communicating effectively, for managing stress, and for successful decision making. As Nancy Gibbs writes in her *Time* magazine article, "The EQ Factor," "IQ may get you hired, but EQ gets you promoted."

What happened to the concept of the magical child? It left when the amount of time was diminished for children to "space out." Remember the far off look in the child who intuitively accessed "their own world"? This allowed children time to rest and reflect internally (meditation, centering, focusing, visualization). Imaginary play, tuning in and visualizing inner worlds where all was possible. Children were allowed, even encouraged, to test what they heard, saw, and felt in the real world. If we had more time and used the same natural tools we automatically accessed as children, we could again live in a time of deep imaginings where many solutions to our problems would intuitively surface and we could investigate their viability.

Stress Management Techniques

Stress reduction education is essential to maintain our current life style. Between stress and a lack of access to our intuition, we will continue to burn out with stress related malfunctions. It is necessary to learn we can direct our life and that we possess tools for exercising this control. Stress management is based on the practice of allowing self to sense connections which consistently emanate from the subconscious; trusting the body, mind, and spirit to successfully problem solve. Stress management will enhance accessing our intuition. Intuitions are "fleeting" and "subtle" messages more easily heard when both the mind and body are calm.

We have created our schools in the image of adults with type A personalities—too little time and too much to do, for students and teachers. We expect our children to juggle six to eight classes at one time. The subjects are in separate compartments and time periods, with very little relevance to each other. We expect our children to excel in all subjects, instead of honoring that each person has strengths and weaknesses. We insist solely on busy, productive work, while allowing no time for synthesizing and assimilating new information via silence and reflection. Our children talk of pressure, no time for self, no time left for play, or daydreaming or solitude and stillness which we know are the most fertile grounds for intuition which in turn nurture creativity and growth.

Life in the fast lane. We joke about it. We live in it. And some of us will die in it. But most often, when lacking a consistent, natural stress-releasing valve, many people become like the active volcano, ready to blow. This is poignantly so for our children. Stress-related dysfunction, both medical and psychological, have been showing up earlier and earlier in our children.

Ironically, television and computer technology have also contributed to our stress. Before the TV and the computer age, which brought with it the fragmented, quick, visually-oriented media world, we learned in a slow, methodical, logical, linear fashion. This is not a cry to deny technology, but is a plea for balance. The use of computers by children so young has produced people more capable of multidimensional thinking, whose systems have the capacity for more integration and whose neural pathways have been expanded to hold, assimilate and synthesize new and massive amounts of concepts and information. This necessitates an equal and opposite addition. Each side of the scale must be equal or one side becomes overemphasized. Like the breeze in a sail boat, too much wind in one sail ultimately capsizes the boat.

Since there is an equal and opposite effect for every cause, we can help to smooth out the results of what John Naisbitt calls "high tech with high touch." The more we interact with computers, plastic, heavy metal and enormous intellectual concepts, the greater our need to be touched—by people, by nature and by our own intuitive self. If our being healthy, intelligent, excelling individuals is to continue, intuitive information and skills must certainly match technological intelligence. The latter only insists on storing more and more information. Our feeling, intuitive side is left out of this equation. Curriculum which includes a model of intuitive intelligence is key to creating a healthy future.

Learning is also greatly affected by how students feel and what thoughts and emotions are busily vying for their attention. Thoughts and feelings which produce stress hinder the learning process. Some anxiety is normal because the right amount of tension allows a child to stretch, to challenge himself. Thus the introduction of reflective tools is paramount to the well-being of our children because visualizations, meditation tools, body/mind practices like Yoga, Akido, and Qigong (chee -kung) are relaxation and focusing tools designed to diminish stress build-up. The arts are also used as safe, non-threatening exercises for emotional release and help to express outwardly what is reflected in this internal quiet time. The arts, emotional release work/play, and reflective techniques set the tone for all other learning and renews and replenishes the body, mind, and spirit so the body can maintain optimum wellness and communication. I offer an anonymous prayer:

> We who have lost our sense and our senses—our touch, our smell, our vision of who we are; we who frantically force and press all things, without rest for body or spirit, hurting our earth and injuring ourselves: we call a halt.

> We want to rest. We need to reflect and to rediscover the mystery that lives in us. That is the ground of every unique expression of life, the source of the fascination that calls all things to communion.

> We declare a Sabbath, a space of quiet: for simple being and letting be; for recovering the great, forgotten truths; for learning how to live again.

> Today we know of the energy that moves all things; the oneness of existence, the diversity and uniqueness of every moment of creation, every shape and form, the attraction, the allurement, the fascination that all things have for one another.

> Humbled by our knowledge, chastened by surprising revelations, with awe and reverence we come before the mystery of life.

Can we do it? Can we learn to sit in the mystery? Can we tolerate and embrace without fear, the unknown that will be revealed to us if we clear the muddy waters and still the ripples of the mind? Survival in the future presupposes that we learn to trust ourselves at the deepest level where the mind's eye has the power of synthesis and sound judgment. Can we put our faith into exploring the consciously unknown, a vast region of ineffable knowledge bigger than ourselves, yet, inherent in us all? We can learn to do this easily and successfully if we begin to acknowledge, access and utilize our intuitive awareness.

Communication Skills And
Conflict Resolution Tools

Successful communication is the vital link that makes or breaks relationships and includes honesty, deep listening, acknowledgment and an unwavering willingness to discover and implement resolution. At the heart of this work is a unique process called Council. It must become a cornerstone of this new communication system. Adapted from Native American tradition in which one person speaks at a time, Council uses the circle and three basic rules: (a) speak in turn only, (b) speak briefly, and (c) speak and listen from the heart. With a commitment to confidentiality, no interruptions or immediate expressed reactions, safety is assured. With safety in place, and respecting the right of the individual to speak or be silent when it is his or her turn, disciplined and deep listening skills arise naturally. Deep listening to oneself and others includes listening to the 'deep wisdom within' or intuition, and being aware intuitively of the non-physical connection we have together.

Now that we have a global village, linked together with a "techno-network," we are called to rely upon mediation and conflict resolution skills without ill-will. Future harmony depends on this. Circus Earth Foundation is one organization which has created curriculum that quickly, deeply and with fun, help our children to solve problems effectively. Using a variety of single, paired, and group exercises, trust is developed, communication is opened, and solutions to challenges never dreamed of are generated.

Group Problem Solving And Team Building

As our world grows smaller, it is important for schools to emphasize teamwork in the workplace, in community building, and in international relations. This can easily be accomplished with trust, exercises, and problem-solving games, collaborative techniques, outdoor exercises designed to create team problem solving like ropes courses, and using the art of brainstorming and Council. Trust, interactive exercises, brainstorming, and Council are non-linear and hence related to intuition. Intuition is both an input and a result of each of these.

Living with different points of view is a constant in our world. Also constant is our reactiveness to views opposite our own. Affective/intuitive education fosters the absence of judgment, creates safety and acceptance making it easier to take risks and express diverse perspectives. As Shelley Kessler writes in *Holistic Education Review,* "A community can tolerate and even encourage respect for differences only if it has the tools to handle the inevitable conflict that comes from divergent thinking."

Spiritual Development

The end result of this curriculum leads to a natural fulfillment of the fourth part of a whole person—not mind, not body, not emotions, but to our ineffable spirit. Spiritual development is defined as: a sense of connection, meaning, mystery, and wholeness. Allowing ourselves to reconnect to our intuitive side, which inexplicably knows all about our myriad parts, a person no longer can define himself as the victim of circumstance, society or self. When people can understand and direct personal power, have an environment of absolute safety and acceptance, are not limited to one-sided thinking, they will have a reconnection to self, to others and to nature, a sense of meaning and purpose in life, a way to utilize the dimension of non-ordinary experience surrounding life, and the experience of wholeness and renewal. When this system is in place, the mind is strengthened and thoughts are calmed leading to an enhanced and balanced state of mind. This creates open-hearted and open-minded students ready and eager to learn.

Understanding and practicing reflective techniques, cultural ceremony, class trips into nature, storytelling, non-cognitive modalities, meditative and visualization techniques creates the capacity for openness, self-acceptance and full expression—preconditions for self esteem and acceptance of others. By learning to accept both the light and the dark within ourselves, in one another and in nature, we organically build wholeness and holiness, the emphasis of an intuitive curriculum. Peter Senge, author of *The Fifth Discipline,* answers it this way:

> When we give up the illusion that the world is created of separate, unrelated forces we can then build 'learning organizations' where people continually expand their capacity to create the results they truly desire, where new expansive patterns of thinking are nurtured, where collec-

tive aspiration is set free, and where people are continually learning how to learn together.

The benefits of including such an extensive, intuitively creative and complete approach are:

- Enhanced intuition
- Enhanced listening skills
- Increased attention span
- More desire to attend class
- More responsible behavior
- Improved academic and personal achievement
- More centered mental and emotional states necessary for maximum effectiveness in learning
- Increased classroom unity and spirit of cooperation
- Fewer discipline problems
- More creativity and participation
- Greater confidence (self-esteem) and joy
- More awareness, acceptance, and respect for the feelings of self and others
- Improved interracial relations
- Diminished judgmental attitudes
- Reduced stress and anxiety

Let us adopt this philosophy and create a new way by blending the intellectual education already in place with intuitive education which will mend the loss of connection and creativity we have been experiencing. Let us craft a partner "ship" to help guide us to new and exciting frontiers. As Michael Mendiza writes, "To inspire our children only enough to become well conditioned cogs that turn the industrial/technological wheels" worked for awhile. However, that kind of focus has diminished our perception, lowered our SAT scores ("dumbed us down"), restricted our talents to specialized jobs and confined our minds to narrow ways of thinking.

When we ask ourselves what ideas of the human underlie the schools to which our children are sent, the current answer might reveal a strong intellectual bias, the need for control and competition as a way of life and cultural expectations of success, money, power and social adaptation. As we have clearly experienced so far, however, these ideas have not produced the desired benefits. Ultimately, the intellectual/scientific approach alone has had little impact on shifting undesirable behaviors or feelings. The result is a limiting of human potential and complete disregard for the wholeness of life.

I have witnessed and experienced a gradual fundamental shift in a cultural core belief. The industrial revolution outlawed faith (trust) in a process outside of our conscious awareness, one that is unscientific, non-logical and unexplainable in any way we can relate to (with the exception of faith in God). Not too long ago, people were expected to work for the gold watch. Financial survival was paramount. Today, in America, there is more wealth spread over a broader spectrum of the population than in any other time or country. More people today have their survival needs met. This leaves a space just waiting to be filled with the next need: being as concerned with the quality of work as much as the size of a paycheck; sometimes quality even takes precedence over paycheck. The struggle to survive is increasingly being replaced by a striving for meaning and satisfaction in the work arena.

In the past, "education" meant the acquisition of a certain body of knowledge. We now live with overwhelming amounts of information; we cannot possibly teach it all. We need a new educational paradigm to help students learn to think and act with wisdom based on knowledge.

If we are to be completely present to learning, we must approach education as a science and an art. Science is the research and studying of facts: the plant goes up and the roots go down. Art is recognizing the metaphor, concepts which underlie the wisdom of how to live an educated life; being in touch with the whole, thus facilitating survival.

Linda A. Garrett is co-founder and president of Creative Learning Technologies, Inc. (CLT), an Idaho-based virtual networking corporation dedicated to the integration of creativity, continuous learning and modern technologies. Garrett has over fifteen years of experience working in the corporate environment, and consults full-time with both business and education workgroups. She is an enthusiastic supporter of bridging business and education by creating opportunities for each to learn from the other. The Theory of Multiple Intelligences is one of the learning perspectives used by CLT to stimulate mental agility, enhance creative thinking, and expand learning capacity in the workplace.

13

M. I. Intuitive?

Linda A. Garrett

*Reading Shakespeare. Playing a computer game. Danc-
ing. Strolling through a museum. Listening to the wind in
the trees. Volunteering in a nursing home. Setting goals for
yourself. What do these activities have in common? It is
possible that when you do any of them, you can develop
and strengthen your intuition. "How can that be?" you
might ask. What does playing a computer game or volunteering in a nursing home have to do with intuition? Perhaps more than you might think...*

Intuition. It means something different to each of us. At one
level, intuition may mean letting go and going beyond the
individual's inner world (i.e., the "superconscious"). At another
level, intuition may be learning to access an inner wisdom that is
often covered by barriers such as the ego or an overly-active and
critical mind. In work environments, intuition may be called by
different names—gut feeling, insight, creativity, perceptiveness,
or even "good judgment." Often intuition is ignored or disguised,
but the truth is, no matter *what* it is called, and *whatever* its
source, intuition is a necessary part of the decision making
process.

This essay explores new and exciting possibilities for enhancing intuition by stimulating the brain in a variety of ways. It
suggests that the human brain can be developed and exercised so
that the intuitive process is nurtured. It also presents practical
applications of the Theory of Multiple Intelligences (researched

and developed over the past fifteen years by Harvard Professor Howard Gardner) in relation to the development, practice and growth of creativity and intuition.

It is the author's opinion that Professor Gardner's perspective on learning builds an excellent framework for tapping into many intuitive abilities by exercising the brain in such a way that it will actually *feed* the intuitive process. So while the brain *per se* may not typically be seen as a crucial part of intuition, it may, in fact, be the key foundation from which we are able to access this important inner wisdom. Learning to more fully develop the brain by using "multiple intelligences" can provide an ideal springboard for developing intuitive abilities on both individual and group levels.

Multiple Ways Of Tapping Intuition

For intuition to be useful in the work environment, it needs to become more prevalent at the personal level. For intuition to be more prevalent, we must find practical ways to exercise intuition on a regular basis. Building from a framework, such as the Theory of Multiple Intelligences (M.I.), can provide that practical foundation.

Gardner's extensive research indicates that we have at least seven major groups of intelligence *capacities* that can be used and developed throughout our lives: verbal/linguistic, logical/mathematical, bodily/kinesthetic, musical/rhythmic, visual/spatial, intra-personal, and inter-personal. While many of these intelligences are interdependent, research also indicates that they are biologically linked to specific regions of the brain. While Gardner resists labeling the intelligences in this way, one of his initial premises for defining an "intelligence" is that it can be biologically linked. The diagram on the next page is an interpretation of how the intelligences map biologically, as indicated in the book, *Seven Kinds of Smart,* by Thomas Armstrong.

Traditionally, Western society has been biased towards the two "left brain" dominant intelligences, verbal/linguistic and logical/mathematical, while other cultures have placed higher value on some of the other intelligences. For example, African cultures place a higher value on bodily/kinesthetic and musical/ rhythmic intelligences, while the eastern Indian cultures emphasize visual/spatial and intra-personal intelligences. Since intuition is often linked more to "right brain" activities and non-

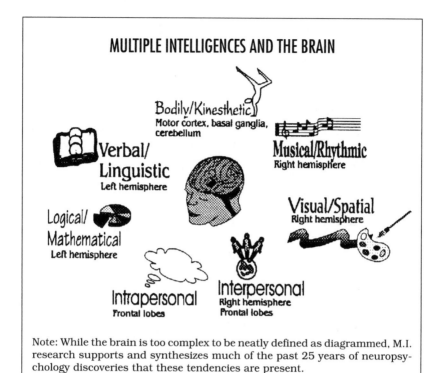

MULTIPLE INTELLIGENCES AND THE BRAIN

Bodily/Kinesthetic
Motor cortex, basal ganglia, cerebellum

Verbal/
Linguistic
Left hemisphere

Musical/Rhythmic
Right hemisphere

Logical/
Mathematical
Left hemisphere

Visual/Spatial
Right hemisphere

Intrapersonal
Frontal lobes

Interpersonal
Right hemisphere
Frontal lobes

Note: While the brain is too complex to be neatly defined as diagrammed, M.I. research supports and synthesizes much of the past 25 years of neuropsychology discoveries that these tendencies are present.

verbal, non-logical states, it is no wonder many people in Western cultures bury or hide their intuitive abilities.

The Amazing Brain

As your brain accumulates the multitude of experiences and sensations gathered throughout your life, it creates a vast storehouse of data that your subconscious mind integrates and connects in a number of ways. Later, when you need to make a decision, you unconsciously access this databank, and sometimes through an elusive means you just "know." That is why it is important to stimulate your brain in ways that will help it expand the data bank and make more of these pathway connections for you to access.

Some of the latest research into the workings of the human brain is finding, in addition to how truly complex the brain really is, new "communications networks that operate within our bodies." A recent report published in the *National Geographic*, for instance, revealed that there is a powerful connection between the brain and the body via chemical reactions and the transfer of energy between cells. These "neuropeptides" are believed to attach themselves to various receptors within our bodies, triggering emotions and other cellular communications. Some are even thought to come from the stomach, validating the expression "gut feeling." This supports the idea that intuition can actually be heightened as we increase our mental agility and the resulting flow of peptides.

The M.I. Journey

The M.I. framework can be used as a guide to accessing intelligence, as well as creativity and intuition, from a whole-person perspective. It can also increase the strength of your neural network, giving both subconscious and conscious minds a higher capacity for drawing connections. In turn, this approach serves to increase your brain's ability to work with the multiple inputs from which revelations and insights are drawn. The "multisensory" thinking acknowledged and stimulated within the M.I. framework is an important part of developing intuition at both personal and professional levels.

Developing intuition by exercising multiple intelligences is a journey—a lifelong process that requires learning how to expand, deepen and integrate these brain abilities. As with any journey, there will be steps which will seem to come easier than others. Here are some general "groundrules" to keep in mind as you travel:

- *Knowing **when** intuition is at work is the first step to **using** intuition at work...* For intuition to become a more accepted part of the work environment, and the decision-making process in general, workers at all levels need to become more aware of how they use (or block) their own intuition. Listening to and trusting your own intuition and that of your co-workers may be the most difficult challenge in putting intuition to work (at work or anywhere!). It requires a conscious intent to listen and to pay attention. As author Gary Zukav asks in *Seat of the Soul,* "How do you get in touch with your intuition, and ultimately your soul? You listen." So listen carefully, and with intent.

- *Fear and ego are pervasive blocks to intuition...* Being

open to intuition requires letting go of your biases, fears, opinions, and ego. Intuition is NOT at work when individuals or workgroups hold on to beliefs in an opinionated, inflexible way, or when the "voice of judgment" is constantly present. As futurist and author Peter Russell once stated, "The voice of intuition is the quietest voice. You have to quiet the voice of the ego to hear your intuition." Intuition can only be accessed when the din of "agendas," hidden or otherwise, and judgment about a particular topic are at a minimum.

- *Timing is critical to making intuition work...* Knowing *when* to "jump" in order to act on your intuition is an important part of the intuitive process. It takes a high degree of confidence and trust to be able to *wait* as well as to *act* when the time is right. Best-selling author Thomas Moore has said, "It takes a lot to do nothing, but it's worth the effort." Intuition, in many respects, is an "act" of faith. A *nondecision* may actually lead to (or manifest) an observable decision.

The Multiple Intuition Workout

It is unlikely that most of us would choose, even if given a chance, to invest in the type of deep retreat that may be necessary to truly tap our deepest intuitive powers. And while any type of capacity building requires an investment, intuition can also be developed slowly, gently, and consistently by starting with some simple activities.

The following activities will help you start the process of exercising your intuition through the use of your multiple intelligences. Most of these can be done individually or in work groups, and can easily be focused on a specific work topic or issue.

Keep in mind, these activities can be used alone or together to stimulate intuition and other forms of creative thought. It is important to remember that each makes up a part of the whole and that the parts are interrelated and interdependent. Exercising the "whole system" is as important as introducing varied techniques that will continue to stimulate your neural connections in specific new ways.

So, start your journey by yourself or invite others in your workplace to join you. Keep track of the steps you take along the way to see what you can learn from each other.

Intra-Personal Intelligence is the ability to know one's inner self. People strong in this intelligence are most likely to be considered naturally intuitive. This is also the most typical area from which to build for "practicing" intuition.

Traditional techniques such as meditation, reflection, dream analysis, keeping a journal, and other inner-directed personal growth strategies, can all be effective for increasing intuitive abilities. For intuition to become more common in the work environment, however, we all must be encouraged to develop this intelligence in the context of the work process as well as in our personal lives. Accessing this intelligence more regularly in work groups can reduce the significance of various mental models as barriers to intuition.

Some companies offer space for quiet time and reflection as a tool for creative thought as well as for promoting health and wellness. There are many ways that intrapersonal intelligence can be cultivated in teams as well. For starters, here are a few simple activities that will build your intrapersonal intelligence and enhance intuition at work:

Incubation Walk. Take a break from a meeting, especially if things are getting bogged down, and have everyone go for a walk. This works best if everyone can walk alone and outside if possible. Before starting, identify a specific issue or question that needs to be addressed, then present these guidelines: *As you walk, let your mind wander to "non-meeting" topics. It helps to focus on the sights, sounds and smells of the surrounding environment. After about five minutes, let your attention be drawn naturally to something. What does this particular object, scene, etc., bring to mind about a work issue?* When everyone returns, use any insights to begin a dialogue session about the work topic.

Mandala Watching. Find a book of mandalas—complex shapes that work naturally to stimulate different parts of the brain—that can be found in most bookstores. Get in a comfortable position, take a few deep breaths, and look at the *center* of the mandala. Keep your eyes "soft," continue breathing deeply, and let your mind relax. While there may be some initial tension as your left brain tries to absorb all the details, your right brain should take over as it gets drawn into the whole image. After a few minutes, take a pencil in your "nondominant" hand and write whatever comes to your mind. You can also color or draw mandalas for this activity. What images or feelings do you experience as a result of this exercise? What insights come to you about your work?

Note: Intrapersonal intuition exercises can also be used to

accelerate the decision-making process by focusing on which data to create, study, etc.

Inter-Personal Intelligence is the ability to understand and work with others. People who are gifted interpersonally may be less inclined to focus on their own intuition since their primary preference tends to be on interacting with others. Intuition can still be cultivated through this intelligence domain, however, and working with others is one of the places where intuition is often most used. Since most people have experienced some form of intuition about other people, acknowledging this dimension of the work/decision-making process may help intuition become more prevalent in the workplace. Try the following activities together to see how you can activate intuition through your interpersonal intelligence:

> **Hero Sharing.** As a warm-up for a team meeting, have everyone list three personal "heroes" and the main attributes which they admire most about these heroes. Then, encourage everyone to share; pay attention to similarities and notice how the trust and compassion builds. See if the discussion stimulates any intuitive understanding of each other or a business issue at hand. (This can also be an intrapersonal activity, as the things we admire in others are often qualities we have or would like to build in ourselves.)

> **Shared Story Writing.** Choose a topic and have each group member start writing a story about that topic. Encourage the use of a real story format, not just business writing. Also encourage cursive writing instead of printing. After two minutes, have everyone pass their story to the right or left and continue writing. Continue this rotation until every person has contributed something to every story. Then share the stories as a group and see what insights you develop.

Musical–Rhythmic Intelligence is the natural ability of rhythm and sounds. The positive effects of classical music on learning, creativity, and general well-being have been validated by numerous research studies. Music and sounds are commonly used to trigger our emotions, to accelerate learning, to create atmosphere, to reduce stress and promote relaxation, and for pure enjoyment. Most people like to listen to music in some form, but those who are truly gifted in this intelligence take this appreciation to a much higher level. People strong in this intelligence may also employ their talents in other ways, such as diagnosing and treating machine performance by detecting sounds and rhythms. We can all use music and sound much more effectively in our lives, including letting it help stimulate our natural intuitive abilities. Here are a few activities to stimulate your intuition through this intelligence:

Music Breaks. These can range from "simple listening" breaks where you use appropriate music to move you into or through various emotions, to more complex uses of biofeedback or "bioentrainment" equipment that help you use music to reach incredibly deep levels of intuitive awareness. When selecting music, be conscious of using music that has been "proven" to work best for various purposes; but most importantly, choose music that is not out of sync with your own body rhythms. This may be difficult to determine for an entire group. However, classical music usually provides the best range for providing focus, enhancing creativity, stimulating learning, and increasing relaxation. If you want to focus the Music Break on a specific issue during a meeting, have everyone close their eyes and visualize while listening; then discuss the various images and how they might relate to the topic or issue at hand.

Nature Walks. Listening to sounds in nature can be a wonderful way to heighten this intelligence as well as to develop your "musical intuition." Similar to the Incubation Walk, this activity should be done alone, and can then be focused back on a work issue. When you do go on a Nature Walk, remember to concentrate on sounds rather than sights. If you work or live in an area that does not allow you to easily venture into a natural setting, there are many audio tapes or CDs which will provide opportunities to experience those sounds. Try playing these sounds while you are working and notice what intuitive inspirations they evoke.

Visual–Spatial Intelligence is the ability to perceive with the "mind's eye." This is the primary intelligence used by the artist, architect, photographer and others who visualize in detail and think in three or more dimensions. Using images to arouse creativity and intuition is a well-established technique and has been used extensively for creative visualization as well as for personal growth and healing. Using art as an outlet has helped many corporate executives ease the stress of a hectic work schedule. Using it specifically as a tool to help access intuition is gaining popularity as well. Here are a few visual–spatial activities which can stimulate your intuition at work:

Collage. From a wide variety of magazines and pictures, have everyone in your group cut out images or words that grab their attention. Then, using poster board and glue sticks, have the group combine these elements to form a group or team collage. The process should initiate a plethora of intuitive thoughts, and discussion of the final product will stimulate even more, especially if judgment is suspended during the entire process.

Visual Connections. Randomly associate various pictures or images with an issue of concern to see what intuitive thoughts arise. You can look around the room, use the collages you just created, use images from a variety of photo books or magazines, watch a video/movie, and so forth, to create catalysts for making intuitive connections.

Mindmapping. Use this effective nonlinear visual technique to let your ideas and thoughts flow randomly and be stimulated from a variety of angles. If you elect to do this as a group, first create individual mind maps to encourage each participant to experience the technique on a personal level before the group process begins (see sample mindmap on next page).

Bodily–Kinesthetic Intelligence is the natural gift of movement. When intuition is accessed through this intelligence, it means paying attention to physical responses, moving spontaneously, and "getting out of your head." Using your body to monitor the decision-making process can help you identify issues and redirect the process where necessary. To cultivate intuition from this angle, you need to get your body moving and keep track of the signals your body gives you on a regular basis. Here are some activities that can be used in the work environment to help you do this:

Camera Walk. Pair up with another member of your work group and be prepared to take turns role-playing the parts of "camera" and "photographer." The photographer will stand behind the "camera" with hands on the camera's shoulders. The camera will keep its lens (eyes) closed until the photographer takes a picture (taps the shoulder). The photographer can develop a theme or take random pictures, and it will be the camera's job to capture these and share any insights with the group at a later time. After the first photographer has taken ten shots (or more, depending on the "roll of film" you are using), trade places and repeat the activity. This is a great trust-building activity that can also be intuitively linked to a topic or issue of interest to the group.

Reach Out and Touch Something. Fill a container with a variety of small, random objects. Write a work issue on a flipchart or piece of paper, then have someone select an object from the container and say the first thing that comes to mind about how the object relates to the work issue. It is important not to take too much time to think, but to listen to the first voice that comes to mind.

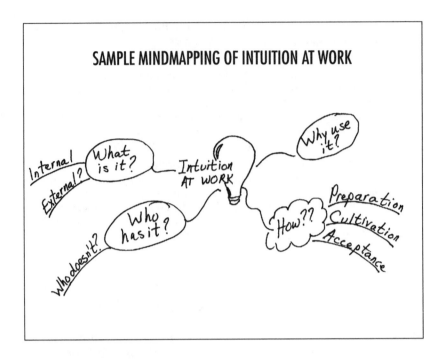

SAMPLE MINDMAPPING OF INTUITION AT WORK

Linguistic Intelligence is the ability to use words and language skillfully. One of our most "over-used" and over-valued intelligences, language can be used to stifle intuition or to heighten it. People who regularly keep a journal—writing about feelings rather than merely the events of the day—will build intuition by paying attention to the intricacies of their writing. Try these techniques:

> **Free Writing.** Spend time every day writing your thoughts without judging them. You don't have to save them or share them, but you need to be able to write everything to begin to see what is beneath the surface. This takes a lot of practice. To use this activity in groups, you may want to start a weekly meeting with even two minutes of free writing to see what surfaces. Focus the writing on a specific topic if you like. Try writing occasionally with your nondominant hand to see what interesting thoughts arise!

> **Poetry.** Read, write or listen to poetry. Take the time to hear beneath the words to find new insight to some challenge you are currently facing. Encourage co-workers to use poetry as a metaphor for their work experience and to recognize that everyone is a poet (even if they don't know it!).

Logical–Mathematical Intelligence is the ability to think in abstract and logical, sequential processes. Perhaps thought to be the least likely intelligence to be used for accessing intuition, this is probably at the foundation of all of our intuitive thoughts. In effect, our database for feeding the intuitive process is created and maintained using this intelligence. The dynamics of neural networks have been found to follow certain "laws" governing mathematics and quantum mechanics. The more you feed this intelligence, the more information you will have available from which to draw intuitive insights and build your intuitive capacity. Try this:

> **Attribute Listing.** Break your topic or issue into pieces by listing every specific characteristic. Then write down any thoughts that are stimulated by each attribute. When you break a topic into this level of detail, your intuition can be accessed at many different levels because you are consciously increasing the number of potential connections that can be made.

> **What If Analysis.** Examine your topic or issue by generating alternative scenarios stimulated by the "what if" prompt. This process can be exercised manually (in writing) or with computer-assisted routines, such as spreadsheets, process flow charts, simulations, etc. What do the results of these manipulations suggest "intuitively" about your situation?

Some of the activities described in this essay obviously stimulate or draw from more than one intelligence. The important thing to remember is to nourish the whole human system. The M.I. perspective involves the whole system in a way that recognizes and even celebrates each person's strengths. This, by itself, may help people put their intuition to work for the benefit of both their work and personal lives, since people often tend to begin to utilize their "sixth sense" more when they become more confident.

So, R.U. Intuitive?

Everyone has the capacity to be both creative and intuitive. Some of us may have more natural capacity than others, as instruments like the Myers-Briggs Temperament Indicator will suggest. However, as with anything, when you cultivate your natural abilities, they grow stronger. While there are many ways to nurture intuition, the Theory of Multiple Intelligences may be the most comprehensive framework available for applying creativity and intuition.

As creativity becomes more of a necessity in this quickly changing and diverse world, intuition, as a critical part of the creative process, must be developed, nurtured and reinforced. Learning to use our whole brain to develop intuition can help us become better learners and creators, both individually and collectively.

• • • • •

So... Read Shakespeare. Play a computer game. Dance. Stroll through a museum. Listen to the wind in the trees. Volunteer in a nursing home. Set a goal for yourself. Exercise your multiple intelligences. You are sure to find some new ways to access your intuition and to develop your full creative potential.

Gigi Van Deckter has achieved much in her life, including being an award winning director/producer for television, theatre, and film. Her extensive European conservatory opera training led her to her latest project as executive producer for the Peace Symphony Week to be held as part of the world reknown Salzburg Music Festival in 1999—marked to benefit young, talented artists for commissions and study in the new millennium.

As president of New York City-based The Van Deckter Company, Inc. she travels the globe extensively working as an intuitive business consultant and reshaper of international economic policy in association with leaders of industry in Japan, India, Europe, and Silicon Valley, as well as sitting on the board of a multinational venture capital firm and working with government leaders.

14

Intuition At Work: A Question Of Balance

Gigi Van Deckter

A client of mine, who runs a multi-billion dollar company in Asia, says he gets his best ideas in bed, in the bath, or while on a break. His mind races along at top speed all day long, focusing upon one goal after another; when his pace finally relents and he relaxes, his entire system slows down and he begins to feel—to intuit, not think. This deceleration sets the stage for a shift into the meditative or peaceful state from which all truly creative ideas flow.

It is only after prolonged endeavor of intensive thought that a break in the flow of consciousness occurs and new ideas begin to surface. Suddenly, as Henry James observed, "things seem to fall into composition." Accessing intuitive capacity in this way is something anyone can learn to do. It is important to realize however, that the development and utilization of one's intuitive capacity has nothing to do with luck. Like most achievements, it requires preparation and practice. As no less an observer than Louis Pasteur has noted: "Luck favors the prepared mind." It is the thorough, in-depth understanding of one's subject that en-ables one to make optimal use of fallow time—to turn sitting in the bath, lying in bed, or taking a midday break into a creative occasion. The intuitive process requires that we learn to set our minds adrift from their usual moorings, let them float unfettered into uncharted waters.

The concept of gravity revealed itself to Newton as he sat in the shade of an apple tree, his logical super-egoed self suspended in abeyance. In much the same fashion, you, too, can revolutionize your conception of your current projects, world, or enterprise. Most major scientific breakthroughs occur when the mind is in a semiconscious, dream-like state; while entering REM (rapid eye movement) sleep, while walking in the woods, or while soaking in the bubble bath. Few "Eurekas" are uttered in the middle of drone-like calculations.

Once ascertained and realized, intuitive creativity takes on a momentum of its own. Once you access it and grasp its function it stands ready, available for use on demand. Crucial to this development is an awareness of how to set up one's life to allow for the requisite ruptures of settled routine that will consequently allow you to readily tap into this spiritual state. When we wish to encourage others to produce desired results, it is generally counterproductive to insist that they drive themselves until they drop. A short series of breaks can serve to regenerate an employee and stimulate her to produce new thinking.

Some people say that such an attitude towards stress is comparable to the dynamics of addiction: "I produce better under stress." Those of us who believe we function well under stress create it in the hope that it will enable us to bolster our productivity. Leaving a project to the last minute is one way in which we provide ourselves with the necessary productive stimulus. While extreme, such an approach is not necessarily a bad thing. Not everyone requires the same conditions in order to give rein to their intuitive and creative impulses. Even when certain approaches carry an element of danger, it is necessary to respect such differences.

No matter what your particular habits are, learning to acknowledge them is what is most important. Successful entrepreneurs will tell you that once they succeeded in mastering the technical base of their enterprise's endeavors, they began to search for a way to accommodate their preferred productive styles. They will also tell you that they began to place greater reliance upon their gut instincts or intuition.

Using Intuition

A partner in a prominent New York City investment bank once told me that he relies almost entirely on his gut feelings about a project. He allows his intuition to serve as his primary guide; an intuitive sense fully informed by a wealth of practical experience has provided him, over time, with consummate confidence and a broad understanding of his field. How does one get in touch with this thing called intuition? Is it difficult? Is it something that ordinary people can do? The response is no and yes. No, it is not difficult, and yes, ordinary people can do it. Needless to say, the greater your grounding in your primary field of endeavor the easier it will be for you to immediately tap into this abundant source of creativity and apply it to your various undertakings.

Three things are required to do this. First, you must be well prepared in the basics of your field. Second, you must be prepared to discard your reliance upon the methodical (scientific) approach. Third, you must realize that intention is everything and be willing to take full responsibility for how you react to all that happens in your life. In short, you must embrace a whole self/whole world view.

Intuition is letting yourself listen to answers from within. Asking a question in a peaceful environment—bed, bath, break—and listening to the thoughts that float to the surface. It could be that, after several days of asking for an answer, a solution may manifest itself in your daily activities. Being aware and trusting that an answer will come is key after asking the question. Intuition is clearing the mind of your daily noise and letting yourself hear more deeply than one does during our normally overfilled days. Using one's intuition is a matter of asking. Focusing, asking, and peacefully listening without effort or strain. Intuition is allowing the universal knowledge to inform you. There is a world of knowledge we can all access if we practice doing so. But one must practice being still and taking the time to ask and listen.

We listen better to our intuition if we are trusting and aware of our own subject and of our own ethics and morality as well. We do not necessarily behave any more morally because of using our intuition. However, we can create a much more productive, financially successful and happy, time-efficient work and home environment if our personal moral beliefs are in alignment with our economic purpose.

Responsible Livelihood

Several months ago one of my clients showed me a photo of himself smiling proudly in the presence of his one-year-old granddaughter. She is a beautiful little girl with a serious countenance. I am confident that she will bring much love and light into his life over the years. Upon displaying his granddaughter's photo, my client proceeded to tell me how concerned he was about a large investment that he had recently made in a game parlor outfit. Kids and young adults spend endless hours in these places playing computer games, zoning out, sometimes associating with drug dealers and other misdirected people who haunt the margins of society. Needless to say, he realized that this was not the most constructive environment for young children. This prompted me to ask my client if he would like to see his granddaughter in one of these places. He immediately responded with an emphatic "No! Of course not!" So I went on to ask, "Why is it that you invest in these parlors if you disapprove of them?"

It is imperative that we at least take responsibility for the things we create and earn our money from. Such an approach makes us aware of how our individual and collective projects might adversely effect other people and their children. We should make it our business to protect the young offspring of others as we would our very own. The development of this type of consciousness will enable us to divest ourselves of many of our more worrisome investments and live in greater harmony with our intentions. Our intuition can guide us to understand how to best accomplish this.

For instance, our intuition might suggest that there is also another way of coming to terms with investments of this sort. We might ask ourselves how they can be redeployed to provide kindred services or products in a healthier environment; one that reflects our best productive intentions, and aims to generate positive results in the lives of both producers and consumers. To bring our investments in line with our good intentions and more humane impulses, one need not throw the baby out with the bath water. There are ways, wholly consistent with sound business principles and the profit motive, of rethinking and reconfiguring existing products to make them work in ways consistent with the best interests and well-being of those who utilize them. However, shifting our thinking in this way poses a creative, intuitive challenge, forcing us to ask ourselves how we can structure our projects differently or better.

The international corporate elite remains wedded to the past. It needs to shift to a new intuitive, positive paradigm that will allow all of us to enter the new millennium with our heads held high. It is essential to begin the process, to acknowledge the importance of change and assume responsibility for our individual and group actions.

Leaders, whether they are teachers, managers, or CEOs need to take a long hard look at how they are living their lives both at home and in the workplace, by asking for intuitive guidance. Each of us needs to begin to take note of where and how we are falling down on the job. Increasingly, interdependence is an essential and inescapable element of the architecture of our lives. As with any building, the collapse of one sector destabilizes the other parts as well.

A Question Of Balance

For instance, if one is not happy at home, the discontent which the situation generates inevitably renders efforts to focus on one's work more difficult. Loss of the ability to focus decreases one's ability to access one's intuition. As a consequence, one begins to experience stress on the job as well as at home. It is essential to accept responsibility for cultivating a more holistic approach to one's life in order to be focused and productive both on the job and at home.

There must be an element of consistency in a person's life for that person to function well. Today, functioning well does not carry the same meaning it once did. As we shift to a new paradigm, it increasingly means that your inside must match your outside; what you do and produce must be good for you and your bottom line, as well as for your customer and the workers who make and sell your product.

Intuition also means growth without rigidity, opening up boundaries of possibility. Allowing all the world to be a part of the family, which also means taking responsibility in business, producing with concern for others and allowing new forms to grow, as they will anyway. Seeking to be more responsible requires a new kind of realism. If we all know more through trust and intuition, and technology provides us with a more or less barrier-free information environment, our choices cannot be hidden or disregarded as in the past. We make choices now based on better information than ever before, and these choices must satisfy more than just our old personal or corporate needs.

In order to be our most productive, creative, successful selves, we must be willing to look at our lives at work and at home and allow them to change in terms of contemporary needs. We must honor all people, rather than exploit one another. Intuitive living can create a world where there is more of a sharing of ideas and cultures for growth and enlightenment. This will create the kind of world society where we earn well, and feel that success is our given right because we walk sure-footed on a path whereby our intentions are honorable and economically sound.

One cannot feel free to use one's intuition without allowing for the possibility that some of the answers may not be pleasing to hear. For example, we may intuit that producing a product in an unsafe environment is working against the interests of the ones we love the most. When we hear the little voice within, we need a clear conscious to follow it.

This new paradigm is incompatible with selling running shoes for $150 a pair in the USA while paying the Indonesian workers who produce them a paltry wage of $30 a month. The world today is entirely too small to permit investors to maintain a clear conscious about such practices.

Recently, I was in New York's Harlem district, listening to the Reverend Calvin Butts of the Abyssinian Baptist Church decry just such a company about its exploitation of a Third World population. He noted how the company in question used famous and well loved African-American sports figures in a series of ads that aimed to seduce kids into buying their brand rather than another. I was amazed and pleased to see the pulpit being used for this sort of deconstruction of popular culture and myth. Unfortunately, few kids in Harlem attend church services. Therefore, it was incumbent upon the parents and grandparents in the congregation to return home and talk to their style-conscious offspring about this latter day repetition of the dynamics of slavery, and make plain exactly what the purchase of these coveted sneakers implied.

Human beings are creatures of habit and can easily fall back on old forms and prejudices as an easy way of doing business. It is this rigid conformation to the past and its expecta-tions that is inconsistent with listening and trusting one's intu-ition. Holding onto form without regard to the content, or ignoring the original content and relying solely on form denies that inside/outside balance necessary for wholeness and humanity in our lives and work. Without this balance we cannot function intu-itively. All life is a set of balanced opposites and we must embrace them all in order to be in an optimum condition to access our intuitive state.

Vitality

To remain vital, every expressive form must be adapted to the needs and ideas of ensuing generations. Such adaptations allow each form to retain its communicative power and better reflect the shifting needs of an ever-changing world. The Catholic Church, to take but one example, is, in many ways, the embodi-ment of a deposed form. Although the church still has many excellent lessons to teach and a significant residual capacity to transform and inspire individual lives, its dogged adherence to static and unbending doctrines has resulted in a sharp curtail-ment of interest in its principles among the youth from which it must draw its new members, nuns, and priests. It is essential to understand just why this type of calcification occurs.

Recently, a young dancer, just back in New York from a world tour with a popular modern dance troupe, related to me how common it is for dance techniques to go stale. He described how an obsession with form comes to replace the vitality that made the dancers inspired to move in a given style when it was pioneered. He noted, by way of example, that the technique created by Martha Graham originally dealt with the interrelation-ship between movement and breathing; with how the intake and expulsion of oxygen propelled the dancer forward. The breathing process gave enormous impetus to the movement and meaning of this internationally famous choreographer's work.

This understanding is now rarely conveyed by Graham's disciples. In fact, in her last days, even Graham herself had become so engrossed with the formalistic aspects of her work that she began to neglect the philosophy behind her form.

Once the importance of adaptive fluidity is discounted, a form or product becomes less meaningful to contemporary needs and is ultimately rendered obsolete and replaced by something that has greater relevance. The rigidity that most forms gradually take on is what ultimately ensures their demise. We will progress much more rapidly in the new millennium if we can learn to both acknowledge this fact and harness certain of our egotistical impulses such as our lust for the notoriety associated with having created some new form. We should be honored to innovate within a tradition, grateful that whatever we offer is deemed worthy of adoration, adaptation, or use (however short-term) and go on from there.

Our success in the new millennium and beyond will require that we seek a level of enlightenment that is open-handed, intuitive, and responsible; a sense of enlightenment that is informed by an intentionality that aims at the well-being of all people, not just oneself or one's immediate world. We must prepare ourselves to live in an increasingly barrier-free environment where we are free to take the best elements of a plethora of cultures and incorporate them naturally in our work and play. Embracing rather than excluding will be the key. Increasingly, East, West, North, and South will reach out towards one another, each taking the best from its counterparts, and modifying it in a manner consistent with its own values and traditions.

John Pehrson is president of Creative Change Technologies, a consulting company that is focused on managing organizational change, developing powerful teams, and accelerating performance through the disciplined use of intuitive technologies. He is a former executive with DuPont and a graduate of Iowa State University, with a BS in Chemical Engineering.

Pehrson has served as a director of the New York Open Center, Inc., the largest urban holistic learning center in the world. He is a founding member of "UP on the Mountain," an innovative community-based organization for teenagers "at risk" in our society. He is a published author of various articles on innovative business practices, and co-author of the books, *Community Building: Renewing Spirit and Learning in Business* and *Intuitive Imagery: A Resource at Work.*

15

Creative Imagery: Harnessing The Power Of The Intuitive Mind

John Pehrson

It's in every one of us to be wise.
Find your heart. Open up both your eyes.
We can all know everything without ever knowing why.
It's in every one of us by and by...

—from a song by David Pomerance

As the song says, "It's in every one of us to be wise." But wisdom is not born out of the rational mind alone. Our left-brain reason filters, orders, and analyzes. It is a powerful part of the intellect that has led to tremendous scientific and material achievement. But it does not give us wisdom. That requires engaging the heart, which the ancient Chinese considered the seat of spirit or higher consciousness. It is the heart that opens us up to our right-brain intuitive faculties and expanded human capabilities. Without engaging the heart, we see out of only one eye. We lose depth and perception.

If we are to solve some of today's most pressing problems, it is clear that we must once again become whole. We must become whole-brain thinkers. We must learn to integrate the head and the heart.

The song goes on to say, "We can all know everything

without ever knowing why." This seems to sum up something important that we need to learn in our Western culture. Some things are intellectually *un-figure-outable*. Our rational minds often don't give us the clearest, most reliable direction to follow in our businesses or in our lives.

But if we allow ourselves to go beyond our reason and use all of our abilities, we can still find the answers we seek, even if we don't know why we know. This integration of the rational and intuitive is a critical skill for businesses in the 1990s. In fact, it may be the key to our future sustainability.

Life, as we approach the new millennium, is characterized by accelerating rates of social, political, and business change. We live with rapidly increasing complexity, uncertainty, environmental stress, and global conflict. Most of our ecosystems are in decline. Our cherished institutions are under attack. These are signs of the times. Anyone who has reflected for more than a moment on the state of the planet knows we have some tough problems to solve if we are to create a sustainable future. And it falls upon business, as the world's most powerful and adaptable institution, to come up with many of the solutions.

Yet, business itself is not immune from the larger forces at work in the world. If it is to be our hope for the future, business must successfully deal with its own sustainability issues. Many companies are emerging from the turmoil of "rightsizing, restructuring, and reengineering" to find temporarily-improved profitability. But now, with a smaller and often less-experienced workforce, they must continue to reinvent themselves while grappling with the ongoing issues of employee commitment and productivity, workforce diversity, tightening quality standards, environmental stewardship, and a host of other challenges. It is a time when the need for flexibility and rapid response has pushed our forecasting, planning, development, and decision-making systems to their absolute limits.

To paraphrase Einstein, neither the problems of the world nor the issues facing businesses today will be solved at the same level of thought at which they were created. Responding to today's challenges requires a willingness to be open to new, creative ways of thinking. Indeed, *we must begin to shift our beliefs about how we know what we know.* For this will also restructure how we do what we do.

For three hundred fifty years we have exalted our "outer knowing" through objective reason. We are like the proverbial crazy man who keeps on doing what he's been doing all along, expecting each time to get different results. Clearly, we are at a point where something must change. Something important is missing.

It's time to reintegrate our "inner knowing" or intuition into the equation.

The Intuitive Approach

Intuition may be defined as *knowing spontaneously without the conscious use of logic or analytical reasoning.* Intuition is so powerful because it gives us direct access to knowledge. It operates independent of the rational mind and is neither logical nor sequential. It can operate as a hunch, a flash of insight, or even a gut level feeling. It is like taking a shortcut to our destination without being given a road map that shows us how we got there. Its strength is that it allows us to know something directly. Zap! We know it. The uncomfortable part is that intuition takes us through unfamiliar territory. It beams us, like a character on Star Trek, through a dimension beyond our understanding that bypasses the normal mental process of logic and reason. It gives us direct knowledge but leaves us without an understanding of how we got the answer.

But if we can't understand it, how can we trust it?

The famous Swiss psychiatrist Carl Jung once said, "It is fashionable stupidity to regard everything one cannot explain as a fraud." We all trust lots of things every day that we don't understand. For instance, I don't understand how my telephone works, or my television either. But I'd be lost without them. Learning to trust in our natural intuitive ability is no different. We simply must begin to use it.

In fact, the most successful people in business draw heavily on intuition because they realize that the rational mind doesn't always give the best or most timely answers. A recent worldwide survey of business executives sponsored by the International Management Institute in Geneva, Switzerland, showed that fifty-four percent use intuition in their business about equally with logic. And thirty percent of these successful business people said that they use intuition *more* than logic and reason in their personal lives.

The issue in applying intuition on a practical basis in business is not whether it is powerful or effective. It is both. The real issue is how to make it reliable. Intuition may come in a flash. But it may not. And if it comes at all, it may not come on command. Moreover, intuitive knowing is easily colored by strong emotional attachments to outcomes, habits of perception, as well as stress, fear or anxiety about an issue under scrutiny. How do we minimize this effect? To top it off, an intuitive flash is not easily verifiable like a cause and effect analysis or mathematical proof. How do we harness the power of intuition in a disciplined way and test its reliability through empirical results?

The SWAT Team

In February 1989, a group of us at DuPont became interested in the potential of an intuitive process to break through the "Let's-run-the-numbers-one-more-time" analysis/paralysis that gums up most businesses. We knew that if we could find a process that could slice through the chaos of information overload, simplify decision-making, and tap into deep levels of inner knowing in a *reliable* way, that it would enrich the business and improve profitability. That's why we were excited when we encountered and began to work with an imagery process that seemed to be just such a tool.

Five of us from several businesses within DuPont formed a small cross-functional team to work with the practical application of intuition as a tool for business. We had no formal company charter. But with open minds, we were ready to do something different. We shared a conviction that new approaches were needed for DuPont to keep pace and remain competitive, and a belief that intuition could be harnessed for practical use. And from 1989 through 1992, we tested the disciplined use of an intuitive imagery process for its effectiveness in a broad variety of business applications compared to traditional, logical processes.

We called ourselves the SWAT team, an acronym for our use of "special weapons and tactics" in our study. The growing body of information on the efficacy of imagery processes in other fields, such as sports, medicine, and learning, provided the grounding for our own investigation.

At that time, *intuition* was still a word that was not spoken in polite business company. It's beginning to change. However, we still prefer to give our credence to computer models and spreadsheets that organize data so our powers of rational analysis can extract meaning and make decisions. Indeed, the job we've given to the rational mind of filtering and organizing *is* a critical capacity. But when everything gets filtered through our beliefs, over time, this screening process traps us into habits of perception.

Habits of perception become like grooves in the mind that channel our thinking and limit our creativity and potential. In a very real way, we perceive only what we believe. Our rational mind is like the Captain of the Guards, testing perceptions against our acculturated beliefs and turning away anything that doesn't fit. So, instead of saying, "I'll believe it if I see it," it's much more accurate to say, "I'll see it if I believe it!"

The use of an imagery process removes the "mind funnels" so that we are able to access a vast storehouse of inner knowledge. In fact, most of what we know already comes through images and sensory input, not through written or spoken words.

The Power Of Images

The word "tree" in English, "baum" in German, or "dyériva" in Russian all represent an image of one of those green leafy things in the forest. The image is constant. The words change. That's because words are what we make up to represent a more fundamental image. It is our inner images that are *primary.* They are the natural language of the mind. At the most basic level, we think and dream in images, which is why working with our inner images is so powerful. They dive deep. They go to the source of what we know and who we are.

Moreover, images are not only informative, they are creative! Working with inner images has the power to inspire action and change outcomes. Humans have believed from the earliest times in the power of the image to affect reality. And modern science is beginning to support this view. *Working to change outcomes in the image reality produces real effects in the physical reality!* Yet few people today are aware of the power that our inner images have on our lives.

Simplistically, your brain is like an incredibly powerful bio-computer, where the operating system program is written in images. These image programs affect our feelings, our individual capabilities, our health, the decisions we make, and the level of success we achieve.

We learned all this as the SWAT team worked with a process called Creative Imaging, discovered by Magaly Rodriguez Mossman.

We didn't understand how it worked at the time, but committed to apply it in a disciplined way and test the knowledge we gained. To our delight, over a period of several years we achieved impressive results in both our business and personal lives.

Creative Imaging

Creative Imaging is a whole-brain process that harnesses human intuition in a reliable and disciplined way. It uses the power of inner images to gain deeper insight to questions than the rational mind alone can give. It is fast, flexible, uncomplicated, and fun. It is portable and can be used anywhere. In fact, the SWAT team effectively used it when members were separated by hundreds, even thousands of miles.

The process can be done either solo, or interactively with a partner. It can be used in a simple and straightforward manner, or in increasingly rich and sophisticated ways as confidence and proficiency are developed.

Like other forms of guided imagery, Creative Imaging engages right-brain imagination to produce images. Then, left-brain analysis and discrimination are used to provide image interpretations and validation.

It differs from traditional forms of guided imagery because it incorporates an intuitive, or "translogical," process to temporarily circumvent the rational mind and bypass the ego. *Creative Imaging takes advantage of the fact that our minds are linked at levels beyond our normal conscious awareness.* This is its unique contribution and the source of its power.

Specifically, in the process, "guide questions" are used to evoke images that are linked to silent instructions and symbols called "silent keys." Instructions are given on two levels: verbal or written guide questions and silent, non-verbal instructions that are not known until the exercise is over and these silent keys are shared. The inner images that emerge are uncontaminated by frozen belief systems, old logic, attachment to outcomes, or anxiety over specific issues under scrutiny. This yields two major benefits: greater reliability and greater ease of learning.

In the three years that the SWAT team worked with this process inside DuPont, we found the results to be accurate, reliable, and sometimes amazing. As we taught the process to others in the company, we also found that anyone can do it as long as they have three things: (1) the desire to learn, (2) an open mind, and (3) a determination to practice long enough to build personal confidence. No special intuitive gift or set of skills is required. It appears to be a natural, human ability.

Getting Started

Getting started is easy. No major purchases are required. You already have within you all the equipment that is necessary to unlock the vast storehouse of inner knowledge. All you need are some colored 5" x 7" index cards and something with which to write. Then just follow the following steps:

1. Define your question. Write a series of questions on the back of your index cards. Formulate at least three questions, but *only one per card.* These become the *Silent Keys* to interpreting your images. Make sure your questions are clear and specific. And make sure your question is not really a compound question where more than one answer is required.

2. Shuffle. Turn your cards face down and shuffle them until you have no idea which question is on which index card. Now, number the cards to identify them.

3. Choose a guide question. Choosing a guide question in advance gives your mind a focus for the imaging. It's like giving your mind a helping hand in getting started. Good overall guide questions to start with are: "Open a door, what do you find?" And for those who are more auditory, "Get a message."

4. Relax and receive images. Take each card in turn. Without looking at the question on the back, relax and open a door in your imagination. Let an image come to you about the unseen question. It's important not to edit what comes. Even if it seems strange. The image can be a symbol, a person, an animal, or a structure. Describe the image and tell what it means to you. Or get a message in your mind about the image as if someone wise were speaking to you. Then, record your images, feelings, or messages—either on the front of the index card or on a separate pad on which you have written the number of the question.

5. Interpret. When you are done getting images, messages, or stories for the series of questions, turn over the cards and match the silent key questions with the images. Then work on decoding and interpreting your images. Remember, even when consulting references on images and symbols, the most important factor is your *own* interpretation.

6. Date and record your imaging information. A suggested format for this is:

Guide Question: (The imaging guide such as: "Open a door.")

Silent Key: (Your question—underlined.)

Image: (Your inner images and feelings.)

Interpretation: (Add your interpretation.)

Results: (Record actual results at a later date.)

Applying what you learn from your imaging is important. Application leads to deeper levels of meaning, validation, and confidence. Examine the information you receive. Act on it if appropriate. Trusting the images and applying what you learn tells the mind you are serious and keeps the imaging channels open.

Examples Of Creative Imaging In Business

The following examples are short excerpts from imagery done inside DuPont. The imaging was used in parallel with traditional analytical techniques. To maintain the confidentiality of the actual people doing the imaging, they will be referred to as *Travelers* in the examples shown below.

1. Competitive Intelligence: This is an excerpt of some imaging done by the SWAT Team for a large polymers business. It makes a nice example because the results were so dramatic.

Date: June 21, 1989

Guide: See a person and describe. Comment on their strengths and weaknesses. Imagine a brief, year-end headline.

Silent Key: Competitor 1.

Traveler: It is a thin woman with red hair. Although she has the ability to overcome most difficulties, her weakness is that she is too sensitive. She is easily hurt and vulnerable. *Headline:* "Woman dies of a heart attack."

Interpretation: This is the weakest of the competitors. There is a potential that they will exit the market by year end 1989.

Result: This competitor *did* exit the market by the end of 1989! They sold their converter-based business.

2. Team Purpose: This next image was done to clarify the purpose of a team of four managers given the responsibility to make a group of forty-four employees more cohesive, and simultaneously more flexible.

Date: March 12, 1989

Guide: Open a door. What do you find?

Silent Key: An image of the Technical Service and Development management team purpose.

Traveler: A close-up image of a black strap with a gray buckle fastener, much like the strap and fastener on a book bag. Then the image shifted to ballet dancers, *four* of them. They all had on matching costumes, and were dancing in perfect synchronization.

Interpretation: The strap and fastener meant to *band together tightly.* The four dancers (managers) need to coordinate efforts so they can be in perfect synchronization and harmony. Dance is a feminine symbol of emotional expression of inner feelings. A caring approach by the managers is indicated. [Notice that the image picked up on the four managers (dancers), even though it was done without knowing the silent key.]

Result: The management team did bond tightly, closely coordinated efforts, and managed with a participatory and empowering style. The results were an impressive increase in group productivity.

3. Human Resource Applications. Creative imaging is very successful in helping managers understand the deeper needs of the people in their group. Here's one example from my own experience as a manager when I was still with DuPont in Wilmington, Delaware.

This excerpt concerns a black woman in her early thirties who was transferred into my technical group in 1990. For the purpose of this example, I'll call her Reanne. She had a Master's degree in Chemical Engineering. She had a background in research were she was not treated well by her previous managers. She was looking to catch up on what she felt was lost time in her career. After a brief time in the group, she asked for a transfer to California to become part of a plant technical organization to be closer to family on the West Coast.

Date: May 13, 1990

Guide: (a) See a person and describe. (b) See a structure. (c) Snap. What happens to the person/structure now?

Silent Key: (a) A person who symbolizes Reanne. (b) More information about Reanne. (c) Will she be successfully transferred to California in the next three months?

Traveler: (a) An image of a firebird. It is like the symbol of the United States with the eagle holding the arrows. But, it is landing in a cloud of smoke from its rocket thrusters. And, at first, it has a space helmet on. (b) As a structure, I see a powerful rocket ship blasting off. Its course has been set, yet the rocket has a mind of its own. (c) The firebird is being shot at. He is in danger, and is afraid. All pride is gone under fire. He quickly dons his space helmet to take off for outer space, but his helmet has been damaged. He is stuck.

Interpretation: (a) The image of the firebird landing in a cloud of smoke, clenching arrows in its talons is simultaneously an image of power, and of anger. The helmet covers her true face. Something is not being spoken. (b) The rocket ship shows Reanne's desire to leave the company. She may have already set this as her course of action. (c) The transfer is not likely to happen in the next three months. This is likely to increase Reanne's desire to leave the company (take off for *outer* space).

Result: For Reanne to be successfully transferred, a job had to be specially created for her. We ultimately could not find a way to do this. So Reanne actually did feel stuck. Despite efforts to move her into an assignment in Wilmington which offered a high profile and growth opportunities, she found a way to leave the company. She took a job on the West Coast with a competitor.

4. Changing directions: This was the imaging series that led to my leaving DuPont to start my own business. It was during a period of turmoil amidst aggressive downsizing activity—the *outgoing tide* seen in the image below:

Date: September 29, 1992

Guide 1: Go to a place in your life. Describe it, and how you feel there.

Silent Key 1: A place that represents your business organization.

Image 1: I am in a boat, a cabin cruiser. It is headed out to sea in the wake of a turbulent outgoing tide. I am turning the wheel furiously, attempting to turn the boat around and head back into shore. The rudder is not responding. The boat is still being carried out to sea. I have to choose whether to be carried out with it, or jump into the surf and swim for shore. The shore is not that far away but I'm not sure I can swim well enough to make it. I am afraid but I have to decide quickly.

Interpretation: There is a good deal of turbulence in the business. I have to decide whether to be carried along with it or to jump ship and swim toward freedom even though I'm afraid. I'm not sure I can make it on my own.

Guide 2: Meet a person or entity in this place. Describe them and what you know about them.

Silent Key 2: A person/entity that is a symbol of your Higher Purpose in Life.

Image 2: A dolphin jumping out of the water. She is swimming near the boat. I know she will help me get to the shore.

Interpretation: Dolphins are traditional guides and saviors of the shipwrecked. They represent safety in troubled waters. I am being told that my Higher Purpose lies in jumping ship. I will be guided to safety.

Result: These images resulted in my asking for and receiving a separation package from DuPont. I left at the end of 1992 to start my own consulting business. Since leaving, I have felt gently guided to take each new step.

Practical Applications

The results that the SWAT team achieved with Creative Imaging in the period between 1989 and 1992 were outstanding. During that time, each of the team members integrated the process not only into their business lives, but also into their personal lives.

From a business standpoint, the SWAT team found this method of accessing our intuition to be particularly useful in situations requiring rapid responses, where little data existed and answers were simply not available through traditional means. It is especially useful for breaking free of limited thinking patterns, establishing a group vision and purpose, establishing priorities, discovering latent customer needs, and gaining insight into relationship issues with customers, employees, and peers. We found Creative Imaging to be a practical way to harness that "direct knowing" part of each of us and discipline it for daily use.

Specific applications where Creative Imaging has been found to be useful can be seen in the chart on the next page.

I have found in my work with the SWAT team, and with the many people to whom I have taught the process since then, that everyone has the ability to access their "inner genius" using this process. It requires no special power. It appears to be a natural human capability that is independent of race, gender, or social status. Moreover, the success that people continue to have in accessing information of which they had no previous knowledge says something fundamental about how reality is "wired together" in interdependent and "unknown" ways.

Using this type of imaging helps the practitioners to understand the interconnection of all things, and the holographic nature of reality in which, as individual pieces of the hologram, we are each able to access the whole.

Creative imaging goes deep into the fundamental essence of who we are. It generates an inherent understanding and value for our deep levels of connectedness and interdependence with others. Because of this, it is a powerful tool for building a spirit of community among people of all backgrounds and cultures.

Summary

The use of the whole-brain Creative Imaging process has proven its reliability and power in the work of the SWAT team inside DuPont, and with the many other people who have applied it since then. While its boundaries are still being explored, it has produced excellent results in the areas in which it has been applied in a disciplined way.

It is a process that honors both intuitive and rational ways of knowing. Images are simultaneously the strength and the weakness of the process. The process evokes inner images that provide a richness and power the logical mind cannot match by itself. However, images must be interpreted by the logical mind.

APPLICATIONS OF CREATIVE IMAGERY

Organizational	Personal
• Creating or clarifying a shared vision, mission, or purpose.	• Finding or clarifying your life purpose, creating a personal vision, and discovering your personal gifts.
• Optimizing organizational structure and work flow.	• Identifying and removing the blocks to productivity and creativity.
• Providing insight into personnel development needs, and checking assignment fit.	• Promoting increased confidence, hope, health and well-being, growth, and faith.
• Designing events, meetings, and/or conferences; preparing travel agendas and approaches.	• Resolving interpersonal issues; improving the quality of relationships.
• For better understanding and meeting the needs of customers, clients, or patients. Discovering latent needs.	• Reducing or removing the obstacles to greater success such as confusion, fear, and anxiety.
• Prioritization and allocation of efforts and resources; reviewing budgets.	• Making choices and prioritizing effort.
• Evaluating research, product development and marketing options, and decisions, or generating new options and alternatives.	• Anticipating or discovering the probable outcomes of decisions, and identifying paths around potential barriers.
• Market research and competitive intelligence. Discovering and prioritizing market needs.	• Testing perceptions and different approaches to issues.
• Business forecasting; evaluating strategies; reviewing business ideas or hunches.	• Discovering the nature of underlying problems before they fully surface.
• Preparing presentations, materials, and speeches.	• Verifying hunches.
• Building a stronger sense of community and respect for diversity.	• Discovering your connectedness with others; gaining a renewed sense of the sacredness and wonder of life.

This takes practice and is subject to error. The power of the logical mind to design the imaging frameworks and experiments, and then to interpret the resulting images, is also critical. Success is based on a balanced approach between both right and left brains.

The effort of the SWAT team to harness intuition as a practical tool was as deeply rewarding as it was successful. But perhaps the most rewarding experience has been the personal transformation for which Creative Imaging has been a catalyst.

Each member of the team, through the disciplined use of intuition in both our business and personal lives, came to understand reality differently, more holistically. Each of us also came to experience ourselves as more than separate individuals living in a disjointed world. We became aware of the invisible interconnections between ourselves and others, and experienced instances of knowing that transcended linear time and space. It was a deeply transforming experience for each of us. And, quite literally, it changed the course of my life.

What is most encouraging is that I have seen a glimmer of the possibility that business may also experience this kind of transformation in years to come. It will happen through a reintegration of the rational and the intuitive into a more unified and brilliant perception. *If we can change our beliefs about how we know what we know, then we will begin to restructure how we do what we do.* This is our critical task for business in the 1990s and beyond. Indeed, it may well be the key to our future sustainability on the planet.

Part Five

THE CONSCIOUS WORKPLACE

Making The Workplace Safe For Intuition
Nancy Rosanoff

The Intuitive Organization
Kymm Harvin Rutigliano

**Introverted Intuitives:
Managing Diversity In The Workplace**
Laurie Nadel

Nancy Rosanoff is an authority in the field of intuition. Over the course of seventeen years, she has counseled, trained, and inspired thousands of executives and individuals to realize their goals by harnessing their intuition. She became a pioneer in the field of intuition after several dramatic personal experiences revealed that we often know much more than we think we know. She has developed exercises which strengthen the link between intuition and everyday thinking, which, in turn, makes it reliable, accessible, and understandable.

Rosanoff is the author of *Intuition Workout,* the first "how to" book on intuition, and is a columnist for *Intuition* magazine. She is a sought-after speaker for corporate and association audiences and conducts seminars for the general public. Her clients include First Union National Bank, IBM, Inset Systems Software, NatWest Bank, Marriott Hotels, and Pepsi. She is also on the board of directors of the Intuition Network and was president of the National Speakers Association, New York Tri-State Chapter (1995-1996).

16

Making The Workplace Safe
For Intuition

Nancy Rosanoff

Twenty years ago Herbert Kelleher acted against the current wisdom of how to run an airline. As Chairman, President, and CEO of Southwest Airlines, he eliminated First Class, limited the type of aircraft used to one, refused to use a "hub," and only scheduled flights to cities on a non-stop basis. These are just a few of the innovations he instituted based on his "gut feeling." Herb Kelleher is renowned for being an intuitive maverick. The stock of his company has grown 23,000% since it started, making it the number one U.S. company in growth of stock price over the past twenty years. Going with his intuition has paid off big time for Mr. Kelleher and Southwest Airlines. Like all great corporate visionaries, he now faces the next great challenge. Can he sustain this level of innovation and growth and, perhaps more importantly, can he transfer his intuitive approach to the next generation of leaders? Unless he actively trains and encourages others in his company to develop and use their intuition, my experience tells me that he will not.

Individual entrepreneurs and innovative managers have successfully used intuition since the beginning of business history and continue to do so. These individuals are often forced to work independently and isolate themselves from co-workers in order to find and follow their "inner guidance" on how to proceed.

Company leaders and managers who have great instincts tend to put on mental helmets and blinders so they can force their way through the system in order to get their ideas realized. As a result, these highly intuitive and successful individuals often have difficulty encouraging and utilizing the intuitions of team members and have a hard time communicating their intuitive approach.

With the current business climate demanding ever faster product development, increased customer service, tighter fiscal responsibility, and global responsiveness, intuition, now more than ever, is an essential tool. This holds true not only for individuals within a system, but for the system itself. Individual leaders have been able to inspire others to follow their vision based on personal power and charisma. The challenge has always been to translate vision and commitment to other leaders when a company grows beyond the manageability of one person. To stay with the customer and ahead of the competition requires more than one intuitive wildcat navigating new ideas through the system. Success requires intuitive thinking at all levels of a company, communicated and implemented as part of the system. This essay discusses why it is important to bring intuition openly into the workplace, how the intuitive process can be incorporated into business systems, and some steps to begin to open your workplace to intuition.

What Is Intuition?

Intuition is when you know something without knowing *how* you know it. Intuition is an internal guidance system which is part association and memory, part experience, and part unknown. It is one of those things in life that we know exists by experiencing its results, but we don't know how it works. Conrad Hilton, in his autobiography, tells this story: "My first bid, hastily made, was $165,000. Then somehow that didn't feel right to me. Another figure kept coming, $180,000. It satisfied me. It seemed fair. It felt right. I changed my bid to the larger figure on that hunch. When they were opened, the closest bid to mine was $179,800. I got the Stevens Corporation by a narrow margin of $200. Eventually the assets returned me $2 million." How did he know what to bid? Some might say his experience told him, although this happened at the beginning of his career. Some might say that he was just lucky. According to his own experience, he "had a feeling," which we can try to analyze and justify.

The bottom line is that we don't know how he knew it. He just did, and that is intuition.

Business thrives on the willingness to take risks, and the ability to venture into an uncertain future. There is no tool more valuable than a sharp intuition because of its ability to reduce uncertainty while providing insight about the future.

A recent two-year study of senior managers by Daniel Isenberg of the *Harvard Business Review* concluded that senior managers seldom think in ways that one might simplistically view as rational. Yet, ironically, he also found that although the majority of managers favored the intuitive over more analytic approaches, most believed it was not how decisions were normally handled by other successful managers. This last statement tells us that intuition is used, but seen as "wrong" or "not normal" by the managers who use it. Managers use intuition and feel isolated in their practice.

The bad news is that, because many people use and value their intuition but do not talk about it, it rarely gets trained, evaluated, and improved. It is a valuable tool, especially in the complex decisions and judgments made in the business world every day. How many times have people said, "I knew that was not going to work," or "I knew that business idea had merit," but it was too late. The window of opportunity had passed. It is like the old V-8 commercials where someone finishes a soda, slaps his head, and then says, "I could have had a V-8!"—We slap ourselves and say "I could have listened to my intuition—if only I knew how"—and *if* it was openly valued within our work group.

The bottom line here is, just about everyone has hunches and gut feelings. The problem is what to do with them, how to turn those vague sensations into information that can be communicated to, and acted upon by other team members within corporations.

The main complaint heard about using intuition in the workplace is that there is no empirical verification. While empirical data are one piece of the information gathered in the decision making pie, they are still just one piece. The rest of the pie involves future trends, customer needs, preferences and appeal, all of which require intuition to determine successfully. So the problem with intuition in the workplace is not one of empirical verification, it is that the corporate decision-making structure has not incorporated intuition openly into the process. Intuition can be made "corporate friendly" when corporations become "intuition friendly."

Is Your Workplace Safe For Intuition?

Modern business is faced with a life-or-death paradox: While trying to maintaining a stable, systematic process of planning, implementation, and control, it is also necessary to practice frame-breaking management, in which managers conflict, question, learn, and make new discoveries. The paradox, in the words of Ralph D. Stacey, author of *Managing the Unknowable,* is "that the structures and behavior appropriate for stable management have to coexist with the informality and instability of the extraordinary form of management that is necessary to cope with the unknowable." Intuitive thinking plays an important role, but the traditional hierarchical structures found in most businesses don't allow for "fuzzy" thinking. Even the new wave of Quality Management and Re-engineering, while providing ways to rethink systems and improve work processes, doesn't have room for "hunches" and "gut feelings." If a team member has a feeling that there is a better way to do something, but cannot articulate the new way precisely, many work groups won't or don't know how to support the gestation of what may turn out to be a breakthrough insight.

For example, a product development team launched a new product which failed, costing the company millions of dollars. Each person on that team told me personally that he "knew intuitively" that the timing was not right for this product before it was launched, but no one said anything to the rest of the team because they had no facts to back up their intuition. This is not an isolated incident. Work groups and management need to learn how to encourage, respect, develop and communicate intuitive knowledge. I am not suggesting that a company turn it's approach around based on someone's hunch. What I am suggesting is that there are ways to develop, train and encourage employees to talk about their hunches and together discover the evidence to support or refute the hunch.

For example, while speaking to a group of credit managers, I was told the following story by a credit manager for a large chemical company who was working with a new client who happened to have an immaculate credit history. The job of the credit manager is to determine whether a customer can afford to purchase large amounts of chemical products on credit. Before the company releases the product to the customer, the credit manager needs to approve the transaction. According to all the corporate guidelines, this person was a good risk. Yet every time the credit manager tried to get the client on the phone, he was difficult to find. And every time the manager hung up the phone, he had an uncomfortable feeling about this client. Eventually, the customer called on a Friday afternoon, asked for the product to be released, and said that he was putting the check in the mail right this minute. The credit manager did it, felt uncomfortable, and, sure enough, the check was not "in the mail." It took a long time, with many calls and letters, before full payment was received. This cost the company both time and money. Now, if intuition were valued within the workplace, this manager could have gone to his supervisor or team members and shared his discomfort. If the manager had a track record of "accurate intuition," then the supervisor could back him up in his decision and they could work together to find another way to service this client. Perhaps another team member would have made some other observation which, alone, was meaningless, but, coupled with the "uncomfortable feeling" of the first manager, would begin to build a picture. More questions could be asked, more information could be gathered until the manager felt "comfortable" with the plan.

Too often in companies, the rules or structure override individual instinct and intuition. Intuition is our internal guidance system which needs to be matched and fed by "data" which are our external guidance system. When these two systems are giving different signals, then more research needs to be done, both internally and externally, until the systems match. This requires an ability to distinguish between external and internal information, tools to articulate both, and methods to gather more information within both systems.

Our educational system has focused mainly on training for the gathering, analysis, and articulation of external information. Making the workplace safe for intuition requires that internal, intuitive information be gathered, analyzed, articulated and integrated openly within the business setting.

Putting Intuition Into The Decision-Making Process Openly

Gathering Intuitive Information

Intuitive information can happen at anytime, whether it is consciously asked for or not. It is an internal sensing which needs to be translated into thoughts and words. Intuition utilizes all of our sensory experience to communicate, so feelings, words, images, dreams and physical sensations are all tools used by intuition to communicate. In the above example of the credit manager who felt uneasy when his client was difficult to reach by phone, intuition used an uncomfortable feeling attached to an event (hard to reach) as a way of getting the attention of the credit manager. The fact that someone is hard to get a hold of on the phone is not reason enough to deny credit, but in this case, intuition was using that event, coupled with an uncomfortable feeling as a warning signal—communicating "LOOK OUT!"

Intuitively, the credit manager knew something was not right with this deal, but could not articulate it as it was intuitive information and in a language that was not understandable to his supervisor. Since the language of intuition is not acknowledged in most businesses, much intuitive information and insight gets lost or ignored. Here are some suggestions on how to cultivate an awareness of the language intuition uses within the workplace:

Pay Attention:
— At the beginning and end of team meetings, take a breath and ask yourself "How am I feeling?" Get the team comfortable checking in with their own intuition with a key phrase such as: "Now that everyone is here, take a moment to bring in your logical and intuitive minds." At the end of a meeting, take an intuitive pulse by asking: "On a scale of 1–10, how complete or agreed are we on this issue?"

— Take a Time Out: It takes less than five minutes to reflect on the current situation and to sense whether the direction you are going in is still the most appropriate one. Ask team members to take a moment to write: (1) an issue statement; (2) what is known; (3) what needs to be known and is currently unknown.

— Think peripherally: Notice the little details that, in and of themselves, are inconsequential, but which may add up to an intuitive message. Ask team members to remember something that has occurred during the project, but seemed completely unrelated. Then make up a story about how it might be related.

Ask:
When researching and gathering information for a project, ask many questions, as far afield as possible, and listen

deeply to the answers, paying attention to signals received from the speaker, as well as yourself. If something makes you uncomfortable, ask more questions, until a clear and comfortable direction is reached. Here are some ways to ask questions and receive intuitive answers:

— Ask a question and then flip a coin: Watch for the internal reaction of "yes, that's it," or "no, that's not what I want" for the answer, not whether the coin is heads or tails.

— Ask someone in the workplace who is not involved in the decision about a current issue: Intuition is non-hierarchical. The position someone holds is unrelated to her intuitive ability. During intuitive training, an advertising group focused on a current client for one of the intuitive team building exercises. Two people on the team knew nothing about the client and held receptionist and secretarial positions. The insights they added to the resolution were at least equally as valuable as those of people who were most involved with the client, if not more insightful. Another result of working with the team in this way was that everyone, within a matter of minutes, was synergistically on the same page about how to approach and handle this client's needs.

Pretend:

Pretending to be able to listen to your intuition is probably one of the most beneficial tools I've used. Perhaps because of our desire to be "right" and to "not make mistakes," we avoid making "foolish guesses" or un-thought-out statements. In this process, many intuitive insights can get lost and remain hidden. Pretending that intuition exists and that it can be perceived can take away the stigma of needing to be "right" and allow for innate intuition to emerge. Try these tricks:

— Ask yourself or your colleagues to fill in this blank: "If I did have an intuition about this issue, it would be _____," or "_____."

— "If I had to make a decision right this instant, it would be _____."

Evaluating Intuitive Information

Once intuitive information has been gathered, it needs to be evaluated. Evaluating intuitive information is like putting together a jigsaw puzzle. Each piece of intuitive information has a place, exactly where it belongs, and how it all fits together takes time and skill to figure out. Once the right fit is found it is unmistakable. Two isolated pieces of a jigsaw puzzle may look unrelated, as isolated pieces of intuitive information often seem. With a jigsaw puzzle, there is usually a picture of the completed puzzle to work from, while with intuition, the discovery of the big picture occurs when more and more little bits of information fit together. Evaluating intuitive information, determining what, how and when intuitive information can be used, is also an intuitive process.

Intuition communicates through gut feelings, physical sensations, emotions, symbols, images, and hunches. Intuition is validated through a similar process. An intuition may begin as a vague hunch or feeling, and through acknowledging, nurturing, and stimulating that feeling through some of the exercises suggested above, the meaning of the communication will make itself clear. This is validated by another intuitive feeling—it feels right. Here is an example which will clarify my point. A friend of mine is a forensic accountant. He is brought into situations as a detective, looking for accounting errors and determining criminal intent. He shared with me his process, as follows: Immediately upon opening the books a feeling comes over him. Something feels fishy about these books—he knows something is wrong but he doesn't know what. He keeps looking and looking until he finds something, then there may or may not be an "aha" feeling of "that's it!" If there is the feeling, he knows he has found the major problem. If there is no feeling, then he knows he has to keep looking. Intuition has validated itself with an intuitive feeling. It begins with a feeling and is verified with a feeling. When electricity makes a complete circuit and is attached to a light bulb, the light goes on. Intuition is the electricity and the light represents our understanding. We know electricity exists and has made a complete circuit because we see the light. We know intuition exists because of the "aha" feeling which indicates that what was "intuited" at the beginning of the process has been found and validated.

Evaluating whether intuition is getting mixed up with intellectual and emotional patterns takes some experience to determine. Here are some warning signals that intellectual and emotional interference is going on:

Attachment To Outcome: This can be a difficult signal to pay attention to, especially for business people who have been trained to focus on results and always to be goal oriented. Goals and vision are not in conflict with intuition. But when we become too focused on a particular desired outcome, the ability to perceive intuitive information that may be in conflict with that outcome will be ignored.

Rejection Of External Data: When you hear phrases such as "I don't need to look at that report, I know what is in it," or "They don't know what they are talking about, I've been in the business for years," or "What do you mean such and such is happening. That's impossible," watch out! There may be intuitive information being rejected by intellectual snobbism. It can also be a sign that there is an attachment to a particular way of thinking and proceeding, so that any new information is ignored.

Lack Of Clarity: Sometimes an issue just won't make sense. Nothing helps to gain clarity. It could be that it is not the right time to make the decision, and it also may be that the issue is fogged in because of emotional confusion and attachments. This may be the time to give the issue to someone else—get another opinion or three—to help clear the fog.

Needing To Make It Happen: Whenever you hear yourself say, "I can make this work," watch out! Disaster may be right around the corner. To make such a strong statement and to need to generate so much energy is clearly going against intuitive information, usually for emotional attachments to a certain set of results, which will most likely not happen in this scenario.

Articulating Intuition

The most effective way to communicate intuitive information is to acknowledge that it is intuitive. Intuition loses its ability to be flexible when there is a need to make it sound more solid and concrete than it is. When working with a group of people who do not generally acknowledge and talk about their intuitions, it is useful to add a phrase that anticipates their reaction. For example, "This may sound vague to you, but I have this very uncomfortable gut feeling about this situation. Have *you* ever had a strong feeling about something that you couldn't articulate precisely?" This opens a door to communicate with clear expectations of the type of information that is coming. It also invites the other person to share a story about an intuitive experience he might have had. Simple, direct and honest is always the best approach.

Sometimes intuitive information is on such a feeling level that words are inadequate to express it. In intuitive teamwork sessions, participants work with many simple creative tools to help articulate intuitive knowing, such as colorful markers, clay, story telling, toys, etc. Communicating through art helps relate intuitive knowing to symbols and metaphors, which, in turn, helps articulate the practical meaning. In one training session, a copywriter was blocked and could not come up with anything. I asked him to close his eyes and pick up something from his desk. He picked up a pencil and focused on the eraser. An immediate recognition came that the block was related to his need to be "good" and not to have to "erase" what was written. This was an experienced writer who had struggled through blocks before only after an intense waiting period. His teammates, also in the training, watched in amazement while he began to write freely after a few minutes. Sometimes just articulating intuition releases blocked energy.

Integrating Intuition In The Workplace— Where To Use It

Although intuition is used throughout the business process, there are a few key times when it is beneficial to actively incorporate intuitive thinking into the process:

1. Troubleshooting. When a project keeps running into dead ends, slow or no energy, problem after problem, it is usually a signal that there is intuitive information and/or insight which is being ignored. One of the ways intuition communicates is through external circumstances. When the more subtle signals of gut feelings, hunches, and emotions are ignored or bypassed, the message finds more concrete messengers. To keep trying to do what is not working is stubborn. This is an excellent time to get the work group together, ask for an intuitive evaluation of where the project may be blocked, and to employ intuition to discover where the "open door" to successful completion is located. This method is also very useful when there is extreme tension and frustration around a particular situation or work group.

2. Planning. Whether a team or work group is conducting a long- or short-range planning event, intuition plays a key role in assuring that a wise and complete decision focused on the future will result. When preparing for a planning session, make sure participants are prepared to think intuitively as well as analytically. At the beginning of a planning session, ask the participants to share their "sense" of where the project or company is headed before digging into reports, figures and ideas. If it is a long planning session, take a couple of "intuitive" breaks, where the intuitive "pulse" of the situation is taken. Once a decision has been made or a conclusion drawn, ask participants how it "fits." Get their intuitive sense of appropriateness and rightness of the decision.

The owner of a construction company told me that after he looks at a potential job analytically and determines whether or not it is worth his time, he always is successful if he takes a few moments to "try on" the decision and notice how it feels. At that point, he may turn down a deal that "looks great on paper," or he may decide to do a job that doesn't look so good. In construction, as in any business, there are factors that can make or break a job that cannot be determined analytically at the outset, weather and labor issues being just two examples. We do, however, possess an intuitive muscle which can "sense" the success or failure of a situation before it happens. It is truly foolish to not develop and use that ability.

3. Tracking Progress. Once a project is underway, intuition still plays a valuable role. It is important to revisit the "sense" of a project as well as the "numbers" to determine whether the pursued course is still on target. Encourage team members to look for and articulate "yellow lights"; warning signals which, in and of themselves, mean nothing, but, put together with an intuitive understanding, can anticipate problems before they become disastrous. As in the new product fiasco described earlier, intuition, if encouraged and articulated, could have turned a failure into a success through fine tuning the product and in intuiting optimum timing for its release.

4. Follow-Up/Evaluation. Once completed, it is valuable to ask "How do we feel about what we accomplished with this project?" Asking this question can give a whole new perspective. Instead of moving forward after looking at financial results, intuition can help evaluate the impact of the project on customers and employees, insights for improving future projects, and loose ends to complete which may look unimportant now, but which can make a significant difference in the future.

Checklist For Making Your Workplace Safer For Intuition

There is no one formula which will work for every workplace. Each group will develop their own unique way of inviting and using intuitive information. It is important not to use a "cookie cutter" approach of imposing an "intuitive structure" onto an existing group. Each group is made up of individuals who each have a personal style of receiving and reporting intuitive information. That needs to be discovered and developed first. Then a team approach which incorporates intuition more systematically can be created. Once created, it can be improved, modified and grown to fit changing needs. The following is a checklist of ideas which, once implemented, will begin to integrate intuition into your workplace:

- Make a commitment.
- Start small. Determine where the business can incorporate intuition easily.
- Determine measurement factors within each department and measure baseline.
- Train and educate.
- Allow group process to emerge with encouragement and attention;

  -disclose personal intuitions;

  -ask questions and then more questions.
- Track and follow-up on intuitions—create a record/keep logs.
- Measure results.
- Share results and extend into other parts of the company.

When attempting to incorporate intuition into the workplace, it is important to recognize a few basic underlying truths about intuition, people, and corporate structures. Many in the work force have become habituated to leaving their wisdom at the office door as they enter, and picking it up on the way out. There have been few rewards for voicing "intuitions" and taking risks. Asking people to all of a sudden reveal their insights will not work. Making the workplace safe for intuition does not require a huge reorganization effort or the implementation of new systems and structures. Those changes will happen naturally once individuals feel free to talk about, trust, and act on their intuitions. Begin one person, one department at a time and let a natural evolution take place.

Intuition is a natural human gift. When the environment allows for it, intuition grows naturally. With involvement, trust, open communication, fair and consistent management practices, and shared vision, intuition will also be present. The key is to be willing to talk about it and share it. By allowing and developing intuitive thinking in all phases of decision making and product development, companies will solidify their chances for success in the future while utilizing more of the current talents of their workforce.

Kymn Harvin Rutigliano, PhD, has spent the past thirty years conveying a singular vision: Life is all about love. During the course of her distinguish career, she has worked as a journalist, political speech writer, corporate change champion, relationship coach, management consultant, speaker, and author. She is internationally known for her groundbreaking work at AT&T and with other Fortune 100 companies committed to nurturing the hearts and spirits—as well as minds and bodies—of their employees. Her work provides a "wake up call" for her clients to discover and integrate into their professional lives their own inner resources of love, clarity, and spiritual expression.

17

The Intuitive Organization

Kymn Harvin Rutigliano

> Dig up all the information you can, then go with your instincts. We all have a certain intuition, and the older we get, the more we trust it....I use my intellect to inform my instinct. Then I use my instinct to test all this data. Hey, instinct, does this sound right? Does it smell right, feel right, fit right?
>
> —General Colin Powell

When I first read that quote in Colin Powell's best-selling book, *My American Journey*, I giggled. I envisioned a board meeting somewhere in corporate America where a courageous soul says, "Hey, group, does this decision smell right to you? Does it feel right? Does it fit right?" In my mind's eye, the group is stopped dead in its tracks. Silence. Utter silence. Then, with an incredulous voice and an arrogant smirk, someone says, "Did you say, 'Does this smell right, feel right?' 'Are you for real?' 'What's that got to do with anything?' 'The numbers prove we are on the right track.' 'What more do we need?'"

Well, if you ask me, General Powell, or a growing number of highly successful people, the answer is clear. In our high-speed, high-risk, highly-changing business landscape, we need a lot more than data and facts to make decisions—in our organizations as well as in our own individual lives. We need to trust our instincts. We need to trust our gut feelings. We need to allow all our senses to inform us. We need to embrace our intuitive nature as well as our intellectual mind.

Simply put, in my view, the organizations that will thrive in the 21st Century will be *Intuitive Organizations.* They will be organizations that trust the hearts and the souls—not just the minds and bodies—of their employees, their customers, their partners, their owners. They will not simply be "learning organizations," to use the phrase Peter Senge promoted in his best-seller, *The Fifth Discipline.* These organizations will not rely solely on giving people new theories, new skills, or even new paradigms. They will not simply look for ways to do more with less, to beat the competition, to gain market share. All this will be insufficient; in fact, all this already is insufficient. Rampant layoffs, low morale, and high stress levels in many organizations make this clear.

What is called for is *going within,* embracing what can't be seen, can't be proven, can't be viewed through the lenses of a microscope, a marketing plan or a balance sheet. *Going within* is more about *being* and less about *doing.* It is about being still, entering silence, asking what's there, listening openly. It is about tuning into the guidance, the messages, the wisdom springing from our hearts, bodies, souls/spirits, not just our minds, our intellects, our brains. *Going within* is the key to becoming—and being—intuitive.

This Makes Sense For A Person, But What About For A Business?

In many ways, a business is like a person. A business is an entity, passionately conceived out of a need, a desire, an insight or a dream. Fueled by others' life energy, it gestates rapidly and creates its own life energy in the process. In time, all systems say "go," and with blood, sweat, tears, and love, it is birthed. Typically, the "new creation" is celebrated and draws widespread attention. In the early days, like any new being, it is filled with wonder, with curiosity, with endless possibilities. Dedication and loyalty help shape its existence and generate great promise for the future. All those involved are viewed as precious, necessary, and valuable. TLC (Tender Loving Care) is mutual—given and received. The growing entity continues to progress, thanks to the steadfast care, wisdom, and creative energies of those who nurture and contribute to it. Any downs are shared as generously as the ups and there is a sense of learning a great deal from risking and, sometimes, failing.

Education is viewed as a worthy investment. As the entity goes through growth spurt after growth spurt, it eventually thinks it has a life of its own, and resists recognizing the contributions of others. Arrogance rules. People are viewed as expendable commodities. The "older crowd" can't be trusted and is no longer worth investing in. The bottom line beckons: Build me up, build me up. Nothing else is important.

Who cares about others? Focus solely on me. I'm your ticket to the top. Forget that mushy, TLC stuff. Kick ass, take names. Win at all costs, otherwise you are out of the game. Cut here, cut there. We don't need this one or that one. Look, the bottom line is better already. Let's cut some more. This is really working. Those guys on Wall Street love us. Lean and mean they say. An adolescent's dream.

Better cut a bit more...oops! Hit the aorta! Call for help! What do you mean no one's answering the phone? This is URGENT! Call back! I'm bleeding to death...hurry!!!!!!!! "Thank you for your patience. You are now seventh in line for assistance...please hang on. While you wait we will tell you about our upcoming holiday specials."

The above scenario may be an oversimplification, but it sure makes the point clear: People are the lifeblood of business. It is therefore vital that we treat them as such, honor them as such. One important way to do this is to recognize the wisdom that they bring not only on a mental/intellectual level but also on physical, emotional and spiritual levels as well.

Can This Really Work In Business?

Yes, I promise you it can. I've seen it work wonders in Fortune 100 corporations, family-owned businesses, as well as education and health care enterprises. Let me share a recent experience with you.

Shortly following the "trivestiture" of AT&T—the announcement that this prominent telecommunications company is going to split into three separate companies by the end of 1996—I was invited to work with a small group of nine people who were charged with advising one of the new entities on how to transform itself in order to stay successful in an ever-changing marketplace. This group of highly-skilled, successful, versatile leaders had been given an arduous task and very tight timeframes in which to achieve it. In order to meet this deadline, they asked one of the Big Six consulting firms to work with them. Almost immediately, this group began to produce results, to develop possible strategies, to grapple with the future of their enterprise. While the group was very successful in meeting the "content" demands of their task, the members knew that something was missing. Just what that was wasn't clear, yet they had a sense that the missing ingredient was vital not only to their success as a team, but also to the success of the new enterprise. Unfortunately, they weren't discussing this collectively since the content work had urgent deadlines. Each member, in his or her own way, was searching to discover what was missing.

One of the leaders recalled meeting me a year earlier when I was about half-way through my doctoral program in Organization Development and Spirituality. At the time, he had been intrigued by my studies in these seemingly contradictory disciplines. He was beginning to see evidence in his own life and work that spirituality was a driving force for many business leaders, including him. He noticed himself, a physicist by both training and profession, making decisions not based solely on facts or empirical data. He noticed his own search for "something more," though he had few words to describe the gnawing hunger he felt. He began to see a need to infuse this vital project with spirit, but had no idea what that really meant or how to do it. He asked himself: "Could it be that Kymn, that consultant with a heart in her company logo, is an appropriate resource for this team? Would the group accept a consultant so outspoken about bringing love and spirit into the workplace? Or, was this too far outside the box for even this creative, innovative group of leaders?"

Much to my surprise, this courageous man and his colleagues invited me to work with them. They decided to venture into the unknown, to try something that admittedly was risky. But not taking the risk felt worse to them. They chose to go for it...and they did.

Nicknaming me "Dr. Love," this group shared the frustrations of their journey with me. They all considered the work they were doing to be of utmost importance to this organization with nearly 100,000 people. They were in the enviable position of helping architect the future, not merely react to it. They considered themselves to be the right people at the right time for the right project—and in my view they were. So what was happening? What was amiss? What was missing?

In less than two hours—following introductions and some ice-breaking discussions—the missing pieces of the puzzle became obvious. This group of accomplished leaders was suffering from mental flooding, while the group's hearts, spirits, and bodies were suffering from persistent drought. Data and information were crashing in on them like tidal waves. There appeared to be no room to move, no way to turn down the noise of the ticker tape of facts and figures, no way to stop the mounting uneasiness and fear. Yet, the posing of four simple questions changed the entire scene. It was, even for me, the eternal optimist, hard to believe. I asked:

- What is your *mind's* message to this team right now?
- What is your *body's* message to this team right now?
- What is your *heart's* message to this team right now?
- What is your *soul's—your spirit's—*message to this team right now?

Each person first wrote their responses on a piece of paper and then the floor was open for anyone to share. What occurred could best be described as a "wake-up call." People shared their candid responses. It was not surprising that the "mind" was encouraging the team onward, was highlighting the progress made, and was pointing out how much the business was relying on this team. While these comments were well received, it was the comments from the body, heart, and spirit/soul questions that seemed to "awaken" the group. There were pleas to be listened to, to be noticed, to be considered. Care, concern, and love were expressed for colleagues. Several members—men and women alike—spoke of what it was like to leave their heart on the kitchen table when they said good-bye to their children each morning. A sense of being a part of something very big and very wonderful was expressed—but also the frustration of feeling like a misfit. One engineer spoke eloquently of the lack of synergy and the sub-optimization of the group's collective behavior. He spoke of his struggle to give 150 percent only to have 30 percent of his effort and contribution considered valuable by the rest of the team.

In the hours that followed, as people shared from these four "quadrants" (as we came to call them), the mental flooding was stemmed. The parched hearts, spirits and bodies received their due. And as these different dimensions of the team members themselves were voiced and validated, the team "came to life." It was as if the fog had lifted. Clarity abounded. People began to see each other not just as colleagues on this project but as whole, human, spiritual beings who genuinely wanted to make a differ-ence with their lives. It became clear that these are people who not only wanted this project to be successful, but for their journey together to be successful—characterized, they said, by learning, growing, and having fun together. "This isn't just about growing a business; it is about growing individually and collectively as well," they said. "And it is about having fun in the process."

I learned a lot by working with this group. I learned not to underestimate peoples' willingness to venture outside the box, outside the conventional culture, outside business as usual. I learned the power of creating opportunities to tune in to our bodies, hearts, spirits/souls and allowing them to speak with the same validity that we give our minds, thoughts and empirical data. I learned that real team-building comes from people expressing *all* of who they are.

These learnings shed light on becoming an *Intuitive Organization*. The ways are many; these are just a few. There is no formula, no list of how-tos, no collection of seven easy steps to follow.

As Colin Powell says, let your intellect inform your instinct. Then trust your intuition. Let this wisdom be your guide. The very best teacher is your own intuition. I invite you to become its student. Rich, revealing, rewarding lessons are in store, for you and your organization.

Laurie Nadel, PhD, is the author of the international bestseller *Sixth Sense*. She has appeared on "Oprah," "Sightings," "Sonya Live," "Good Day, New York," and dozens of other television and radio programs around the country. Her work has been featured in *New Woman, Cosmopolitan, Ladies' Home Journal, McCall's, The Los Angeles Times*, and United Press International.

Nadel develops and presents seminars on intuitive leadership and decision making. She is a trainer for the American Management Association. Holding doctorates in psychology and clinical hypnotherapy, she maintains a private practice in New York City. She is also on the faculty of the American Institute of Hypnotherapy in Irvine, California.

A professional writer for more than twenty years, she has worked for such major news organizations as CBS and ABC News, *Newsweek*, and United Press International.

18

Introverted Intuitives: Managing Diversity In The Workplace

Laurie Nadel

Simon M., 53 years old, is a senior vice president of a Fortune 500 company. Serious and thoughtful, Simon's strengths are his ability to troubleshoot problems and develop ingenious solutions with relatively little data. He is able to express his ideas well in writing but often has difficulty communicating his ideas verbally. Simon prefers working alone in his office to attending meetings. "Even though I am successful, people tell me I think too much," Simon says, adding, "Ever since childhood, I have been hearing that I am different in a way that makes me think there is something wrong with me." Simon describes how he has had to learn to model other people's behavior in order to be accepted. Underneath, he believes that he is living through a mask and that if people at work really knew him, they would not like him.

Ingrid L., 38 years old, is the CEO of her own public relations company. Outgoing and articulate, she operates on her gut instinct about people and projects. "I could not function in a large corporation. My ideas were not valued because they did not fit into the standard mold. I went for the big picture while everyone else was analyzing details," she says.

Michael H., 45 years old, describes himself: "I failed math in second grade. Even though I got the right answers, I could not show the steps. In engineering school, I excelled at problem solving but did not score as well in technical subjects." Now a civil engineer,

237

Michael works best on his own and often feels frustrated when his attempts to present creative strategies are often rejected and put down by his superiors.

These three cases contain several common elements. Simon, Ingrid, and Michael function best when they can use their intuition at work. Although each is successful in his or her field, all three perceive themselves to be outside the mainstream. Simon and Michael describe long-standing patterns of feeling "different" from other people. Ingrid and Michael have had to struggle for their ideas to be accepted in their respective companies. Ingrid's response has been to start her own company.

Along with a strong sense of their individualism, creative problem solving strategies, and a desire for autonomy in the workplace, Simon, Ingrid, and Michael have introverted intuitive (IN) personality types, as measured by the Myers-Briggs Type Indicator.

Myers-Briggs Type Indicator And Intuition

Based on Carl Jung's theory of personality, the Myers-Briggs Type Indicator is a self-validating instrument that measures personality preferences across four scales. The scales focus on an individual's attitudes and orientation to life, as well as cognitive behaviors, including intuition.

The original version of the Myers-Briggs Type Indicator was developed by Katherine Cook Briggs and her daughter Isabel Briggs Myers in the 1920s. Neither Katherine nor Isabel was a psychologist. Their interest in personality patterns evolved as a result of their reading biographies of famous people. When meeting people in their everyday life, Katherine and Isabel would often provide them with an informal sheet of questions about favorite activities, habits, decision-making patterns, and work. From the responses given by their friends, relatives, and guests, the mother–daughter team started a data bank which formed the basis of Katherine Cook Briggs' 1926 essay on four personality types in *The New Republic*. Synchronistically, and unknown to Katherine and Isabel, psychiatrist Carl Jung had begun to publish his theory of personality which corroborated the findings of Myers and Briggs.

Katherine and Isabel incorporated Jung's work into theirs, refining their personality instrument several times before launching it officially in 1947. Since then, millions of people have taken the MBTI, making it the most popular personality profile in the world. The MBTI is used throughout the United States government, including the military, as well as private industry. More than one million MBTIs have been administered in Japan. The instrument is also available in French and Spanish. With an underlying purpose of helping people understand themselves and how they differ from others, the Myers-Briggs' primary applications in business include the fields of career counseling, recruitment, and placement.

An unsurpassed source of statistical information about intuitive functioning in the workplace, the Myers-Briggs findings show fascinating cross-cultural similarities. Among the most significant principle findings is that people with similar personality preferences in different countries are attracted to the same professions. For example, computer engineers from the United States, Brazil, India, and Nigeria, will report out with similar Myers-Briggs personality types. When examining intuition at work, therefore, the Myers-Briggs provides a global foundation for insight, although the percentages of individual personality types may vary in different countries. Perhaps equally significant is the research into the triune brain conducted by Dr. Paul MacLean, Chief of Brain Evolution at the National Institute of Mental Health. The triune, or three-in-one brain, consists of the primal, or reptilian brain, which corresponds to Jung's sensing function; the limbic system, which corresponds to the feeling function; the left neocortex, which corresponds to thinking; and the right neocortex, which corresponds to intuition. The existing physiological correlation between the Jungian model and the human brain reinforces the usefulness of the Myers-Briggs Type Indicator as a means of understanding intuition.

Carl Jung's model of personality identifies intuition as one of four mental processes, called psychological functions. A function helps each of us absorb information, process it, and navigate through the inner and outer worlds. A function is defined by Jung as "a particular form of psychic activity that remains the same in principle under varying conditions."

There are two types of functions: *perceptive* and *judging.* Through the function called perception, one gathers information about the world of people, places, events, and things. Data is absorbed from both external and internal (mental) environments. Through the function of judgment, one evaluates or judges the data perceived in order to reach conclusions and establish choices.

The *perceptive* functions, through which one gathers information, are called *sensing* and *intuition*. Carl Jung described them as "irrational" functions because they operate best without conscious, rational guidance. The *sensing* function refers to how one uses his or her five physical senses to gather data and absorb information. Its opposite function, *intuition*, uses the unconscious mind to perceive insight, anticipate possibilities, and associate disparate elements and pieces of information. (The term unconscious mind refers to that part of the mind which lies below the threshold of consciousness. It is also called the subconscious and the nonconscious.) The intuitive function is capable of anticipating future patterns, possibilities, and events. Although intuition is often believed to be a nonlogical ability, within the framework of the Jungian/Myers-Briggs model, intuition is not contraposed to logic, which is a judging function, used to evaluate incoming data. One may prefer intuition to sensing, but one combines intuition (or sensing) with logic (thinking) or feeling. In other words, one can be an intuitive thinking type or an intuitive feeling type.

The *judging* functions, *thinking* and *feeling*, are used to evaluate whatever the sensing and intuitive functions have perceived. The judging functions organize information and assign meaning to it. The *thinking* function makes logical, sequential connections and analyzes consequences using a cause and effect model. In contrast, the *feeling* function uses emotional response and subjective criteria to evaluate information. Whereas the goal of the thinking function is to achieve an *objective* balance, the goal of the feeling function is to achieve a *harmonious* balance. While the thinking function tends to be impersonal, the feeling function tends to be oriented toward the needs of people, rather than an abstract concept.

The Myers-Briggs Type Indicator also examines individual preferences across two other scales: Extroversion/Introversion, and Judging/Perceiving. The Extroversion/Introversion scale determines how someone focuses his or her energy: outward, toward people, places, activities, and things; or inward, to the world of concepts and ideas. To help determine that preference, ask yourself whether you need to be around people to regenerate, or whether you need time alone. The Judging/Perceiving scale examines how someone orients to the external world by asking the following question: After you have taken in information using your five physical senses or your sixth sense, and you have evaluated that information, using your thinking or feeling functions, do you spend more time evaluating or judging that information, or taking it in and being perceptive? A judger tends to be someone who finds it necessary to reach conclusions about the information gathered, whereas a perceiver prefers to keep absorbing data and may avoid making decisions.

The Myers-Briggs Type Indicator gives compelling evidence that not all intuitives are alike. The personality profile shows how your intuition functions in combination with your other three functions. It provides you with a hierarchical structure for understanding when you use your sixth sense as part of your information gathering and decision making process. Moreover, it distinguishes between different types of intuitive personalities. Intuitive thinkers (NT) are distinct from intuitive feeling types (NF).

Susan S., 37, (NT), supervises a department of 15 people. She has strong preferences for seeing the big picture and using analysis to reach conclusions. She likes to make reasoned, equitable decisions. Susan reports to Bob L., 54, (NF), who also looks at the whole when making a decision. However, Bob tends to combine his intuition with a subjective sense of what is right. In sorting criteria, Bob aims at decisions that will bring a sense of harmony and cooperation to the department. He is likely to be empathetic in situations where Susan wants to be objective.

When a position opened up in their department, Susan and Bob had to choose between two evenly qualified candidates. Sandy, 28, had been filling in at that job for two months. His background and performance were excellent. Mark, 30, was working in a similar job in a different department where his performance was equally highly rated. Mark was single and had no dependents, whereas Sandy was married to a woman with a medical condition that would require surgery and possibly ongoing hospitalization. Susan reasoned that hiring Mark would be more cost-effective because he would be available to work longer hours when necessary. Sandy would cost the company money because he would need time off to take care of his wife. Bob saw the picture from a different perspective. Since Mark was single, he did not need the job as much as Sandy did. Bob also factored in Sandy's need for medical insurance and decided that since Sandy needed the job more than Mark did, he would be more committed, making Sandy the better choice.

The Myers-Briggs Type Indicator also discriminates be-tween intuitive types who are methodical and organized (NJ) and those intuitives who tend to be more flexible and open-ended (NP).

As a commercial real estate broker, Helen M., 48, (NP) has built a successful career by following her gut when putting deals together. "I know immediately whether I will get a particular listing. Then I gather as much information as I can about the property. Sooner or later, the person to whom I will ultimately sell the property pops into my head," she says. "Then I start to work the deal." Because of the volatility of her market, Helen places high value on being open-ended and spontaneous. "When a buyer asks me to meet him later that afternoon, I will be there, even though it means rearranging things at the last minute," she says, adding that, "I do my best to obtain any information, answer any questions, and resolve any obstacles." Her partner, Josephine B., 43, (NJ), also follows her intuition when acquiring properties and packaging deals. But Josephine does not enjoy the abrupt, last-minute meetings and open-ended negotiations that can take years to wrap up. "I simply don't have the same patience and tolerance that Helen does," says Josephine. "On the other hand, Helen is great at nurturing the deal but she feels pressured when it's time to close. We are now, after several years, developing a formula that uses our respective strengths. I step in for the close after she has worked out the basics."

Intuitive Vs. Sensing

Even a quick look at the statistics displayed in Table 1 shows intuitive types to be in the minority in the United States. According to Consulting Psychologists Press, Inc., only 25 per-cent of the adults surveyed reported a preference for their intu-ition. In contrast, Table 2 indicates that 42.6 percent of American children who have taken the Murphy-Meisgeier Type Indicator, a children's version of the Myers-Briggs, prefer intuition to sensing. (This corroborates my findings. As a trainer and consultant, I have worked with hundreds of professional adults who say that they "used to have more intuition" and that they would like to be able to access it in their business and personal lives.) Jonathan S., 35, is a dispatcher for a news organization. "My job requires that I pay attention to details and scheduling. But there are times when I have a gut feeling that a flight is going to be delayed or that something is going to get lost. Whenever I act on those feelings, I'm almost always right." But Jonathan is afraid. "People in my

Table 1. Statistical Preferences of the Four Scales

Scale	Percent
Extroversion	75
Introversion	25
Sensing	75
Intuition	25
Thinking	
Male	60
Female	40
Feeling	
Male	40
Female	60
Judging	60
Perceiving	40

Table 2. Murphy-Meisgeier Type Indicator Statistics

Function	Percent (%)
E	74.2
I	25.8
S	57.4
N	42.6
T	20.4
F	79.6
J	34.3
P	65.8
IN	11.9
EN	30.6
IS	13.8
ES	43.6

office will probably think I'm weird if I start making decisions based on hunches instead of schedules."

Fear of being considered "weird" or "different" in a culture where looking and acting like everyone else is a highly valued criterion appears to be the biggest impediment to adults who want to become reacquainted with their intuition. James P., 54, is a vice president of a hotel chain. "There have been situations where my gut feeling has contradicted the numerical data," he says. "But I have learned to camouflage my decision so that my superiors believe that I have thought it out in a logical manner." James has observed that "the higher up you go in a corporation, the more intuitive the executives are." But larger corporations have installed structures which make it extremely difficult and uncomfortable for middle managers to rely on their intuition. "There is not much leeway in these companies," he says.

The intimidation and social pressure which prevent people from relying on their natural intuitive abilities often stems from the educational system. Students who are rewarded for presenting facts in a linear way soon realize that those flashes of intuition will not help them score well on the SATs that lead to scholarships at Harvard. "In tests, I performed well in the essays. I was able to write about concepts and historical background. I found it harder to deal with the technical nitty-gritty," says Michael M., adding, "My teachers used to say that I was smart but I got the sense that they were somehow disappointed in my work." The feeling that teachers and parents are somehow "disappointed" in them is a fairly common theme among intuitives. In a society where three quarters of the adult population believes, "If I can see it, hear it, smell it, taste it, or touch it, then it is real," the other twenty-five percent are at a distinct disadvantage when they say, "My intuition tells me this is real, but I can't really tell you how I know it."

The One-Percent Types

The difference in perception between a sensing-oriented and an intuitive-oriented person becomes highlighted when a preference for introversion is combined with intuition. Extroverted intuitives (EN) focus their energy toward people, activities, and things while using their sixth sense for acquiring information. Because their behavior is outgoing, and their intuition functions as a kind of radar for anticipating possibilities, extroverted intuitives appear confident in public, and often occupy high profile positions. In contrast, introverted intuitives (IN) focus their energy on the internal world of concepts and ideas while using their sixth sense for acquiring information. They appear to be reserved, even reticent in public. Because they have a strong internal frame of reference, need quiet and concentration, and dislike telephone interruptions, introverted intuitives are often perceived as poor team players. "The strengths of an IN include the ability to make decisions without small talk, and a talent for seeing the outcome and expressing it well in writing, as well as being able to handle autonomy," says Nancy Garbett, president of Transition Management, Inc., in Park City, Utah. "They don't care about company politics and won't play, which can be a benefit or a drawback, depending on the context." One advantage may be the IN's ability to cut through red tape, although an IN who has difficulty communicating his strategy may well alienate others in the process.

"The biggest problem for an introverted intuitive in the workplace is that he or she is, quite simply, outnumbered," says Garbett, noting that 75 percent of U.S. adults surveyed show a preference for extroversion and sensing (ES). (The ratio of extroverts to introverts is almost equally reversed in Japan.) Introverted intuitives (IN) comprise only four percent of the U.S. population, breaking down further into four IN types, each of which represents one percent.

What follows is a short description of the four introverted intuitive types:

> INTJ (Introverted Intuitive Thinking Judging): "I never enjoyed watching Star Trek because I thought that Mr. Spock was too emotional," was the self-description offered by one INTJ who is the CEO of a financial services company. In business and in their personal lives, INTJs are, at the same time, brilliantly logical and original thinkers. In business as well as in their personal lives, they set high standards for themselves and others, are quick to voice criticism (internally as well as externally), and can maneuver with forceful independence.

INTP (Introverted Intuitive Thinking Perceiving):
Skeptical yet curious, the INTP spends most of
his or her time in an internal dialectic or debate.
Whereas an INTJ tends to think in abstract,
conceptual terms, an INTP engineers complex,
cognitive structures of fluctuating criteria. In
business, an INTP would rather organize concepts for a presentation than organize a team of
people. In his or her personal life, an INTP may
find it difficult to enjoy relationships.

INFJ (Introverted Intuitive Feeling Judging): The
INFJ brings a sense of vision and commitment to
any project or organization, but only as long as
he or she believes in the intrinsic value and
integrity of the endeavor. In the workplace, an
INFJ can quietly motivate and inspire others but
an inherent reserve may keep him or her from
presenting creative ideas to a wider audience.
The INFJ tends to idealize people and often
experiences disappointment when friendships
and relationships fail to meet his or her high
standards.

INFP (Introverted Intuitive Feeling Perceiving):
Tact, tolerance, and empathy are the natural
gifts that an INFP brings to any organization.
But those same gifts may make it difficult for the
INFP to give or accept criticism. Flexible and
adaptable, the INFP makes a wonderful facilita-
tor and can unify others around a common goal.
It is important for an INFP to reconcile that goal
or vision with the realistic steps needed to attain
it, and this is where he or she may encounter
problems. In the workplace and in relationships,
the INFP has difficulty saying "no" to people and
may go overboard in his or her efforts to appease
others.

A Soul In A Body:
The Special Case Of Introverted Intuitives

Unlike sensing types, who believe that they are their respective bodies, intuitive types generally believe that they inhabit a physical body. This pattern is even more pronounced among introverted intuitives who connect so strongly with their non-physical essence that they often describe themselves as "not belonging in a physical body" and "not wanting to be here," meaning in physical form. The poet John Keats described this state when he wrote, "I feel as if I had died already and am now living a posthumous existence." Such malaise does not reflect pathology or suicidal tendencies among introverted intuitives, per se, for they tend to have a strong conceptual framework which often includes a belief that there is a spiritual purpose for this lifetime, along with a belief in reincarnation. "I don't want to be here, but if I choose to end my life, I know I will have to come back and learn these lessons again," is another belief system common to INs.

This feeling that he or she is, essentially, a soul in a body is inherent in the nature of an introverted intuitive. Other driving modalities include having a restless intellect, a need to know, and an ongoing quest for insight and information. Many great leaders, visionaries, mystics, artists, philosophers, and scientists have been introverted intuitives (see IN Hall of Fame, below). Because these traits are *innate*, rather than acquired, introverted intuitives recognize that they are quintessentially different from the majority of the other people around them. "My family was always telling me that I spent too much time alone, that I thought too much, that I read too much, and that if I would just act like them, everyone would like me," recalls Ingrid L. "I imprinted that there was something wrong with me because I did not think like they did. I realize now that simply because my way of thinking and expressing myself was different, they punished me."

Pressured into family, educational, and other social activities in which they are surrounded by extroverted sensing people who believe "everyone should" act in a particular way, a naturally introverted and intuitive child will often retreat even further into his or her favorite world with concomitantly increasing disapproval from parents, siblings, relatives, and teachers. "When my mother went to meet my fourth grade teacher, she was told that

I was always wasting time, looking out the window, and not paying attention," Simon M. chuckles. "I wish I had known enough to tell her that this was how Albert Einstein discovered the theory of relativity." Undervalued and often denigrated by others, introverted intuitives learn how to model extroverted behavior in order to succeed. Sandra Hirsch, PhD, a Myers-Briggs seminar leader, says that because extroverts believe everyone else should be like them in this culture, there is an abundance of courses on how to develop extroversion skills: how to flirt, how to date, how to speak in public, how to be popular and outgoing. "But does anyone tell extroverts that they need to take courses in how to shut up and listen?" she asks.

Even if they did, it might not make enough of a difference. By the time most INs reach adulthood, they carry with them a sense that there is something undefinably wrong with them. They feel as if they don't belong anywhere. In his play, "John Bull's Other Island," George Bernard Shaw expresses this sentiment through a dialogue between two characters, Broadbent and Keegan:

> Keegan: You feel at home in the world then?
>
> Broadbent: Of course. Don't you?
>
> Keegan (from the very depths of his nature): No.

Reserved, often guarded about their feelings, with a strong tendency to internalize feedback, introverted intuitives are often at a loss to explain how and why they are misunderstood. As there is relatively little information about the statistical minority to which they belong, introverted intuitives lack information to confirm what they have felt throughout their lives: that they have experienced prejudice which is as strong as any form of racism, sexism, or religious intolerance. This, in turn, reinforces a sense of aloneness that has been analyzed extensively by Colin Wilson who in *The Outsider*, writes, "At first sight, the Outsider is a social problem. He is a hole-in-corner man." Wilson goes on to quote French author Henri Barbusse, whose protagonist in the novel *L'Enfer* describes himself: "Again, I am on the pavement, and I am not at peace as I had hoped. An immense confusion bewilders me. It is as if I could not see things as they were. I see too deep and too much."

It is this quality, this seeing "too deeply and too much" which is both the blessing and curse of the IN personality. Without this enhanced quality of perception, an introverted intuitive would have a different character and identity, perhaps a different genetic code. The ability to see deeply and greatly brings depth to one's vision, passion to one's heart, and strengthens one's connection to that unique place inside each of us which connects us to something greater than ourselves, the soul. To be an introverted intuitive is to know beyond any rational sense that these inner realities are at least as important, and sometimes more important, than the external world, even though there may be little or no sensory data to support that belief.

Challenges For Introverted Intuitives

The main challenge facing introverted intuitives in the workplace, then, is one of integration. For the individual, it is important find an office and working environment where it feels safe to express what he or she is thinking or feeling. "To be an IN in the business world is an exercise in frustration," says Ilene D., 42, a sales manager and department head of a retailing chain. "Every day, you wake up, look in the mirror and ask yourself, 'Am I going to be me today, or am I going to play the game?'" Years of prejudicial thinking may have conditioned an IN to expect disapproval. This, in turn, can easily inhibit an IN from producing original solutions and strategies which could be energizing and profitable to an organization. For management, the biggest challenge may be encouraging and supporting introverted intuitives so that they can contribute their best work. "When I started working as an investment banker, I tried to act like everyone else," says Jack S., 38, an INTJ. "But when I moved into a management position with my own office, I was able to be myself. Now that my job calls for strategic planning, I can work to the best of my ability." Jack acknowledges that if one of his bosses had not made it a priority to help Jack find a position where he could work with autonomy, he may have quit investment banking, dissatisfied.

It is essential that an introverted intuitive find a friend or ally within his or her organization, preferably someone who will be supportive of the IN's strengths and contributions without casting negative judgments (verbal and nonverbal) on his or her social patterns. Jung has described a "successful introvert" as someone who knows how to put his or her energy out when necessary. In order for the introverted intuitive to discover an ally within the workplace, he or she will have to put out feelers and initiate conversations *at his or her own pace.*

Challenges For The Organization

Lewis L., 43, is an attorney in private practice. "When I graduated from law school, I was approached by several of the big law firms. The recruiters asked me if I knew my Myers-Briggs personality type. When I told them I was an INTP, they stopped talking to me. In fact, three of them never returned my phone calls."

Many people have the unfortunate misconception that INs make lousy employees because they are poor team players. While attitudes such as this have undoubtedly driven many introverted intuitives into self-employment, they represent commonly held beliefs rather than facts. In fact, INs have a strong sense of integrity and will work through the night, if necessary, as long as they believe in the inherent value of any project assigned to them. They detest busywork and find it demeaning. In the widely-used survey developed by Gordon Lawrence in the book *People Types and Tiger Stripes,* INs are likely to do their best work when they are given the freedom to work on their own ideas, and the time and space to work out solutions in their own way. They need opportunities to be creative and to set their own standards of quality. An IN also needs to be able to pace himself or herself, and does not respond well to heavy-handed supervision. Above all, an introverted intuitive needs to be able to follow his or her curiosity, to act on hunches and gut feelings, and to work in depth on projects which the IN considers meaningful. INs tend to be abstract, conceptual thinkers. Therefore, supervisors who manage introverted intuitives may want to develop a team which will include both the IN and a sensing type or an extroverted intuitive who will assist the IN in working out the steps and schedule for different stages of a big project. This may help the IN to communicate more clearly about the composite elements of a project.

While it is neither necessary nor desirable to change the work environment to accommodate the IN, shifting the prevailing mental model about introverted intuitives would be beneficial to the "one percent" types, as well as the other 99 percent. Supporting an introverted intuitive may mean providing him or her with a quieter office, limiting attendance at nonessential meetings, and assigning him or her to smaller teams which will make it easier for the IN to interact. In terms of company activities, INs should not be pressured or manipulated into attending social functions. Nor should they be ostracized for choosing not to attend. When an introverted intuitive believes he or she is ac-

---

INTROVERTED INTUITIVES' HALL OF FAME

Albert Einstein (INTP)

Vincent van Gogh (INFP)

T.E. Lawrence (INTP)

Nijinsky (INFJ)

Fredrich Nietzche (INFJ)

Richard Nixon (INTJ)

George Bush (INFP)

Jimmy Carter (INTP)

---

cepted and does not have a play games in order to hold a job, he or she is more likely to outperform a manager's expectations. By understanding these differences, and acknowledging the difficulties that they cause for INs, supervisory management can provide support and access to working conditions that will motivate any introverted intuitive to excellence.

Part Six

WALKING THE TALK

Suzie Hightower has a comprehensive and highly successful background in government relations, and investor relations. She is a strong advocate of personal empowerment and has had a lifelong interest in intuition, both as a spiritual path and as a tool for decision making in business and government. Her most recent contribution has been in promoting a cooperative spirit and creating partnerships between a national trade association and regional associations in the promotional products industry. As a recognized change agent and visionary leader, she intends to expand her efforts to promote self-mastery and organizational renewal in other business arenas.

She is a member of Renaissance Business Associates, an organization of like-minded people committed to demonstrating the power and effectiveness of integrity in their lives who want to expand their influence in the business environment. She is also a member of the Institute of Noetic Sciences which comprise a multidisciplinary study of the mind, consciousness and diverse ways of knowing, focused especially in the fields of science, mind-body health, psychology, the healing arts and sciences, the social sciences and spirituality.

19

Embrace Intuition

Suzie Hightower

> *The intellect has little to do on the road to
> discovery. There comes a leap in conscious-
> ness, call it intuition or what you will, and the
> solution comes to you and you don't know how
> or why.*
>
> — Albert Einstein

In each life there comes at least one moment which, if seized when recognized, transforms the course of that life forever. For me, that moment came on January 2, 1995. Upon examining this life-altering experience, I have been given insights on ways to change the way I do business and help others through transition. There are many messages in my story. Perhaps you will identify with some of them. Perhaps there are experiences in your life that have already prepared you to welcome change and move smoothly through transition. Some of our greatest teachers and guides come disguised as pain and limitations. It has been said that only at the point of greatest darkness do we become aware of the light within us. May my story help you connect more closely with your light and enable you to embrace your intuition as your best and most cherished friend.

Now here's my story: It wasn't your typical Monday morning. Most offices were closed in observance of the New Year holiday. However, there were a few of us working that day, and I was one of them. It was extremely cold that morning. The temperature was below freezing and, unbeknownst to me, some of the roads were icy. Had I turned on the news that morning or listened to a weather report, I would have known that. But I didn't. You see, I'm one of those people who just refuses to start the morning off with hearing any bad news. No drunk driving stories or shootings over the holidays for my ears! So off to work I go without realizing there are patches of ice on the roads.

Shortly after 8:00 a.m. and less than two miles from my house, I lost control of my car and crashed head-on into a telephone pole. I was traveling between 40 and 50 mph in a small sports car without an air bag. This was my moment. This was my gift. Incredible things began to happen and I began a new journey. My accident contained the seeds of opportunity. It brought about the process of self-change, a personal transformation. A transformation that was so radical that I no longer continue to live the "ordinary life" in the ordinary way. My accident became my teacher. Everyone that I came in contact with became my teacher, and I was able to go deep within myself—much deeper than ever before. As I connected with my "Inner Knowing," I took a leap in consciousness.

The entire experience—from the moment the car hit ice, the plowing into the telephone pole, the people at the scene of the accident who helped me, the doctors and nurses in the hospital (I could go on and on)—was incredible. The first "miracle" was that I didn't die. I did sustain some pretty serious injuries though. I had a contusion to my heart, separated my sternum, crushed all the cartilage in my chest, sprained my neck along with the upper and lower back, smashed my knees, and took a very bad blow to my right leg. I never lost consciousness or my sense of humor. You see, I didn't scratch my face or break a fingernail! I'll never forget how time distorted. A second seemed like minutes. I'll never forget that "Inner Knowing" of exactly what was going to happen. I knew I wasn't going to die, but I also knew it was going to really hurt. It would take another chapter in another book to share with you all the incredible insights and blessings I received by remaining present in each moment and recognizing each experience as a gift. But on to Miracle #2!

> Only when we learn to see the invisible, will
> we learn to do the impossible.
> —Frank Gaines

How many people really get the opportunity to walk their talk? How many people actually put their faith and belief system to the test? It was obvious that I was pretty beat up from the collision. I was told by doctors and nurses that I was lucky to have survived the accident. They indicated that the blow to my chest could have easily killed me, and that my legs were probably just inches away from being crushed beyond repair. Fortunately, both of the medical doctors who cared for me have known me for years and respected my belief that the power of the conscious mind could bring about healing. Whether they subscribed to my holistic philosophy or not wasn't important. What was important is that they made me feel that they believed that I believed my body would heal itself given time. They made me feel that if a miracle was possible, I was a great candidate for it.

For years I have studied mind–body medicine and the relationship between spirituality and healing. I also knew how important it was to have doctors who would participate in and help influence the course of healing. Bernie Siegel, MD, in his inspiring and powerful book, *Love, Medicine & Miracles,* shared with us the critical role doctors can play in the healing process of patients. Dr. Siegel helps make us aware of our own healing potential and explores the link between mind and body. It's important that our doctors give us the option to participate in our recovery. Our understanding of the spirituality and healing relationship is vastly incomplete. There's a great mystery here. Some things are just beyond human understanding and can't be scientifically explained. At least not at this point. My advice is to reach beyond the rational mind. Miracles don't come from the intellect. They come from feeling and connecting with your authentic self.

I utilized the two months after my accident to heal. I accepted the accident totally and completely so that I could learn from it. Pain can be quite helpful. Instead of feeling angry towards it, I acknowledged and loved it. As I experienced my pain, the sensations became more articulated. The pain helped me to go deep within to a new level of consciousness. My Inner Knowing, my intuition, guided me through the healing process. I just knew what to do. It wasn't a struggle. It was an exciting journey experiencing the body and the mind working together to repair my injuries. I utilized many alternative methods throughout the process of healing—meditation, visualization, prayer, massage, music therapy, aromatherapy, herbs, and laughter.

I wore a leg brace for two months and went to physical therapy three times a week. Each visit to the doctors brought surprise and smiles. I was doing so well and appeared to be healing at an unusually fast pace. Two months after the accident, the right leg was still very swollen and bruised and without feeling to the touch on the knee. However, my range of motion was returning to normal and I just knew everything was being repaired internally. I was sent to Baylor Hospital for an MRI. I'll never forget two days later when I called for the results and was told, "Ms. Hightower, we can find NO ABNORMALITIES in your right knee!" Wow! Another MIRACLE!

After a two-month absence, I returned to work on March 1, 1995. For the previous three years, I had been on staff at the Promotional Products Association International, formerly known as the Specialty Advertising Association International. I was hired to develop a proactive government relations program for the industry. My focus has been on enhancing volunteer involvement in the political process and empowering individuals to take action. The ultimate aim of the program is to keep markets open for the sale of promotional products. Our effectiveness has been a unified industry with one voice speaking for the many.

When I returned, I was asked to take on additional responsibilities in the regional relations area. The Association is currently embarking on a new quest to strengthen the promotional products industry by forming cooperative partnerships with the 29 regional associations across the country. I had the privilege of serving as the visionary leader of this effort. Just as my Inner Knowing, my intuition, guided me through the healing process, it also guided me on a daily basis as we created programs to build partnerships, assist members, and strengthen the industry. The utilization of intuition was critical in the decisions we made to promote a cooperative spirit and build an infrastructure that promoted growth.

Promotional products marketing has a long and honored history in the United States. Traditionally, promotional products have been called "ad specialties," but with a natural evolution in the industry, a new name arose—promotional products. This description embodies all the modern aspects of the industry, and encompasses all items given away by businesses to their customers to create goodwill, name recognition, and to thank them for their patronage.

While many of the 5,500 companies represented by the Association are family owned and operated small businesses, they produce and sell over $7 billion of promotional products every year in the United States alone. The growing interest in this very effective method of target marketing is reflected in the expanding size of the industry. Promotional products marketing has exploded, enjoying a 75 percent growth in the last eight years alone. Another way to envision this astounding figure is to realize that the industry has grown from a $4 billion industry in 1987 to over $7 billion in 1995, an increase of over $3 billion in just eight years. Additionally, international members are increasing tremendously, with Mexico and Canada becoming important promotional products marketing business neighbors.

As business owners look to find more efficient and economical ways of reaching their customers with a personal message, they find promotional products marketing a natural solution. As other forms of media become too expensive, more and more businesses are turning to direct marketing, a type of marketing exemplified by promotional products.

One of the original and most enduring promotional items is the *Farmers Almanac.* Political campaign buttons are also a long-standing example of promotional products marketing at work. Today the industry has expanded to add a multitude of items including shirts, writing instruments, mugs, aprons, balloons, jewelry—just about anything. The only limit to the type of product used is the imagination!

Intuition is used frequently in this industry. Those who succeed in this business must be able to anticipate client needs and create promotions to meet those needs. The promotional products industry, which is based fundamentally on creativity, is the perfect place to encourage the recognition and utilization of intuition. Intuition, in any situation, opens up an infinite number of possibilities. When creativity is involved, intuition is invaluable as a resource.

> *To keep our faces toward change, and behave like free spirits in the presence of fate, is strength undefeatable.*
> —Helen Keller

As we continue to deal with uncertainty and change, the utilization of intuition is being recognized as an essential management tool in business. Today, we live in a world of uncertainty. Just look around. Change is everywhere. There are changes in your home, your workplace, your community, the country. The entire world is changing. New technology is constantly emerging. Social changes are ongoing. Our lifestyles are influenced by shifting values. Our environment is changing and we're witnessing political changes across the world.

Let's take the Association as an example. Change is occurring continually. Every year a new Association chair is elected. One third of the board of directors rotates annually. Committees vary as terms expire and new leaders emerge. Just in the short four years that I've been associated with the Association, numerous changes have occurred. Our name has changed. We have a new logo. We've gone from volunteer-driven to staff-managed. There's a newly implemented strategic plan. New departments and positions have been created. We've changed legal counsel. There's been a reorganization of staff. New programs and member services have been added. A new president was hired in January, 1996 since Ted Olson, the Association's president for 17 years, retired.

As the world changes, the challenge will be to make sure the Association stays current with member needs and the needs of the industry. Proactive powerful leadership must constantly monitor environmental and sociological change and provide the force necessary to organize resources in the right direction. How do we cope with all these changes? How can we make these shifts and what tools do we have to help us? Simple...INTUITION!

At the Association and among the volunteer leadership, there are highly creative individuals with compassion and integrity who recognize and value the use of intuition in decision making. Let's explore intuition for a moment. For you "Analyticals" who have a proclivity to live in your head rather than your heart, let's read Webster's definitions—"immediate apprehension or cognition; knowledge or conviction gained by intuition; the power or faculty of attaining to direct knowledge or cognition without evident rational thought and inference." For the "Compassionates" that hang out in their hearts rather than their heads, they refer to intuition as "Inner Knowledge" and would probably prefer Webster's alternative definition—"quick and ready insight."

> And what is as important as knowledge?"
> asked the mind. "Caring and seeing with the
> heart," answered the soul.
> —Flavia Weedn

Let's explore some ways to tap into your intuition. Meditation is a wonderful way to quiet the mind and allow the Inner Knowing to speak to you. There are many ways to meditate and many spiritual groups teach the various techniques. In addition to the many Christian churches there are metaphysical churches such as Unity and Religious Science. One of my favorite spiritual groups is Self-Realization Fellowship founded by Paramahansa Yogananda. The beauty is that there is no one right way. No one method or one group has all the answers. What's important is that you know there are many avenues you can explore. Try one and if it doesn't feel right, try another. You will intuitively know the right one for you when you find it.

My hero is Deepak Chopra, M.D. If you were to ask my closest friends, who currently living on earth would I like to share a day with, their answer would be "Deepak Chopra." They would probably tell you that Sean Connery or Mel Gibson run a close second and third, but my first choice is definitely Dr. Chopra! I have had the opportunity to personally thank Dr. Chopra for sharing so much of his knowing concerning mind–body medicine through his many books and lectures. His teachings helped guide me to awaken my Inner Knowing so that my body was able to heal from within. Dr. Chopra is a world-renowned leader in the field of mind–body medicine and human potential. He is currently the executive director of the Sharp Institute for Human Potential and Mind–Body Medicine in San Diego, California. With his permission I share with you the Mindfulness Meditation that he explains in his book, *Journey Into Healing.* The Mindfulness Meditation technique is a simple meditation procedure that can create a deep state of relaxation in your mind and body. As the mind quiets down but remains awake, you will experience deeper, more silent levels of awareness. The Mindfulness Meditation may be a stepping stone on your pathway to awakening the wisdom within you.

1. Start by sitting comfortably in a quiet place where you will have a minimum amount of disturbance.

2. Close your eyes.

3. Breathe normally and naturally, and gently allow your awareness to be on your breathing. Simply observe your breath, trying not to control it or alter it in any conscious way.

4. As you observe your breath, you may notice that it changes of its own accord. It may vary in speed, rhythm, or depth, and there may even be occasions when your breath seems to stop for a time. Whatever happens with your breathing, innocently observe it without trying to cause or initiate any changes.

5. You will find that at times your attention drifts away from your breath and you are thinking about other things or listening to noises outside. Whenever you notice you are not observing your breath, gently bring your attention back to your breathing.

6. If, during the meditation, you notice that you are focusing on some feeling, mood, or expectation, treat this as you would any other thought and gently bring your attention back to your breath.

7. Practice this meditation technique for fifteen minutes.

8. At the end of fifteen minutes, keep your eyes closed and just sit easily for two to three minutes. Allow yourself to come out of the meditation gradually before opening your eyes and resuming your activity.

It is recommended that you practice this Mindfulness Meditation technique for about fifteen minutes twice a day—in the morning and evening. You may also use this technique for a few minutes during the day to help center yourself if you are feeling upset or agitated.

Here's another technique I find extremely useful when making a decision—both on the personal level and professional level. This simple two-step process can sometimes be accomplished in a matter of seconds to a matter of minutes.

Step 1

Sit quietly. Focus on the decision you are trying to make. Look at your intention behind the action you are considering taking. Ask yourself two questions. Are your intentions honorable? Does your decision hurt anyone? If you find your intentions honorable and the action hurts no one, then immediately proceed to Step 2. If you find your intentions less than honorable and that your action will hurt others, continue to sit quietly and review other options.

Step 2

Visualize the decision you've made in Step 1. Go into your heart where the intuitive knowledge resides and see how it feels. Does it feel good? If it feels good, then proceed with your decision. If it doesn't feel good, then your intuition is directing you to seek another way.

What other methods might we utilize to access our intuition? Remember when you were a child. We were so beautiful, so innocent, so connected. We just knew things. Connecting with our Inner Knowing came naturally. As we grew older, we began to look outside ourselves for direction, for guidance, for the answers. We forgot who we were. We forgot that all we needed to do was to tap into the wisdom that resides within us. With time, we anesthetized our feelings as a protection against disappointment and hurt. We stopped honoring ourselves, our emotions, our feelings. We just stopped listening. The good news is that the wisdom hasn't gone anywhere. It's just patiently waiting for you to reconnect with it. Getting in touch with your own deepest source will allow the wisdom and creativity to flow freely again.

I recommend becoming childlike again. Play and laugh again. Feel free. Remain immune to criticism. Remember, what other people think of you is none of your business! Relinquish the need to judge anyone or anything. There is a prayer in *A Course in Miracles* that states, "Today I shall judge nothing that occurs." Love dearly the Earth and all its creatures both great and small who call it their home. And by all means, share your toys!

Take a few minutes each day to spend with nature. Watch a sunrise or a sunset, take a walk in the park, sit under a tree, perch yourself on a mountain top, curl your toes in the sand, watch the tide roll in and out. Spending time in nature will help you draw upon the wisdom of instinct. Go within and honor the receptive side of your Inner Knowing.

Spend time in silence. The quieter you become, the louder the voice of intuition. Your intuition is like an intelligent and compassionate friend who perceptively articulates your inner-most thoughts.

I have shared with you my most recent personal triumph, along with ways that you might also find useful to access the wisdom that resides within, in hopes that you will journey with me to a deeper appreciation for the use of intuition in our daily lives. I encourage you to embrace intuition and cultivate your own path to connect with your Inner Knowing. Listen intently. You will find a resonance within.

> *To leave the world a bit better, whether by a healthy child, or a garden patch, or a redeemed social condition; to know even one life has breathed easier because you lived. This is to have succeeded.*
> —Ralph Waldo Emerson

Jaime T. Licauco is considered the Philippines' foremost authority on inner mind development, creative and intuitive management, paranormal phenomena, and Philippine mysticism. He has written eight best-selling books and numerous articles on these subjects over the past fifteen years.

He is the president and founder of the Inner Mind Development Institute which conducts public and corporate seminars and workshops on intuitive thinking and decision making, stress control, self-healing through visualization, the psychology of peak performance and inner awareness.

He is a frequent resource for the Young Presidents Organization (YPO), a member of the International Board of Advisers of the Intuition Network, and a Visiting Faculty Member of the Rosebridge Graduate School of Integrative Psychology.

Licauco has had twenty years of middle and senior management experience in various firms in the Philippines, mainly in the areas of human resources, management consultancy, and management development.

20

Remote Viewing And Intuition

Jaime Licauco

What Intuition Is For Me

Intuition in our daily life manifests in multifarious ways and is called by different names. For example, intuition is when I bring an umbrella during a hot and dry summer walk, and it rains. Or when I tell a fully-clothed acquaintance she has a mole under her left breast, and it is correct. It is intuition that tells me that a well-known TV host's chronic cough is coming from her hyperactive thyroid, rather than from her lungs. It is also intuition that tells me to stop at a "blind" corner only to have a speeding car barely miss me.

So what is intuition? Definitions of it are tricky and are, at best, inadequate because they are all attempts to verbalize and rationalize something essentially nonverbal and nonrational. It is, as good old Charlie Brown wisely pointed out, like "using an old math mind to solve a new math problem."

Intuition is simply "inner knowing" and we don't even know where that inner knowledge comes from. We only know it comes from within and not from any external source or data. We also know it is correct and true.

Consider the following examples taken from real life situations: When Ray Kroc asked the brothers Richard and Maurice

McDonald to quote him a price for the entire McDonald's hamburger chain in 1960, he was not prepared to buy it at the price the brothers wanted for it—$2.7 million. His lawyer thought the price to be exorbitant. Nevertheless, Kroc took it. "I'm not a gambler and I didn't have that kind of money," Kroc recalled. "But my funny bone instinct kept urging me on. So I closed my office door, cursed up and down, and threw things out the window. Then I called my lawyer back and said, "Take it." The rest is history.

A second example involves Meliton V. Salazar, then executive vice president of a nationwide appliance marketing company in Manila. One day he called a meeting of his department heads for noon. About an hour before the meeting, he suddenly asked his secretary to call it off. He could give no rational explanation for his change of mind. He only had a sudden urge to go home, although he had earlier told his wife he would not be home for lunch because of the meeting. Before leaving the company premises, he passed by the office of the company's medical director and asked him to have lunch with him at home.

When they reached the executive's home, they found his wife lying unconscious near the kitchen in a pool of blood. She had had a miscarriage. The doctor quickly administered first aid and then declared afterwards, "If we had been late even for one minute, your wife would have been dead, for loss of blood."

A third example comes from the *Philippine Daily Inquirer* of February 7, 1991. The story headline was "Hunch Leads to the Arrest of Renegades." It seems that police intelligence knew only that rebel leaders would be in a certain area of Manila that day. The police agent on guard in that area saw a car and had a "hunch" that it was carrying the men they were looking for. They stopped the car. The driver gave a false name, and looked different from his pictures since he had subsequently gained weight and let his hair grow. The hunch led to the man being questioned and being identified as the rebel leader, Colonel Victor Batac.

These three examples have one thing in common: the individuals acted on information that sprang spontaneously from somewhere inside themselves and not from external data. It was as if each tapped a hitherto unknown reservoir of knowledge within themselves.

What Is Intuition?

It has been called instinct, gut feeling, a hunch, business sense, and even a lucky guess, but few can offer a precise definition. Because of this, many others shun it. CEOs are not supposed to say, "I feel." They are supposed "to know." Hence, many CEOs call it "judgment." Whatever they call it, CEOs rely heavily on their intuition. Professor Henry Mintzberg of McGill University says that a CEO is a "holistic, intuitive thinker who is constantly relying on hunches to cope with problems far too complex for rational analysis."

Intuition is commonly regarded as being a function of the right hemisphere of the neocortex, while that of logical, linear thinking is a function of the left hemisphere. Although this may be true in its most general sense, it has been pointed out by neuroscientists that such a dichotomy is a gross oversimplification of what really takes place in the brain. Nonetheless, conceptualizing the left brain as being concerned primarily with verbal, logical, analytical, and objective thinking, and the right brain as non-verbal, visual, intuitive, and subjective is useful.

Personal Experiences With Intuition

I have never considered myself to be highly intuitive. That's why I never paid too much attention to certain extraordinary experiences I've had throughout these many years. I was convinced that everyone must have it. Two specific examples will serve to illustrate my point.

In 1974, the Miss Universe Beauty Pageant was held for the first time in the Philippines. One evening I met a friend near the hotel housing the contestants. He is a well known cardiologist. As he said "hello," he asked if I could guess who he escorted to dinner the evening before. "Miss Japan" I blurted out. An incredulous look came across his face. "How did you know?" he asked. I do not know how I knew. But the moment he asked the question the thought "Miss Japan" came to me. I will never forget the look on my friend's face.

Another unforgettable experience I had with intuitive knowing happened in the late 1970s. I was in my library one Sunday morning talking with a Swiss doctor and a Filipino businessman when a friend, Tony, unexpectedly came for a visit. Tony said he was in the area and since he was having a severe headache, he decided to just rest for a while in my house. He and I had been doing psychic research together for a year or two. I introduced him to the others and I sat on the floor across from him in the room. He apologized for barging in unannounced and for his headache.

At that point I asked him, "Would you like me to see what's causing your headache?" Actually I didn't know why I said that, because I had never done any psychic diagnosis before. Tony said "yes." I closed my eyes, took several deep breaths and focused on Tony's head without knowing exactly what I was doing, nor what I would see. Suddenly, I saw very distinctly Tony's skull, as if I were viewing an X-ray picture. I noticed that the bridge of his nose was somewhat crooked and leaning towards one side. Intuitively I knew that that was where the headache was coming from. I described aloud what I was seeing and told Tony his headache was caused by that crooked bone in his nose.

Tony was visibly surprised and excited at what I saw because he said he actually had sinusitis caused mainly by a "deviated septum." He said that he had had surgery a year before but it did not show on his face. I didn't know what a deviated septum was, and the Swiss doctor who was listening to all this was so excited that I had described perfectly that medical condition although I knew absolutely nothing of human anatomy.

After that extraordinary incident, I was able to perform a number of correct intuitive readings of other people's health conditions, but never where they were as visual as the one I did with Tony. These other readings came in the form of feelings or ideas coming to my mind.

Remote Viewing As A Demonstration Of Intuition

Because we don't know exactly what intuition is, we cannot summon it at will, nor apply it deliberately. One technique I have found effective in understanding how intuition works and how to summon it at will with relative ease and little training is through a remote viewing exercise. Remote viewing, as a distinct psychic ability, was first investigated scientifically in the early 1970s by two physicists from the then Stanford Research Institute (now called SRI International) in Menlo Park, California—Russell Targ and Harold Puthoff. At first, the research scientists used a well-known psychic, Ingo Swann, as a subject. Known to have strong telepathic and clairvoyant powers, Swann could zero in on any hidden object and find it psychically. He was even able to read the contents of an envelope hidden by the scientists in the ceiling without actually looking at it.

One of the most important series of experiments conducted by the scientists with Swann has become a model of later experiments in remote viewing. They placed him in a room while another person went to a place as far as fifty miles from SRI. Then, at a given time, the latter was supposed to look intently at any scenery or spot of his own choice for about 20 to 30 minutes. His job was merely to enjoy the scenery and mentally observe everything in it. Meanwhile, back at the SRI building, Swann was asked, "What is that fellow out in the field looking at?"

Swann would describe in detail or draw what he thought the other person was looking at. Then independently, the other person was also asked to describe verbally or to draw what he was looking at. A third party was asked to match the statements of Swann and the person in the field to ensure there would be no prompting or bias introduced into the experiment. When both statements or drawings were compared, they were found to be extremely accurate, something that could not be explained by mere coincidence or chance.

This experiment went on for several tedious years until both scientists were fully convinced that such ability really existed. To find out if remote viewing could be done by persons other than by Swann, they experimented with practically anybody willing to undergo the rigors of the investigation, with surprising results. Practically everybody succeeded in describing accurately what another person was looking at many miles away.

As Dr. Russell Targ told me a couple of years ago when I met him in California, "Psychic functioning is a fact, it is not a rare ability. Practically anybody can do it with very little training." In my Intuition and ESP Development Seminar, I use a modified version of the SRI remote viewing technique that is easier and more fun to perform, while still obtaining immediate feedback of one's accuracy. This is how I do it. I ask every participant to sit beside a person he knows least in the room, or, better still, someone he has never met before. All they are allowed to do is to look at their partner and ask only his or her full name. That is all.

Then they are asked to close their eyes and I guide them

through a ten- or fifteen-minute guided relaxation exercise. When they have achieved full mental and physical relaxation, I ask them to focus their attention on the name and/or the face of their partner. Then I would count from one to three, and at the count of three, I'd ask them to imagine that they are in front of their partner's house. I ask them to describe the house, beginning outside, and then describe in detail the inside of the house including every room.

This trains them to realize the difference between the products of left-brain analytical thinking and those of right-brain intuitive thinking, which they can use as psychic points of reference later on. After about ten minutes, I ask them to tell their partner what they had seen without censoring anything at all, even if they think it wrong or outrageous. The results are often so amazing that the participants can't believe that they did it. The descriptions, more often than not, zero in on some distinct elements found in the house. For example, a woman suddenly saw a tiger upon entering the living room of her partner's house. Because of this she opened her eyes in disbelief and she told her partner what she saw. Her partner smiled at her and told her how accurate she was. "You see," he explained, "when you enter my living room, the first thing you will see is a big tapestry with a tiger's head."

In an international conference of executives where I gave the same exercise, one woman had a foreign partner whom she had never met before. She had not even been to the country where her partner came from. During the exercise, she was surprised to see boats when she entered the living room of her partner's house. So she thought she was completely mistaken and at first refused to tell her partner what she saw. When she finally revealed to her partner that she saw boats in her living room, her partner laughed out loud and said that she lives right at the port and when one enters the living room, the first things she will see are boats outside her big window.

It is interesting what we have discovered about the inner workings of the mind as a result of these remote viewing exercises. For example, we have discovered that, not only the present house of one's partner can be seen, but also the past and the future. On one occasion a participant "saw" and described in detail the house of her partner, although that house had burned down four years earlier and a new house now stood on that same property. The burned house was where the participant, a Catholic nun, grew up. If a person has lived in several houses, the partner will see a combination of the features of the present and previous houses.

We also learned that we are psychically protected in the inner realm. For example, you can't see a woman taking a bath if she does not want to be seen naked by any stranger. If a room remains locked physically, and nobody but the owner is allowed into it, one cannot enter that room psychically, no matter how hard one tries. A man tried to enter the "house" of his partner and found he could only stand outside of it and could not enter. He discovered later on that his partner was a Catholic nun who lives in a convent where no male is allowed to enter.

We found out that more than ninety percent of the participants in a class are able to perform remote viewing successfully. The degree of accuracy differs, but many are able to perform above chance to their great amazement and disbelief.

Applications Of Remote Viewing Ability

Remote viewing, I believe, is very much related to intuition. In a way, one can say that remote viewing is controlled intuition. One knows that he is doing it and the immediate feedback given by one's partner enables a person to develop psychic or subjective benchmarks so that he can repeat the same thing on some other occasion. All he has to do is to remember the feeling and the circumstances he had before when he made a correct remote sensing and he will be correct again the next time.

The range of applications to which remote viewing ability can be put to use are many. In business and industry, one can scan psychically a business environment and detect opportunities, strengths, and weaknesses. An executive vice president for a Philippine airline discovered an employee whose highly developed intuition could identify airplane crash victims who were burned "beyond recognition." In health investigation, one can try to see what ails a person by scanning or remotely viewing his internal organs. In military intelligence, an officer can see ahead what the enemy position and number are before attacking. In our daily life, we can scan our car when it bogs down to see what the trouble is. Before buying a house, one can remotely view it to see if there are negative energies or entities lurking inside.

An interesting example of how remote viewing was used to calm one's nerves happened to a couple who were inside an airborne plane. Halfway to their destination, the passengers heard a very alarming metallic sound coming from underneath the body of the plane. Everybody was alarmed by the sudden noise. The husband became panicky and asked his wife to prepare for the worst. The wife calmly closed her eyes, focused her mind on the underside of the plane and "saw" that a piece of wire got loose and was hitting the side of the plane but there was no danger to the plane at all. "Sit down and relax," she told her husband. "There is nothing wrong with the plane." Then she dozed off. The pilot announced shortly after that there was nothing to be alarmed about and that there was no danger at all to anybody. They landed safely.

Case Of Intuitive CEO

One way to understand how intuition works in an organization is to talk with and observe individuals who use it as a matter of habit in their daily lives. This is usually difficult because most executives will not want to talk about the way they make decisions, much less admit that they use intuition at all in their decision making. One exception to this is William Farley.

Bill Farley is chairman and CEO of Farley Industries, which controls a diverse group of companies, including Fruit of the Loom, Westpoint Pepperell, and various other businesses. The group of companies he heads (as of 1992) had a combined sales volume of about $4.5 billion with a total of 75,000 employees operating in North America, Europe, and, to a small extent, Asia. His companies belong to Fortune's 500 largest industrial corporations in the United States.

I met William Farley at an international conference of the Young Presidents Organization (YPO) held in Taipei in 1992. After my presentation, where I talked about intuitive decision making and remote viewing, we had a brief conversation. He mentioned he had always used intuition in making major business decisions and agreed with me about the need for executives to develop their right, intuitive side of the brain. He said he built his company from a $3 million business to over $4 billion in ten years using his intuition. I got so intrigued by William Farley that I requested an interview with him. He accepted.

Farley's personal and academic background barely prepared him for business. His father was a musician and his favorite subject in college was art. After college he began selling encyclopedias, but found it very frustrating. He read *Think and Grow Rich,* by Napoleon Hill, which got him very interested in intuition, positive thinking, the subconscious mind, and the uses of imagination.

He then worked for National Lead Company in corporate planning and strategy, stopped studying intuition, and soon realized he was not cut out to be an employee. At age 30 he asked himself a fundamental question: "How do I want to live my life businesswise?" He decided that he wanted to be an entrepreneur rather than a business manager. But he had little working capital and no inheritance. That is what led him back to the study of intuition, imagination, visioning, and positive thinking.

It was in this environment that he met an old friend who informed him that Anaheim Citrus Products was for sale. "As soon as I heard that, I knew intuitively that that was the deal I wanted. Something inside me told me to stop struggling and go for it. It wasn't something like somebody coming up to me with a big feasibility study. It just felt right." He needed $2 million but only had $20,000; but he knew the deal was for him. He turned his investment into a $5 billion enterprise!

Bill Farley has learned to trust his intuition or his inner voice because it has served him well. For example, in 1985 he became aware that Northwest Industries (owner of Fruit-of-the-Loom) was for sale. "I didn't know much about the company. I didn't study it very much. I just knew that was the company to go for. It turned out to be one of the best deals that I've ever made."

Intuitive or right-brain decision making is not found in most managerial textbooks, but Farley uses it extensively. He uses it to complement facts. And it seemed to work best when "I was most relaxed, positive, confident, secure, and have gone with those feelings. Where I think I have made decisions that I would have changed today are those where I allowed something to shut those capabilities down."

As is my own experience in business, Farley sees most managers as being left-brained or linear thinkers. "Many of them want more information before making a decision. I tend to say, 'Enough is enough. Let's make the decision and move on!'...Ultimately you have to go with your gut, with that feeling that you are right." When managers are giving him contradictory ideas or information, "I will listen to both managers and think about it for a while, and then make a decision based on my experience and intuition. What feels right is what will determine my decision. You have just got to believe it. You believe it because of past experience, because of the feeling you have. I'm talking about trusting your feelings. Over a period of time, you accumulate experience that tells you you're right. And when I get into a relaxed, positive state of mind, I know I'll make the right decision."

The hundredth monkey theory was first proposed or popularized by biologist Rupert Sheldrake who spoke about the "morphogenic field" to explain the instantaneous spread of knowledge among physically distant beings. The theory states that if a group of monkeys on an isolated island learn a novel way of doing something none of them had ever done before, the moment the one-hundredth learns the technique, another group of monkeys living on the other side of the globe would also learn that same technique with no communication between them. It is as if the accumulation of knowledge by a certain number of monkeys creates a certain resonance in their morphogenic field. This resonance makes it possible for other monkeys, wherever they may be living in the universe, to receive and incorporate that knowledge into their own lives. Of course, this is all done subconsciously. This could also explain what Carl Jung calls the "collective unconscious" of mankind.

The hundredth "intuitive" monkey or whole-brain effect has not yet been achieved in business. Executives such as Farley are somewhere between intuitive whole-brained thinkers number one and number ninety-nine, and making it faster for other managers to reach that way of thinking and making it more of a norm than it is today.

Says Farley, "This right-brain or whole-brain thing is still considered rather offbeat by the average manager in this country. It is still considered to be more in the realm of spirituality rather than reality. In Western culture, you may see one or two articles talking about these things, but not in terms of a norm. In fact, it is regarded almost as bizarre and far out. So it is not commonly accepted. Let me just repeat what Deepak Chopra has recently stated: 'We haven't reached the hundredth monkey yet.'"

Michael Munn, PhD, began his technical career as a relativity theorist at the University of California. He created early models for rotating, magnetic, relativistic stars called pulsars. He later served as an aerospace Chief Scientist at Lockheed. He chaired the research and development activities of Lockheed's Astronautics Division. Munn won the Lockheed "Engineer of the Year" award for his work in cryogenics and outer space optical effects. During his career, he created and managed multi-million-dollar covert projects. As Chief Scientist he helped develop and test a successful space interceptor missile.

Meditation, intuition, and creativity are central to all Munn's work. He has merged human consciousness and advanced business tools. He is also a member of San Jose State University's faculty in the area of total quality.

21

Intuitive Meditation At Work: Solving Science And Business Problems

Michael W. Munn

One dark night
Kindled in love with yearnings,
I went forth without being observed
In the darkness and secure,
By the secret ladder, disguised,
My house being now at rest,
In secret, where none beheld me,
Nor I beheld aught,
Without light or guide,
Save that which burned within my heart,
This light guided me
More surely than the light of noonday
—St. John of the Cross
The Ascent of Mount Carmel

Intuition is an expression,
of the human yearning,
for reunion of the splintered self,
for communion with all beings,
and for Union with the All.
—M.W. Munn

A Road Map For The Journey

As I begin, I have an image of Bob Cratchit sitting at his work bench. He's furiously writing away. He's filling in the ledger. He's getting all the numbers right. If he takes a break he'll fall behind. Maybe there's not even time for lunch today. Ebenezer Scrooge is looking over his shoulder constantly. He is waiting for the first mistake. Then, he'll tell Cratchit what a terrible worker he is. He might even take away his pay.

Does that picture sound familiar? It should. Many of us worked in situations not too different for much of our careers. When I first began working in the aerospace industry, many people still worked in "bull pens." Imagine a giant open room with a twenty- or thirty-foot-high ceiling. Now imagine the entire room filled with rows and rows of desks. They'd go as far as the eye could see. Imagine the boss sitting in a glassed-in room up above. He (and in those days it was a he) looked out over the room. He made sure you were at your desk. He made sure you didn't goof off during the day. At 8:15 a.m., his secretary would check all of us to make sure we were at our desks working. If we weren't, he called us at home to see why we weren't there.

Both Scrooge and the aerospace boss bought into an invisible rule of our Western culture. That rule affects all of us much more than we know or would like to admit. Progress equates to "doing." If we aren't at our desks "doing," we can't possibly be working. It's hard to create when we wrap ourselves up in doing. We just do what we've done before. We do it repeatedly. We never ask the questions, "Why am I doing this?" "Are there other ways to do this?" We are in a terrific rush. We judge everything by precedent and prior practice. "Do it the way you did it the last time." Some people even use the phrase "event driven" for working this way.

When I first started working in TQM (Total Quality Management), I discovered that this came up repeatedly as a major weakness in the aerospace industry. Later, I found it to be part of many American companies. It's more than that. It's a mindset of modern Western culture. It's something most of us learned from the first day we went in the door of a school.

My solution, throughout my career, has been to use intuitive meditation. I learned early on that rational analysis, logic, and "pencil to the paper" efforts can only go so far. Those are the tools I use AFTER the intuitive insights have opened the new doors. I would have failed in graduate school had I followed only the logic path. I learned, with some difficulty, to do physics by use of intuitive approaches. I go down a very different path when I do this. It is a path along which everything I do today may be different from the way it was yesterday. It means I may well toss out cherished beliefs. It is definitely not a path of the status quo. Intuitive meditation opens doors and paths that are invisible to the eyes of logic.

Many illusions populate our world. "Busyness" is one of these. It is the great thief of our true creative selves. The illusion of busyness is the backdrop for my picture of what intuitive meditation is for me. I have used it for many issues during my career. To show how powerful it is, I've written about one such story here. Scientists and those who love the thrill of scientific discovery will love it. Imagine a spacecraft flying high above the Earth. You thought you painted it green on the ground. Up there, it looks red—at least it looks differently than you thought it should. What's going on here? The answer swept aside the prior view of near-Earth space environment and spacecraft interactions. Logic failed here because the voices of logic kept throwing out the "red" pictures. The voice of logic kept the "green" pictures. Those, after all, were the only ones that could be right.

The Skeleton In The Physicists' Family Closet

There was a skeleton in the closet of physics. I didn't know this when I began graduate school. It took me a couple of years to find out about it. Even worse, I had to fail my first round of doctoral qualifying exams to discover it. I'd gone to graduate school thinking I knew a lot about physics. I thought I was pretty great. My first shock happens to many people who come from small universities. I learned, however, that I was way behind folks who had attended the larger schools. I spent my first couple of years trying to catch up with the others. I loved all the Russian books with solved problems. I haunted the library. I pored over these books to find problems like the ones I had in my assignments. Often enough, I found some close enough to get me through that problem set. My professors kept piling it on more and more. Equations filled my head. I learned to analyze and dissect. I could recognize complex differential equations. I had memorized how to plug them into equally complicated matrices and find solutions. I could do wonders with a problem if it matched one I'd done before. If it didn't, I was in big trouble.

In all of this, no one ever mentioned the skeleton. They had hidden it well. I think they might even have been ashamed to bring it up to their students. This skeleton has been in the closets of physicists for years. When I failed my exams, I knew I had only one more chance. What I'd been doing hadn't worked. What was I missing? I had six months. In that time, I had to take and pass the exams. Otherwise, I was out!

It was during those six months that I accidentally stumbled on to the skeleton. Einstein, relativity, and black holes fascinated me. I wanted to follow in Einstein's footsteps. I began to wonder how someone could come up with a theory that was totally new. Einstein didn't have any Russian books of solved relativity problems. What did he have that I didn't know about?

I knew he'd flunked math in school. I knew his parents thought he'd never amount to anything. They were afraid, like many parents today, that he'd never move out of the house. He'd live with them forever. They tried to persuade him to become a plumber. It didn't work because of a dream Einstein had during those years.

He dreamed he was sledding down a snow-packed hill with some friends. They slid down, climbed back to the top, and slid down again many times. After many trips, one slide down was different. Einstein's sled began to go faster and faster. It sped down the hill so fast that light from ahead spread into rainbow colors. He knew he was going almost as fast as light itself. In an interview with Edwin Newman, Einstein said, "My entire scientific career has been a meditation on that dream." Einstein is not alone. Edison, Niels Bohr, and Elias Howe all made brilliant discoveries from the dream world. Authors (Robert Louis Stevenson, John Milton...) and composers (Wagner, Brahms, Puccini...) channeled their works or saw them born in the dream world.

Here was not one, but two skeletons. All my professors had given me the best in logic and analysis. They'd taught me the best techniques and mechanics for solving problems. No one had ever mentioned dreams and meditation. I later learned that Einstein continually used dreams and his imagination. He broke new ground with these throughout his life. I still wonder if my professors felt embarrassed by the intuitive side of physics. Is it also possible that my discovery of this *unmentionable* was the real test?

I began to study differently. I no longer sought books of detailed problem solutions. I began to picture physics. I began to imagine, in my mind's eye, things like a swinging pendulum. I'd hook springs and weights onto the pendulum. I'd watch them bounce and jiggle around in my mind. I *saw* visions of clusters of air rising in the atmosphere. I *saw* them cool and swirl. I discovered that it was easy to solve a problem, and get numbers out, once I had pictured the intuitive physics. In fact, I didn't solve any problems in those six months of study. I'd picture the physics. Then, I'd jot down HOW I'd solve it if I really wanted to do so. I used those six months to change into an intuitive physicist.

I won't say the test was a breeze, but I made it through the second time. Those six months changed my life. It changed my understanding of scientists forever. I'd learned that the big jumps of discovery and creation occur in an intuitive second. The scientist may take the rest of his or her life writing down what happened in that moment. That's the place for the mechanics, the analysis, and the equations. Somehow there is a perception that advances in science are rational and logical. I discovered that they are only that after the leap has been made.

I was lucky. I had to discover the skeleton. Much of life isn't that way. In business, academia, private life, and almost anywhere else, we work like I did before I flunked the test. We enshrine the idea of being rational, objective, and logical people. The skeleton isn't mentioned.

The Illusion Of Busyness

It's very tough for busy people to find the time to reflect on the events swirling around them. I've seen a number of sad things in corporate life in America. One of the saddest is the changes in people as they rise higher in management. Other people place more and more demands on their time. The phone is ringing constantly. Important customers line up for a hearing with them. They become experts at political infighting. They spend the entire day in one activity after another. I have frequently seen these executives interrupted between five to ten times in a thirty-minute period. They felt these phone calls were so important they had to take them.

I've seen secretaries hand a boss a schedule card. He or she doesn't even know for sure what's going on in the meetings. The card says be at a certain place at a certain time. They go. They could take a little time to sit quietly and reflect. They'll get farther behind if they do that, won't they? It's important to keep up with things. Isn't it? How can the decisions get made? How can others go do their jobs if I'm not on top of everything?

Busyness is one of the greatest illusions of all. Busyness robs us of the opportunities for true greatness. The facade of activity is so fascinating. Busyness entraps all of us in its web. It's so illogical to sit and do nothing. That's what meditation is, isn't it? Or is it the source and fount of all real progress? Is it where innovation is born? Is it where the spark of creativity can change directions of whole societies?

I have made time for these quiet periods of reflection for many years. They have changed me in countless ways. They have influenced every aspect of my life. Action comes, but it flows from the times of deep quiet and listening.

I usually meditate three or four times a day. I have no idea what meditation means to you. I know it means different things to people. Some people think it's a far-out oriental practice. It has something to do with India doesn't it? Maybe it has something to do with those people who wear orange robes.

I'll tell you what it is for me. I use meditation to relax. When I need to relieve stress, I'll turn to it first. I use breathing to rebuild my energy (my Chi). I have always used it to solve problems. I listen to my subconscious mind. It reveals so much to me during those times. It changes my path. It changes the ideas in my mind in a matter of moments. I'll emerge with very different directions from when I began my time of meditation.

I always urge people to take time from their busy days for reflection. After one workshop, a senior executive came to my office. Mild anger showed on his face. He said, "Mike, have you been telling people to take time to meditate during the day?" I said, "Sure I have. They need the time. They need to find new ways to solve the problems around here."

He didn't understand. He came back with, "We can't have people doing this. What if an auditor came by their desks? What could they point to on their time cards? What could they say they're charging to for this?"

I tried to tell him this made them more productive. They saved time. They found more clever ways to do their work. It really was part of the job. What I said didn't matter. The illusion of busyness had trapped him well. People who weren't active and busy must not be working. I've seen where the real work gets done. You have to try it (meditation) to realize it.

In different forms, I've meditated for more than thirty years. It is the heart and soul of my work. Even if I am actively at work, I will take the time to meditate. I know that the real source of my ideas lies in my meditations. I spend the rest of my day living out what I saw there.

My Way

I'll begin with some breathing exercises. It's usually a very simple one. Breath in for the count of six, hold the breath for a three-count, and breathe out for a six-count. It's a 6–3–6 breathing pattern. Take your pulse first. Time the counts with heart beats. I'll continue this for seven or more complete cycles. Often, I'll do the breathing for several minutes.

I then relax my body. To do this, I use self-hypnosis and other meditative methods for relaxation. I want to go in to as deep a trance as I can. I want to do it in as short a time as possible.

When I begin, I always have a question to ask. I go in with something for which I need an answer. It could be a problem at work. "What should I tell the boss this afternoon?" It could be an idea I need for writing an article. It could be a technical problem. I had many of those while I was a Chief Scientist. My subconscious mind solved most of those problems while I was in a dreamy, meditative state. I see pictures. I see images of how things work that I never could have gained from weeks, months, or years of hard effort.

As I begin to relax, all sorts of thoughts flash through my mind. Conversations I had that day replay themselves. Do I have bills sitting at home that I have to pay? What will I say to John or Sue this afternoon? You name it. Millions of random thoughts float in to my mind. I let them float right by. "That's interesting," I think. They play themselves out finally. For me, it takes about ten to fifteen minutes for these to quietly leave my mind. It's not blank though. I then begin to have pictures flash into view.

Most often, these pictures are of people. I don't think they're anyone I know—just random collections of one face after another. Sometimes the faces change. Sometimes one just fades into another. They might be male or female, old or young, white, black, or yellow. I've seen them all. Somewhere in here animal faces and forms begin to arise in my mind. Like the thoughts about bills to be paid, I let all these images float in and swiftly float away from me.

I'll often speed up reaching the "picture" state by replaying dreams. Since dreams are images, they help me change from an outer focus to an inner focus. It doesn't seem to matter what dreams I replay. Anything works. I can even use my memories of guided imagery. I'll often jump from dream to dream as my mind connects many of them. I'll even find memories of dreams from years past surfacing during these times.

I also find that another kind of random imagery pops into mind. I see jumbles of Chinese-like letters. They often fill in the shapes of circles or ovals. Often, I'll see random three-dimensional geometric figures. After awhile all of these pass away.

The one constant idea I keep is the problem I want answered. Sometimes I reach this point in ten or fifteen minutes. It'll often take half an hour. Sometimes I never reach it. If I don't reach it, that's okay. Those were great relaxation times. That's important too. When I get to this point, however, I know it's time to begin listening for the answers to the question I asked.

After a little while, I find that answers begin to come. I find that answers to other questions pop in as well. They aren't my target question, but they are areas of importance to me. It's often hard to remember them all. I try to capture them right after the session. I'll create an Awareness Map (see the next paragraph) to make sure I don't forget. I know I'll lose some of these. I have to trust that they'll come back when I need them. Many times they'll return the next time I go into the meditative state.

Awareness Mapping is my expanded version of Tony Buzan's Mind Mapping. It is a two-dimensional map of associations around any central idea, question, word, or image. The associations can be words, phrases, or pictures. At its simplest level, it is a powerful personal or group brainstorming tool.

How do I know the answers are there? I see pictures or movies or dreamlike sequences. I have an immediate inner knowing that this is the answer for which I was waiting. My intuition lets me know, "This is it!"

A Space Science Mystery

As a Chief Scientist I studied many tough technical problems. I couldn't find textbooks that held the answers. We were writing the books. We were at the cutting edge of discoveries.

What most people didn't know is where I got my ideas. Even my friends and co-workers didn't know. Every day I'd go out to my car at the lunch hour. I'd take along the problems of the day. After relaxing to the dreamy, partly sleepy state, I'd let thought images flow into my mind. Almost always I'd go back with fresh insights.

I remember one very difficult problem. We were working on a program aimed at stopping Russian nuclear bombs in space. We thought we could find a way to collide with them. If we could run into the bombs, then we could smash them into millions of pieces. You might think of it as a giant car crash in space. We had to hit a speeding bullet with another kind of bullet. Think of how fast bullets travel. Could any of us reach out a hand to grab a bullet in flight? Perhaps Superman could do this. These bullets traveled ten times as fast. How could we ever stop them?

Our bullet had to be "smart." It had to "see" the other bullet far away. It had to fire its own rocket motors. It had to move directly into the other bullet's path. We successfully did this in a test in 1984. The Russians knew we'd done it. They had spy ships near our test range to watch the tests. I recall that Yuri Andropov was General Secretary of the Communist party then.

I'll never forget ABC-TV's Peter Jennings report the next day. He reported our test. He followed that with a report from Andropov. The Russians had decided to resume nuclear arms reduction talks. They knew America had achieved a technical breakthrough that they could never match.

We didn't know earlier that we'd do so well. We were performing an experiment to find out if this was possible. My boss stated it very well. Our job was to "see it, hit it, kill it!" Our bullet had to decide very fast how and where to collide. We'd built the best telescope and fastest computer we could.

If you or I were there, we could look with our eyes to try to see the other bullet. We might have a picture that helped us with the color and shape of the bullet. How could we make a computer do all that our brains could do?

Our bullet worked in the day or nighttime. If it was night, we couldn't try to see the kind of light our eyes see. We decided to try to see the heat from the other bullet. No one knew for sure what the bullet's heat might be. People made predictions. Another group of scientists measured the heat from one in space. Their pictures didn't agree with the predictions. Most of the scientists thought the pictures must be wrong. They thought the predictions must be right.

We had a problem. We had to put numbers in our computer. The numbers told the computer how warm the bullet would be. They told our computer the shape and color of the bullet. We had to be right or the experiment wouldn't work. I had a tough decision as Chief Scientist. What if the pictures the other scientists took were right? If I said to put in the predictions, our computer might not see the bullet. It would look for something that was pink. If it was really green, it would think it wasn't the bullet. We would miss the collision because our computer would think the other bullet wasn't there.

Was there another way to do the job? Very good radar sets watched the bullet as it flew in space. They could help us predict where it would be at any time in the future. We decided to tell our telescope where to look for the bullet. We told it, "Whatever you see in that spot is it. Go after it." It didn't matter what color it was. It only mattered that something was there. It's good we did this. Our pictures were just like the ones the other scientists took.

We experimented four different times. The pictures were different from the predictions every time. Many of the scientists who made the predictions told us we'd taken the pictures incorrectly. How could their predictions be wrong?

I wondered if maybe the predictions were incomplete. I wondered if something real might be happening in space—something none of us had expected.

My meditations were the key to understanding this problem. The story I'll tell here took place over a couple of years. I'm going to retell it as one meditation.

I knew what the pictures looked like. I decided to assume that they were right. What did that mean? What had to be happening if they were right?

During meditation, I saw the bullet flying through space. It wasn't alone. I saw clouds of stuff around the bullet. I saw dust. I saw wisps of air. I saw electrons and protons flying into the clouds of stuff. I saw the Earth's magnetic field and could see the electrons and protons spiraling along the field lines. I even saw the shape of the cloud as it spread out from the bullet.

We'd noticed that the color of the picture changed while we watched. My meditation imagery told me it had something to do with protons and electrons. It had something to do with the Earth's magnetic field.

I went in to my team of scientists and engineers. The first thing I said was, "Find measurements from satellites for the times of our experiments." The satellites measure how many electrons and protons there are near the Earth. We got the measurements. We discovered that the color changes corresponded to changes in the number of electrons and protons. We could relate the two different kinds of information.

We now had two vastly different pictures of what was happening in space. The old picture was simple. Space is a vacuum. Objects, like the bullets, are as clean as the cleanest Silicon Valley clean room.

The second picture, born in intuition, came to be known by project scientists as the "pigpen" model. Do you remember how "Pigpen" in Charles Schultz's comic strip "Peanuts" always had a dust cloud around him? We saw bullets as very dirty objects. They carried atmosphere with them. They sucked debris from the missiles and carried it along. Even separating from the missiles made junk the bullet carried along. All this gas, dust, and junk flew through a space which was definitely not a vacuum. Positively and negatively charged particles filled space along the bullet's path. These collided with the bullet and its "pigpen" cloud. Imagine your hair standing on end when you touch a big static electricity generator. Everything around the bullet became charged like your hair. The same kinds of forces that made your hair stand on end made dust orbit around the bullet. What a difference in the pictures. What a rich and marvelous book intuition opened.

We didn't understand all the science yet, but we knew we were on the right track. That's how it is with many scientific advances. In a flash of insight, the scientist "knows" a new truth. It takes many years, and much work, to prove it to others. It takes much time to convince others of the new insight. That's still true for our experiment. Many people are still unconvinced. For others an exciting new chapter in near-Earth space physics opened and is still being read.

Closing Thoughts

Intuition guides us slowly, but surely, toward total awareness and freedom. It is not the guiding star, but it allows us to *see* that star. It is the guide in the many times of uncertainty and confusion. It leads us to amazing and unforeseen turns in the paths of life. When we use intuition, we return to our deepest roots. We join, once again, the head and the heart. We do more than return to what was once known. In cycling back to our roots, we also take the step forward in the evolution of humanity. We become more than we were. We become more than we can imagine.

Thoughts To Ponder

1. For the non-intuitive, intuition is a source of shame and embarrassment.
2. For the intuitive, intuition is a door to true freedom.
3. True doing flows from non-doing.
4. Intuition is about being.
5. Stilling the mind is the gateway to knowing.
6. Our blindness is broad, deep, pervasive, and invisible.
7. Intuition is the light that reveals our invisible boundaries.
8. Quantum improvements require quantum mindset shifts.

Michael Ray is the first John G. McCoy–Banc One Corporation Professor of Creativity and Innovation and of Marketing at the Stanford Business School. He is a social psychologist with over one hundred publications including nine books and six state-of-the-art chapters. His co-authored books *Creativity in Business* and *The Path of the Everyday Hero* (picked as the best business self-help book of 1991, New York Time News Service) are based on his Stanford creativity course which has received international attention for its innovative approaches to developing creativity in business and everyday life. The course was also the inspiration for the 1992 PBS television series *The Creative Spirit* for which Ray co-authored the companion book of the same name. His passion over the past decade toward the emerging new paradigm in business has led to the Stanford course Dialogues on Business in a World Transition and his co-edited books—*The New Paradigm in Business: Emerging Strategies for Leadership and Organizational Change* (recipient of a 1994 *The New Leaders* Readers Choice Award), and *The New Entrepreneurs: Business Visionaries for the 21st Century*. He is a Fellow of the World Business Academy and received the Academy's Willis Harman Award in 1991.

22

Sharing The Wisdom: A Report Of An Intuition Network Program

Michael Ray

While some form of intuition variously defined has always been a part of business, there are indications that it is even more important in the present times of turbulence which some have characterized as one of the greatest paradigm shifts in history. Even Barnard in his 1938 classic, *The Functions of the Executive*, said that in conditions of ambiguity or uncertainty, with limited time or inadequate information that especially characterize rapidly emerging situations, people in business increasingly have to rely on non-logical processes. All the current evidence I've been able to gather on changes in business indicate—despite the sharp rise in the volume of information and in the number of decision-making aids—the current situation is exactly like that Barnard depicted so many years ago.

Part of the reason that tools such as intuition seem so important in the present times is that rational approaches are just the start of what is needed. Rosabeth Moss Kanter points out in *The Change Masters* that "change efforts have to mobilize people around what is not yet known, not yet experienced. They require a leap of imagination...a leap of faith that cannot be eliminated by presentation of all the forecasts, figures, and advance guarantees that can be accumulated."

Over the course of the past seventeen years the topic of

intuition has come up often in the Personal Creativity in Business course at Stanford, which I teach with Rochelle Meyers. At first we were somewhat embarrassed when our students would ask visiting speakers about the topics such as meditation and intuition. But we found that the business leaders who came to the class were quite comfortable in talking about these topics. They gave details of the methods they use to bring out their intuition and get ideas.

There seems to be general recognition that intuition has a place in business decision making. But, since there is very little specific research on the topic, most of the discussion of it is at an anecdotal level. Early research by Henry Mintzberg, William Pounds, and Harold Leavitt indicated that it is often impossible for managers to use rational forms of decision making since the situations in which they operate are so chaotic. Business writers point out in various ways that most executives learn early in their career that rationality has its limits. Over and over again we heard in our class, and I have documented in other ways, the experiences of top executives who admit and often are proud to talk about how important intuition is to them in business.

As Mintzberg points out in a 1994 book, however, it is not really possible to assess the use of intuition by purely logical processes:

> It is a subconscious process, which no one really understands, except by certain of its characteristics (such as the speed with which it can sometimes produce answers). Thus the dismissal of intuition as an irrational process is itself irrational, just as embracing it as a process superior to formal logic is itself illogical.

There have been personality inventories and various tests used to measure individual intuition, and scores on them correlate positively and significantly with managerial ranking (higher ranked managers scored higher on the intuition tests) and ability (profit performance of the company or division managed).

Key Questions And Answers

The Sharing the Wisdom project of the Intuition Network promises to fill this need for research on intuition that can help us all to develop faith in our intuition and tools to use it. Those of us involved in the project are collecting case histories from business consultants on the use of intuition in business. We have several hundreds of these cases, but our goal is to collect thousands so that proper analyses can be done. Nevertheless, we already have some answers to the following questions.

What is the nature of intuition as used in business? Our preliminary results indicate that when intuition is used in business it is of the deepest kind. It is possible for business people and organizations of get into a flow of intuitive decision making and living. Of course such widely disparate writers as the consultant and writer Karen Buckley and the Nobel Laureate Herbert Simon point out that there is a kind of intuition that uses our past experience to somehow put things together in new ways and give us "gut hunches" or the "right feel." But our findings and Buckley herself point to other kinds of intuition in business, such as the intuitive ability to tap into the superordinate purpose of the organization or the intuition that comes from deeper dimensions that allows insight or illumination that is beyond what might be imagined by the facts, even those gathered from one's personal experience.

How is intuition used in business? Most of the literature talks about intuition in decision making and highlights insights that have led to new businesses and industries. But we have already discovered from our initial work that there are other areas of application that are really more important in this time of transformation in business. For example, intuition is being developed in such areas as interpersonal skills, stress management, time management, team building, reengineering, mergers, and partner relationships as well as in more common areas such as forecasting, leadership development, company vision, and innovation and product development. People are beginning to see work as an arena of personal development and deep intuition is the key to that manifesting in all these areas.

In what types of situations and industries is intuition being developed and used? Intuition at one level is part of all business. But intensive programs to develop intuition are relatively less common. When we look at where these types of programs are being developed, there are some surprises. Deep intuition work is just as likely to be done at Fortune 100 companies as at small start-ups. It is done in what might seem the most bureaucratic of industries and is celebrated in the more open ones with fewer levels of management.

*At what organizational level is intuition being used within business?*This is really a question about how the use of intuition can most effectively be developed within an organization. Consultants work more often with top management people than with others in these organizations, although the use of intuition eventually turns out to be for everyone. We know of cases in which awareness and use of intuition has bubbled up within the organization. In others it starts by fiat from the people at the top and moves from top to bottom. Sometimes this is successful and sometimes, depending on the commitment of those at the top, it results in initially successful programs that peter out and die or are killed.

How is intuition being developed and used in relation to analysis and traditional decision making in business? The already-existing surface procedures and practices in business represented by our sample thus far consisted of decision tools and analytical processes. These don't go away when intuition is brought more explicitly into organizations. Our questions include: What is the mix that remains or, perhaps more appropriately, evolves when intuition is introduced and adopted? How can the power of these two ways of approaching business issues and problems be used together most effectively?

What are the factors that affect the success or failure of intuition in business? Our cases indicate that there are fits and starts in individuals and organizations developing their intuition. In our first analysis of our data, over a third of our respondents indicated that their efforts in bringing intuition into business had met, in their opinion, with less than sixty percent of total success. More than a few of explorations into intuition come from a crisis situation in which people are forced to resort to their intuition. After such a crisis, or as a result of some change agent within or outside of the organization, there can be a deeper exploration that leads to more consistent acceptance and use of intuition.

Truths About Intuition In Business

Success in bringing intuition into business seems to revolve around acceptance of five truths about intuition that most business people initially have difficulty accepting. Once people begin to live with these truths, however, they begin to develop their intuition in business and life in remarkable ways. The truths:

Intuition is a gift that must be developed. People have to go beyond the idea of intuition as a once-in-a-lifetime lightening bolt and beyond the idea that it is the province of the gifted few or of oddballs. We all have intuition within us and we need to take the responsibility to accept, develop and perfect our own style of it.

Intuition complements reason. No one is suggesting that decisions should be made solely on the basis of intuition. It is the combination of experience, information, reason, and intuition that is so powerful. Our respondents' cases and a wide variety of experts indicate, however, that intuition, as Carl Jung put it, is beyond the province of reason and really more fundamental.

Intuition is unemotional. Listening to intuition is not the act of concentrating on what you think you want. It is not hedonism, a move toward the most pleasurable short-term alternative. It is not giving vent to the inner emotional child left over from infancy. It is simply paying clear attention, without mind chatter and emotions, to the most appropriate alternative that comes from the creative Essence.

Intuition demands action. As R. Buckminster Fuller said, "I call intuition cosmic fishing. You feel a nibble, then you've got to hook the fish." If there is one characteristic that signals success-ful use of intuition in business, it is follow-through. When you don't follow through, your decision or idea dies. Our cases show that lack of follow-through is what kills the development of intuition in business. And follow-through is more than just hard work. It is *timely* hard work. And knowing when to act takes more intuition.

Intuition is mistake-free. It's not easy to defend an intuitive decision, much less an intuitive life-style. But there are always "rational" reasons that support intuitive leaps. And beyond this we must have absolute faith that intuition is a part of us that never makes mistakes. Having this kind of faith takes application of all five truths over a period of time in a consistent way.

Our intuition is that the Sharing the Wisdom project will help all kinds of people to discern their true inner feelings and act on and develop their intuition in business and life. We know that you have something to contribute to this process. Please join us and share your wisdom. [See contact information for author on page 306.]

"People with high levels of personal mastery do not set out to integrate reason and intuition. Rather, they achieve it naturally—as a by-product of their commitment to use all the resources at their disposal. They cannot afford to choose between reason and intuition, or head and heart, any more than they would choose to walk on one leg or see with one eye."

—Peter Senge

Recommended Reading & Resources

Armstrong, Thomas. *Seven Kinds of Smart: Identifying and Developing Your Many Intelligences.* New York, NY: Plume, 1993.

Ashkenas, Ron, et al. *The Boundaryless Organization: Breaking the Chains of Organizational Structure.* San Francisco, CA: Jossey-Bass Publishers, 1995.

Autry, James. *Love and Profit.* New York, NY: Avon, 1991.

Barrentine, Pat (ed.). *When the Canary Stops Singing.* San Francisco, CA: Berrett-Koehler, 1993.

Becker, Robert O. *Cross Currents: The Perils of Electropollution, The Promise of Electromedicine.* Los Angeles, CA: Tarcher, 1990.

Bennis, Warren. *On Becoming a Leader.* Reading, MA: Addison-Wesley, 1989.

Block, Peter. *Stewardship: Choosing Service Over Self-Interest.* San Francisco, CA: Berrett-Koehler Publishers, 1993.

Bolman, Lee G. & Terrence E. Deal. *Leading with Soul: An Uncommon Journey of Spirit.* San Francisco, CA: Jossey-Bass Publishers, 1994.

Bellah, Robert, et al. *Habits of the Heart: Individualism and Commitment in American Life.* New York, NY: Harper & Row, 1985.

Briggs Meyers, Isabel & Mary H. McCaulley. *Manual: A Guide to Development and Use of the Briggs-Meyers Type Indicator.* Palo Alto, CA: Consulting Psychologists Press, 1985.

Brown, John Seely. Address to PC Forum, Phoenix, AZ, March 1994.

Cade, C. Maxwell. *The Awakened Mind: Biofeedback and the Development of Higher States of Awareness.* New York, NY: Delacorte Press, 1979.

Campbell, Joseph. *The Hero With A Thousand Faces.* Princeton, NJ: Princeton University Press, 1949.

Castenada, Carlos. *Journey to Ixtlan: The Lessons of Don Juan.* New York, NY: Simon and Schuster, 1972.

Catford, Lorna & Michael Ray. *The Path of the Everyday Hero.* Los Angeles, CA: Jeremy Tarcher, Inc., 1991.

Chappell, Tom. *The Soul of a Business.* New York, NY: Bantam, 1993.

Chawla, Sarita & John Renesch. (eds.). *Learning Organizations: Developing Cultures for Tomorrow's Workplace.* Portland, OR: Productivity Press, 1995.

Chopra, Deepak, M.D. *Journey into Healing.* New York, NY: Crown Publishers Inc., 1994.

Chopra, Deepak M.D. *The Way of the Wizard: Twenty Spiritual Lessons for Creating the Life You Want.* New York, NY: Harmony Books, 1995.

Cohen, Michael J. *Reconnecting With Nature.* Friday Harbor, WA: Project NatureConnect, University of Global Education, 1995

Collins, Susan. *Our Children Are Watching: 10 Skills for Leading the Next Generation to Success.* Barrytown, NY: Barrytown Ltd., 1995.

Contino, Richard M. *Trust Your Gut! Practical Ways to Develop and Use Your Intuition.* New York, NY: American Management Association, AMACOM, 1996.

Covey, Stephen R. *Principle-Centered Leadership.* New York, NY: Simon & Schuster, 1992.

Covey, Stephen R. *Seven Habits of Highly Effective People: Restoring the Character Ethic.* New York, NY: Simon and Schuster, 1990.

Csikszentmihalyi, Mihaly. *Flow: The Psychology of Optimal Experience.* New York, NY: Harper & Row, 1990.

Cytowic, Richard E. *The Man Who Tasted Shapes.* New York, NY: Warner Books, 1993.

DeFoore, Bill & John Renesch. (eds.). *Rediscovering the Soul of Business.* San Francisco, CA: New Leaders Press, 1995.

Depree, Max. *Leadership As An Art.* New York, NY: Doubleday, 1989.

Dossey, Larry. *Recovering the Soul: A Scientific and Spiritual Search.* New York, NY: Bantam Books, 1990.

Elgin, Duane. *Awakening Earth: Exploring the Evolution of Human Culture and Consciousness.* New York, NY: William Morrow & Company, 1993.

Emery, Merrelyn. *Participative Design for Participative Democracy.* Canberra, Australia: Centre for Continuing Education -Australian National University, 1993.

Foundation for Inner Peace. *A Course in Miracles.* Glen Ellen, CA: 1992

Fox, Matthew. *The Reinvention of Work: A New Vision of Livelihood for our Time.* San Francisco, CA: Harper Collins Publishers, 1994.

Fuller, R. Buckminster. *Synergestics: Explorations in the Geometry of Thinking.* New York, NY: MacMillan Publishing Company, 1975.

Gardner, Howard. *Creating Minds.* New York, NY: Basic Books, 1994.

Gardner, Howard. *Frames of Mind: The Theory of Multiple Intelligences.* New York, NY: Basic Books, 1983.

Garrett, Linda. *M.I. Creative?* Boise, ID: Creative Learning Technologies, Inc., 1995.

Gibbs, Nancy. "The EQ Factor." *Time Magazine.* New York, NY: Time Inc., October 2, 1995.

Gilder, George. *Microcosm: The Quantum Revolution in Economics and Technology.* New York, NY: Simon & Schuster, 1989.

Goleman, Daniel, Paul Kaufman, & Michael Ray. *The Creative Spirit.* New York, NY: Dutton, 1992.

Goodspeed, Bennett W. "Different Styles of Analysis Imperative to Business: More Often Than Not, Intuition, Not Numbers, Tell the Real Story." *American Banker,* November 9, 1981.

Govinda, Lama Anagarika. *The Way of the White Clouds.* Berkeley, CA: Shambala, 1971.

Gozdz, Kazimierz. (ed.). *Community Building: Renewing Spirit and Learning in Business.* San Francisco, CA: New Leaders Press, 1995.

Handy, Charles. *The Age of Paradox.* Cambridge, MA: Harvard Business School Press, 1994.

Handy, Charles. *The Age of Unreason.* Boston, MA: Harvard Business School Press, 1990

Harman, Willis & John Hormann. *Creative Work.* Indianapolis, IN: Knowledge Systems, 1990.

Hawley, Jack. *Reawakening the Spirit in Work: The Power of Dharmic Management.* San Francisco, CA: Berrett-Koehler Publishers, 1993.

Helgesen, Sally. *The Web of Inclusion.* New York, NY: Currency/Doubleday, 1995.

Herrmann, Ned. *The Creative Brain.* Lake Lure, NC: Brain Books, 1992.

Hirsh, Sandra & Jean Kummerow. *Introduction to Type in Organizations.* Palo Alto, CA: Consulting Psychologists Press, 1987.

Isachsen, Olaf, Ph.D. & Linda Berens Ph.D. *Working Together: A Personality Centered Approach to Management.* Coronado, CA: Neworld Management Press, 1988.

Jackson, Phil & Hugh Delehanty. *Sacred Hoops: Spiritual Lessons of a Hardwood Warrior.* New York, NY: Hyperion, 1995.

Jaffe, Dennis & Cynthia Scott. *Take This Job and Love It.* New York, NY: Simon and Schuster, Inc., 1988.

Jahn, Robert and Dunne, Brenda. *Margins of Reality: The Role of Consciousness in the Physical World.* San Diego, CA: HBJ, 1987.

Kanter, Rosabeth Moss. *The Change Masters: Innovation & Entrepreneurship in the American Corporation.* New York, NY: Simon & Schuster, 1983.

Karasek, Robert & Tores Theorell. *Healthy Work: Stress, Productivity, and the Reconstruction of Working Life.* New York, NY: Basic Books, Inc., 1990.

Kiersey, David & Marilyn Bates. *Please Understand Me.* Del Mar, CA: Prometheus Nemesis Press, 1978.

Kidder, Rushworth M. *Shared Values for a Troubled World: Conversations with Men and Women of Conscience.* San Francisco, CA: Jossey-Bass, 1994.

Korten, David. *When Corporations Rule the World.* San Francisco, CA: Berrett-Koehler Publishers and Kumarian Press, 1995.

Kunkel, Franz. *In Search of Maturity.* New York, NY: Charles Scribner's and Sons, 1943.

Lawrence, Gordon. *People Types and Tiger Stripes.* Gainsville, FL: Center for Applications of Psychological Type, 1979.

Lawlor, Robert. *Voices of the First Day.* Rochester, VT: Inner Traditions, 1991.

Levey, Joel. "Consciousness, Caring & Commerce: Sustainable Values for the Global Marketplace" in DeFoore, Bill and John Renesch. (eds.). *The New Bottom Line: Bringing Heart and Soul to Business.* San Francisco, CA: New Leaders Press, 1996.

Levey, Joel. "The Human Heart & Soul at Work: In Mainstream America" in DeFoore, Bill and John Renesch. (eds.). *Rediscovering the Soul in Business.* San Francisco, CA: New Leaders Press, 1995.

Levey, Joel & Michelle Levey. *Quality of Mind: Tools for Self Mastery & Enhanced Performance.* Boston, MA: Wisdom Publications, 1991.

Levey, Joel & Michelle Levey. *The Focused Mind State.* Chicago: IL: Nightingale Conant, 1993.

Levey, Joel & Michelle Levey. "Wisdom at Work: An Inquiry Into the Dimensions of Higher Order Learning," in Chawla, Sarita & John Renesch. (eds.). *Learning Organizations: Developing Culture for Tomorrow's Workplace.* Portland, OR: Productivity Press, 1995.

Lipnack, Jessica & Jeffery Stamps. *The Age of the Network: Organizing Principles for the 21st Century.* Essex Junction, VT: Oliver Wight Publications, 1994.

Loomans, Diane. *The Laughing Classroom.* Tiburon, CA: H.J. Kramer, 1993.

Lorenz, Christopher. "How Ford Used Intuitive Design to Break Free of Committee Cars." *The Financial Times Limited,* September 28, 1988.

McCarthy, Joseph, "The Spiritual CEO," *Chief Executive,* January/February 1996.

Milner, B. "Interhemispheric Differences in the Localisation of Psycho-
    logical Processes in Man," *British Medical Bulletin, Vol. 27,* 1971.
Mintzberg, Henry. *The Rise and Fall of Strategic Planning.* New York, NY:
    The Free Press, 1994.
Mishlove, Jeffrey. *The Roots of Consciousness.* Tulsa, OK: Council Oak
    Brooks, 1993.
Moore, Thomas. *Care of the Soul: A Guide for Cultivating Depth and
    Sacredness in Everyday Life.* New York, NY: Harper Collins Pub-
    lishers, 1992.
Moore, Thomas. "Caring for the Soul in Business," in DeFoore, Bill &
    John Renesch. (eds.). *Rediscovering the Soul of Business.* San
    Francisco, CA: New Leaders Press, 1995.
Morgan, Marie. "Spiritual Qualities of Leadership in Business," *World
    Business Academy Perspectives,* 1993, Vol 7, No. 4.
Nadel, Laurie, Ph.D., Robert Stempson, & Judy Haims. *Sixth Sense.* New
    York, NY: Avon Books, 1992.
Nair, Keshavan. *A Higher Standard of Leadership: Lessons from the Life
    of Gandhi.* San Francisco, CA: Berrett-Koehler Publishers, 1994.
Naisbit, John. *Megatrends: Ten New Directions for Transforming Our
    Lives.* New York, NY: Warner Books, 1982.
Neville. *The Power of Awareness.* Marina del Rey, CA: DeVorss & Co.,
    Publishers, 1952.
O'Neil, John. *The Paradox of Success: A Book of Renewal for Leaders.*
    New York, NY: Jeremy P. Tarcher/Putnam, 1994.
Oshry, Barry. *Seeing Systems: Unlocking the Mysteries of Organizational
    Life.* San Francisco, CA: Berrett-Koehler, 1995.
Paddison, Sara. *The Hidden Power of the Heart.* Boulder Creek, CA:
    Planetary Publications, 1992.
Pearson, Carol S. & Sharon Seivert. *Magic at Work: A Guide to Releasing
    Your Highest Creative Powers.* New York, NY: Currency/Doubleday,
    1995.
Pribram, Karl H. *Brain Power and Perception; Holonomy and Structure in
    Figural Processing.* Hillsdale, NJ: Laurence Erlbaum Associates,
    1991.
Pribram, Karl H. *Languages of the Brain: Experimental Paradoxes and
    Principles in Neuro-Psychology.* Monterey, CA: Brooks-Coles, 1971.
Progoff, Ira. *Jung, Synchronicity & Human Destiny: Noncasual Dimen-
    sions of Human Experience.* New York, NY: Julian Press, 1973.
Rama, Swami, Rudolph Ballentine, & Swami Ajaya. *Yoga and Psycho-
    therapy.* Homesdale, PA: Himalayan Institute, 1976.
Ray, Michael & John Renesch. (eds.). *The New Entrepreneurs.* San
    Francisco, CA: New Leaders Press, 1994.
Ray, Paul. American LIVES, privately published paper of contemporary
    demographic research, 1995.
Read, Sir Herbert Edward. *Education Through Art* (3rd Edition). New
    York, NY: Pantheon Books, 1958.
Renesch, John & Bill Defoore. (eds.). *The New Bottom Line: Bringing
    Heart and Soul to Business.* San Francisco, CA: New Leaders
    Press, 1996.
Renesch, John. (ed.). *New Traditions in Business: Spirit and Leadership
    in the 21st Century.* San Francisco, CA: Berrett-Koehler Publish-
    ers, 1992.

Roddick, Anita. *Body and Soul.* New York, NY: Crown Publishers, 1991.

Rosanoff, Nancy. *Intuition Workout.* Santa Rosa, CA: Aslan Publishers, 1989.

Ross, T. Edward & Richard D. Wright. *Divining Mind.* Rochester, VT: Inner Traditions International, 1990.

Russell, Peter. *The Global Brain Awakens.* Palo Alto, CA: Global Brain, Inc., 1995.

Salk, Jonas. *The Anatomy of Reality: Merging of Intuition and Reason.* New York, NY: Columbia University Press, 1983.

Salk, Jonas & Jonathan Salk. *World Population and Human Values: A New Reality.* New York, NY: Harper & Row, 1981.

"The Search for the Sacred," in *Newsweek,* November 28, 1994.

Senge, Peter. *The Fifth Discipline.* New York, NY: Doubleday Currency, 1990.

Sherer, John. *Work and the Human Spirit.* Spokane, WA: John Sherer & Associates, 1993.

Siegel, B.H., M.D. *Love, Medicine & Miracles.* New York, NY: Harper & Row, Inc., 1986.

Simon, Herbert A. "The Information-Processing Theory of Mind," *American Psychologist,* July, 1995.

Sirag, Saul-Paul. "Consciousness: A Hyperspace View," in *The Roots of Consciousness,* by Jeffrey Mishlove. Tulsa, OK: Council Oak Books, 1993.

"Spirit in the Workplace: A Movement on the Verge of Taking Off." *At Work,* Sept./Oct., 1993.

Stacy, Ralph D. *Managing the Unknowable, Strategic Boundaries Between Order and Chaos in Organizations.* San Francisco, CA: Jossey-Bass, 1992.

Steiner, Rudolf. *Intuitive Thinking as a Spiritual Path.* Hudson, NY: Anthroposophic Press, 1995.

Swerdlow, Joel L. "Quiet Miracles of the Brain." *National Geographic,* June 1995, pp. 25-26.

Targ, Russell, Dean Brown, Jane Katra, & Werdend Wiegend. "Viewing the Future: A Pilot Study with an Error-Correcting Protocol." *Journal of Scientific Exploration,* 1995.

Talbot, Michael. *The Holographic Universe.* New York, NY: Harper Collins, 1992.

Thorne, Avril & Harrison Gough. *Portraits of Type: An MBTI Research Compendium.* Palo Alto, CA: Consulting Psychologists Press, 1991.

Vaill, Peter. *Managing as a Performing Art.* San Francisco, CA: Jossey-Bass, 1989.

Weber, Renee. *Dialogues With Scientists & Sages: The Search for Unity.* New York, NY: Routledge & Kegan Paul, 1986.

West, Thomas G. *In the Mind's Eye.* Buffalo, NY: Prometheus Books, 1991.

Wheatley, Margaret J. *Leadership and the New Science: Learning About Organization from an Orderly Universe.* San Francisco, CA: Berrett-Koehler Publishers, 1992.

Whyte, David. *The Heart Aroused: Poetry and the Preservation of the Soul in Corporate America.* New York, NY: Currency Doubleday, 1994.

Wilson, Colin. *The Outsider.* Boston, MA: Houghton Mifflin Company, 1956.

Zukav, Gary. *Seat of The Soul.* New York, NY: Simon and Schuster, 1989.

Recommended Resources

Associations

Business For Social Responsibility
1683 Folsom St.
San Francisco, CA 94103-3722
tel: 415-865-2500
fax: 415-865-2505

Innovation Network
34 E. Sola Street
Santa Barbara, CA 93101
tel: 805-965-8477
fax: 805-963-8220

Intuition Network
369-B Third Street, #161
San Rafael, CA 94901
tel: 415-256-1137
fax: 415-456-2532

Management Centre for Human Values
Indian Institute of Management Calcutta
Joka, Diamond Harbour Road
Post Box No. 16757
Alipore Post Office
Calcutta 700-027
fax: 91-033-467-8307

Renaissance Business Associates
P.O. Box 197
Boise, ID 83701
208-345-4234

**Robert K. Greenleaf Center
for Servant Leadership**
921 E. 86th Street, #200
Indianapolis, IN 46240
317-259-1241

World Business Academy
1 Montgomery, 26th Floor
San Francisco, CA 94104
tel: 415-393-8251
fax: 415-393-8369

New Academy of Business
c/o Anita Roddick
3/4 Albion Place
Galena Road
London W6 OLT
United Kingdom
tel: (44) 181-563-8780
fax: (44) 171-208-7679

European Baha'i Business Forum
George W. Starcher, Secretary-General
35 Ave. Jean Jaures
Chambery 73000 France
tel: 33-7996-2272
fax: 33-7996-3570

Periodicals

At Work:
Stories of Tomorrow's Workplace
(bimonthly newsletter)
Berrett-Koehler Publishers, Inc.
155 Montgomery St.
San Francisco, CA 94104-4109
tel: 800-929-2929

Business Ethics
(bimonthly magazine)
Mavis Publications
52 S. 10th Street, #10
Minneapolis, MN 55403-2001
tel: 612-962-4700

Intuition Magazine
(bimonthly magazine)
P.O. Box 460773
San Francisco, CA 94146
tel: 415-949-4240

The New Leaders
Bringing Consciousness to Business
(bimonthly newsletter)
New Leaders Press
1668 Lombard Street
San Francisco, CA 94123
tel: 800-928-LEAD (5323)

Perspectives on Business and Global Change
(quarterly journal of World Business Academy)
One Montgomery Street, 26th Flr.
San Francisco, CA 94119-1210
tel: 415-393-8251

How to Contact Authors, Co-Authors, and Co-Editors

JOANNE MARIE BADEAUX
Joanne Badeaux, PC
18333 Egret Bay Blvd., #110
Houston, TX 77058-3200
281-333-0487

JOANNE BLACK
Sphericles
865 - First Ave., #10-D
New York, NY 10017
212-888-6324

SUSAN COLLINS
The Technology of Success
12040 NE Fifth Avenue
Miami, FL 33161
305-892-2702

SHARON FRANQUEMONT
Intuition Enterprises
56 Joaquin Miller Ct.
Oakland, CA 94611
510-531-3842

ROGER FRANTZ
Director
Department of Economics
San Diego State University
San Diego, CA 92182
619-594-3718

LINDA GARRETT
Creative Learning Technologies, Inc.
P.O. Box 418
Boise, ID 83701
208-345-4235

WILLIS HARMAN
Institute of Noetic Sciences
P.O. Box 909
Sausalito, CA 94966
415-331-5650

KYMN HARVIN RUTIGLIANO
Kymn & Company
165 Edgemont Road
Watchung, NJ 07060
908-754-4437

SUZIE HIGHTOWER
5711 Preston Oaks, #442
Dallas, TX 75240
214-458-1392

EDITH JURKA
Wind Song
16 Apple Bee Farm Road
Croton-On-Hudson, NY 10520
212-737-0591

JOEL LEVEY
InnerWork Technologies, Inc.
5536 Woodlawn Ave. N.
Seattle, WA 98103
206-632-3551

JAIME LICAUCO
Inner Mind Development
Institute
106 Legazpi Street
Prince Plaza #308
Green Belt/Makati,
Metro Manila PHILIPPINES
fax: 632-815-98-90

GARY MARKOFF
100 Pond Street, #7
Boston, MA 02130
617-522-8495

JEFFREY MISHLOVE
Intuition Network
369-B Third Street, #161
San Rafael, CA 94901
415-256-1137

MICHAEL MUNN
Gaia Center for Quality
435 Colorado Avenue
Palo Alto, CA 94306
415-326-6402

LAURIE NADEL
56 Seventh Avenue, #7G
New York, NY 10011
212-647-1134

JAN NEWMAN-SELIGMAN
Circus Earth Foundation
7028 Black Mountain Road
San Diego, CA 92130-1609
619-792-6483

ALEX PATTAKOS
P.O. Box 418
Boise, ID 83701
208-345-4235

JOHN PEHRSON
515 Boulder Place
Signal Mountain, TN 37377
423-886-5230

MICHAEL RAY
Graduate School of Business
Littlefield Hall, #356
Stanford University
Stanford, CA 94305-5015
415-723-2762

ELLE COLLIER RE
INEI-RE-The Return Path
714 3rd Avenue E
Kalispell, MT 59901
406-755-3557

CHRISTINE ROESS
Sphericles
212 E. 48th Street
New York, NY 10017
212-308-3283

NANCY ROSANOFF
President
Nancy Rosanoff & Assoc., Inc.
109 Sunnyside Avenue
Pleasantville, NY 10570-3136
914-769-7226

GIGI VAN DECKTER
Psychic Pathfinder
34 Eighth Avenue, #2C
New York, NY 10014
212-242-7314

GARY ZUKAV
P.O. Box 1333
Mount Shasta, CA 96067

Index

THE
INTUITION
NETWORK

The Intuition Network is a nonprofit organization dedicated to creating a world in which people feel encouraged to rely on their inner, intuitive resources—i.e., the deep wisdom of the psyche. In pursuit of this goal, the Network is engaged in a variety of projects including seminars, conferences, tours, television production, computer conferencing, local member groups, publications and research.

• • • • •

For further information, contact:

THE INTUITION NETWORK
369-B Third Street, Suite 161
San Rafael, CA 94901
Phone: (415) 256-1137
Fax: (415) 456-2532
E-mail: intuition.network@intuition.org